PRAISE FOR TEN DAYS W

"Authentic life-stories about grief, perseverance, identity, and relationships. Great insights on perspective and what it means to pursue your passions."

-JESSE ITZLER,

entrepreneur, bestselling author, speaker, father, & an owner of the NBA's Atlanta Hawks

"Mark's superpower isn't ADHD, it's his writing. He goes beyond including the reader as part of the story---we are the story. It is our demons and our obstacles that hold us back from pursuing our passion or purpose. Bravo, my friend!"

-PETER SHANKMAN

entrepreneur, 5-time bestselling author, speaker, podcaster, & single dad

"Mark's story of grief, illness and uncertainty is as familiar as it is powerful. Really though, this is a story about family; what it does to us and what we'll do for it. This is an exceptional book that will stay with you."

-DAN WETZEL

Yahoo! Sports National Columnist, NY Times bestselling author, podcaster, and film producer

Charlie—

Always pursue
your passions with
purpose!

TEN
DAYS
WITH
DAD

[signature]

TEN DAYS WITH DAD

FINDING PURPOSE, PASSION, & PEACE
DURING THE DARKEST DAYS OF
ALZHEIMER'S AND COVID-19

MARK J. RESNICK

FOREWARD BY BOB HALLORAN

MARK J. RESNICK

First paperback edition March 2022

Book design by Alejandro Martin, Bloom Design Agency
Edited by Christina Bagni, Wandering Words Media

ISBN 979-8-9857494-1-0 (paperback)
ISBN 979-8-9857494-0-3 (ebook)
ISBN 979-8-9857494-2-7 (hardcover)
ISBN 979-8-9857494-3-4 (audio)

Published by Mark J. Resnick Media
www.markjresnick.com

In loving memory of Barry Donald Resnick,

my father, coach, best friend, business partner, and hero.

July 24, 1937 - August 3, 2021

TABLE OF CONTENTS

Foreword   xiii
Introduction   1

PART ONE: 16 BEERS AVE
Pork Chop Hill   9
Worst Night Ever   15
Southie   18
Easy-Bake Oven   29
It Started With Mrs. Blake   33

PART TWO: BUILDING CHARACTER
Worst Paperboy Ever   43
Crushed   47
On My Own   51
Best Year Ever   56
Goodbye, My Friend   66
Blinded By Fear   73
The Shirt Off My Back   82
Reunited With Dad   88
Beers Ave   98

PART THREE: DAD'S STORY
Boys From Brighton   107
Doc Resnick   113
Gambling On Love   118
Ten Commandments Of Hockey   121

Papa Smurf   127

Chased By Demons   132

Last Day At Home   139

PART FOUR: TEN DAYS WITH DAD

Day One: London Broil   147

Day Two: Still No Plan   151

Day Three: Time Machine   155

Day Four: The Dog   158

Day Five: Whitney Place   160

Day Six: Flamingos   163

Day Seven: Pain In The Ass   165

Day Eight: Mr. Frank   167

Day Nine: The Emergency Room   169

Day Ten: Cleanup   174

PART FIVE: ASSISTED "LIVING"

First Night   181

Where You Been, Markus?   184

There's Something About Mary   190

Paranoid And Weepy   197

Perspective   201

The Breakup   206

Your Father Needs Help   211

Falling   215

Rising   220

Rock Star   227

PART SIX: FINDING PURPOSE, PASSION, & PEACE   **245**

The Commandments of Life   247

1. Never give up.   250

2. Be kind.   260

3. Forgive others.   266

4. Be yourself.   276

5. Always give more.   290

6. Be mindful.   299
7. Expect less.   311
8. Never make excuses.   317
9. Be grateful.   322
10. Forgive yourself.   330

Epilogue   335
Hat Trick Sponsors   349
Goal Sponsors   351
Assist Sponsors   352
Acknowledgements   353
About the Author   355

FOREWORD

Ironic, I think, that writing this foreword has me looking both back-ward and inward. Mark's fond recollections of his childhood are told with such exuberance and wide-eyed optimism that I'm reminded of a conversation I had with a good friend when we were both still in high school. We acknowledged to one another that we were having wonder-ful childhoods. Good families. Good grades. Good friends. Great times! And it was particularly significant that we were recognizing it in the mo-ment. We weren't waiting thirty years to see it, feel it, and appreciate it. We were aware of it and enjoying life in the moment. My friend and I raised a glass of his mom's God-awful iced tea that was usually the penal-ty for losing a game of ping-pong, and we smiled with a silent agreement that "Yup, life is good!"

And then a different friend of mine died. He fell off a tractor and was crushed by it. He and I had played soccer together, and his father was our coach. They named a trophy after him, and I was the first recipient of it, and I remember thinking: *I don't want this thing! The only reason I have it is because my friend is dead.*

And then a different friend of mine's father died. He had a heart attack in his mid-forties. I was an altar boy, and one of the priests called my home and asked if I would serve at the funeral mass for my friend's father. I didn't want to, but I did it, and I had an up-close and personal view of my friend in the first pew crying for the entire mass.

And then my brother died. I was sixteen. He was twenty-five. Car accident. And I remember friends and family filling up our house, and everyone was telling stories and laughing. Can you believe it? Laughing! I was so angry, and I remember thinking, *What happened to my idyllic childhood?*

And then I read Mark's book and so many memories came rushing back as if they were being carried by a flood. From the memories of inconsequential offhanded comments, jokes, and one-liners to the profoundly inspirational way I witnessed my parents experience the abject sorrow of losing a child, but realize they had six other children to raise and they couldn't abandon that responsibility. Their faith got them through it. They got me through it.

Meanwhile, I'm not at all sure how Mark got through the vastly different, though equally painful, experiences of his childhood, or how his dysfunctional family produced such a highly functioning adult. Mark asks the question: *"But how, exactly, is it possible for me to have such positive feelings about my home when there was so much sadness?"*

It's an excellent question that Mark sets out to answer for himself. For me, it's all about recognizing that as human beings, yes, sometimes we're broken, but by consistently putting one foot in front of the other, we can keep moving forward, and that most times we're able to piece back together a happy and productive life. Personally, I know I've quit a thousand times, but still I've persevered. And I know what has helped me most is the love and support of good people, an inexplicable optimism, and the joy that fills me when I'm engaged in one of my several passions. Oh, and it doesn't hurt to have a sense of humor.

So, I laugh at some of the memories I have of both my parents from when they were full of life, and even as they were dying. The end is never pretty, or clean, or easy. Mark knows that, and he describes the beautiful sorrow and the hopelessness and helplessness of the long, slow, inevitable loss of a dying parent without self-pity, but with honesty and, yes, with humor. It helps you realize there are always reasons to cry, but if you're open to it, you might just find a few reasons to smile.

Like when my brain exploded! In the summer of 2016, I suffered a ruptured brain aneurysm. My wife and I had just taken what we were calling a "bucket list vacation." First, we visited friends in Ireland, and then we went to Wimbledon and the British Open. Within a few days of returning from our "bucket list" trip, I almost kicked the bucket. That's funny, right?

My wife and I talk about the pain and the fear that surrounded the ensuing months of my recovery, but there are funny stories, too, that ease the pain and assuage the fear. Like my parents before her, my wife's faith got her through it. She got me through it.

When I got to the other side of it fully recovered and grateful to the incredible doctors and surgeons who drilled holes in my head and saved my life more than once, I was left with the gift of introspection. Looking backward and inward, I realized I wouldn't change a thing. I know a near-death experience is supposed to change your perspective, but I didn't have "carpe diem" tattooed on my subconscious before the aneurysm, and I don't have it now. I still plan for the future, because I believe I've got a bright one.

Mark's book has me re-examining my past, and I'm good with it. I mean, I wish I had batted lefty in little league (lefties had the coolest swings), but other than that I fully accept my decisions, my mistakes, and my experiences, both good and bad. All of it has led me to where I am, and I'm in a good place. A loving, loyal, generous wife. Four great kids. A good job. Good friends. Great times! Yup, life is good!

Makes me want to raise a glass of some God-awful iced tea, and read a good book: one that evokes memories both recent and distant, a book that invites empathy and compassion from someone like me—and I'd wager, someone like you—a book that encourages kindness, inspires joy, and reminds us that we're all just trying to make sense of it all.

I've read that book. And you're about to.

-Bob Halloran

Bob is an award-winning journalist, accomplished author, movie consultant, and sports anchor. He joined WCVB, Boston's News Leader, in 2003 as a freelance ancho/reporter and was appointed to a full-time position in 2014.

Bob has written several books including *Count the Rings*, which chronicles the first ten New England sports championships of this century and *Irish Thunder: The Hard Life and Times of Micky Ward*, for which he was hired as a technical consultant to the Oscar nominated movie, *The Fighter*.

INTRODUCTION

2014 was a *big* year for the Resnick family. In September, I officiated my younger brother John's marriage to his bride, Kerri, on Nantucket Island. On that spectacular fall morning, there were rows and rows of white lawn chairs, occupied by familiar and strange faces alike—but, except for the bride and groom, only one face stood out to me: my dad's. The rest of the guests seemed miles away; for some reason, I couldn't see their smiling faces, nor could I feel their presence. And even though I tried to look into John's and Kerri's eyes often to convey absolute focus and presence, I might as well have been staring right through them. *Actual* eye contact could have prevented me from fulfilling my promise not to break down and cry during the ceremony.

As I am prone to do before any important event in my life, I had cut my substantially thinning hair too short. Small beads of sweat, warmed by the sun, slowly made their way down from my softball-sized bald spot on the back of my head—though thankfully, the sweat was hidden to all but the cloudless blue sky. Earlier that morning, while shaving, I had nicked one of my sideburns, which I'm also prone to do, and was worried that people were staring at the scabbed-over area.

But I tried not to think about those things as I spoke. Luckily, my remarks, including the wedding vows, were perfectly worded and spaced out on my Kindle—which I held on to for dear life and prayed that nobody noticed my shaking hands. My distracted brain struggled to process the perfect positioning of the chairs, the mixed scents of perfumes and colognes, the busy birds looking on with curiosity. My heart beat loudly. *Wait, are those my heartbeats, or John's?*

Somehow, I persevered.

Honest to God, I cannot say whether the ceremony lasted fifteen or fifty minutes, but I came through on my promise not to cry—which was no easy feat, as I tend to cry watching movies like *Home Alone* and *Christmas Vacation*.

As John had been the last of my dad's three boys to marry, the event should have been one filled with emotion, pride, and jubilation. And it was. Yet, despite the happy occasion, exquisite setting, and flowing drinks, I remember my dad was quieter than usual throughout the weekend. I imagined he felt out of place in Nantucket; his ideal vacations were north, in Maine or Nova Scotia, or west, in Las Vegas or Arizona. But it wasn't just his discomfort with the location that was affecting him.

A month before the wedding, his nurse practitioner sent him to a specialist to determine if his forgetfulness was age-appropriate or something more serious. In hindsight, there were signs that something more was at play. Driving to familiar places became less familiar, parts of jokes and stories went incomplete, choosing a meal off the menu was more difficult, and repetition was omnipresent.

Weeks after the wedding, we were devastated to learn that Alzheimer's found another victim in my dad. What a tremendous burden it must have been, knowing he was diagnosed with Alzheimer's but holding back the news until after John's wedding. That explains my hunch that my dad was not his usual self in Nantucket.

Alzheimer's was not present within our family, which made the initial uncertainty of the diagnosis more stressful. I knew the average life expectancy after the initial diagnosis was seven years, but I didn't know what to expect along the way. No matter how much you research or learn about Alzheimer's, it can't possibly prepare you for the emotional, mental, and physical toll it carries, especially during its advanced stages. I often used to pray that God would take him peacefully in his sleep. Often, as in, multiple times a day.

Within four years of his Alzheimer's diagnosis, my dad could no longer drive, cook, or correctly take his medications. On a routine visit to his home in March of 2019, I took one look at his exhausted and frightened face and immediately knew it would be the last day he would live there—the dementia demons had gotten the best of him. The plan for the morning was to take him to the Omelette Factory for breakfast, not away from his home forever. But that's what happened.

Before moving full-time to assisted living, my dad spent ten days with my family and me in Walpole. The only way to describe these ten days would be 'baptism by fire.' My role as a sandwich parent (caring for a parent—in this case, my dad—and being the parent of my own children) had begun. Need proof? On the ninth day, at dinner with my children, my dad was more than off his game. He was confused and unaware of his surroundings. He put his water glass in the center of his plate, fed his imaginary dog under the table, and dropped his drawers in the dining room because he had to go to the bathroom. It was the first time all week I lost my temper with him. My kids were frightened. My wife, Coleen, was unnerved; this behavior was different. The night ended with a trip to the emergency room, which ended up being one of our best nights together.

During the final two years of his life, my dad and I shared more than 200 meals. Even though the joy of seeing him inevitably turned to sadness, and I regularly cried in my car after visits, I knew it was what we both needed. Despite the pain and exhaustion that came with visiting him daily, I found myself smiling and laughing when we were together. I discovered much more than his humor; I witnessed his kindness, curiosity, and compassion. He inspired me every day. His strength, bravery, and resilience were unmatched. And as strange as it may sound, I was getting to know him better than at any other point in my life. Even though I had lived with my dad for twenty-two years and worked alongside him in business for another fourteen, I didn't truly know who he was until then.

I started writing a story about his Alzheimer's, but it soon morphed into something entirely different. The story paved its path and, despite my intentions, found a way to push me toward an introspection I didn't anticipate—nor welcome. Did his Alzheimer's stem from utter exhaustion, based on his lifelong responsibility of taking care of those closest to him? Or was it the inescapable loneliness he experienced as a child, his on-and-off gambling and drinking habits, or a life of unfulfilled emotional needs that brought it on?

And then it hit me: this wasn't a story about my dad's Alzheimer's. *Ten Days With Dad* was my story all along. I inherited my parents' flaws, limitations, and afflictions, and some demons in me were born out of their struggles—which I used as excuses my entire life, believing they held me back or were in my way, keeping me from achieving the kind of success I had imagined for myself. And worst of all, I had let them control my happiness.

This book is about an emotional transformation born out of my dad's Alzheimer's and a simultaneous, once-in-a-century global pandemic. Together, they could have pushed me into a darkness so deep that I may not have emerged whole again. Instead, they helped me realize, understand, and accept that everyone has demons, flaws, and limitations that need to be faced and overcome.

This book, in a word, is about *progress*.

Alzheimer's robbed my dad of his memory, dignity, and ultimately his life, and yet, out of this darkness, I discovered purpose, passion, and peace. It took me fifty years to get there and some unusual and unfortunate circumstances, but I did it. It is my hope that whether you're trying to overcome adversity, move on from a painful past, find clarity and purpose in your life, or just want to build better habits, my book will help jump-start your transformation.

Upon finishing *Ten Days*, my goal is that you find the morsels of hope, inspiration, and courage you need to embrace a progress-centered mindset that fits your personality, needs, and desires. You can take control of your story at any point. Embrace your past, but don't let it define your present. And most importantly, permit yourself to change, for you are under no obligation to be the person you were five years ago, one year ago, or even a month ago.

-Mark

———

PART ONE:

16 BEERS AVE

PORK CHOP HILL

Before closing its doors for good in 1993, St. Margaret's Hospital in Dorchester was once the largest maternity hospital in Massachusetts. Several notable Bostonians were born there, including Senator Edward M. Kennedy, Former Boston Mayor Marty Walsh, and Alma Wahlberg's nine children. I was born there shortly after 8 p.m. on Monday, March 13, 1972, within fifteen minutes of my mom's arrival.

I was in a rush to be born, and I've been in a rush to do something and be someone ever since.

My parents lived on High Street in Norwell, a thirty-minute drive to Dorchester. Had the drive been any longer, I would have been born in the back seat of my parents' car. My dad had time to park the car, but even that was cutting it close. A scotch at the bar was out of the question. I doubt either of them complained, though—compared to the hours and hours of labor with my older brother, Bill, my prompt arrival was a gift. It was like pulling into a packed mall parking lot at Christmas, only to have someone back out of a spot just as you arrived.

Those fifteen minutes of fame were relatively short-lived; it was no secret that my mom wanted a baby girl. They tried again, but there would be no third-time charm for her. Less than two years later, my brother John was born, cementing my role as the middle child. Bill and I were thrilled to have a brother, but Mom *wanted* that girl.

I have but one photo of my brothers and me from childhood. It was taken at my grandmother's rental cottage near Swift's Beach in Wareham. Bill and I are shirtless, wearing swim trunks and smiling. John, only two at the time, had a full head of beautiful, curly blond hair. He looks just like the girl my mom always wanted—only he's not smiling.

Being born in the middle could have meant a lifelong battle for attention—or worse, a veil of invisibility—but it didn't. I thrived in the role and grew to be more easygoing and extroverted than my brothers were. Bill and John seemed content to keep to themselves, whereas I wanted to share whatever was running through my mind at that moment. I had trouble sitting still and craved action (or, more likely, attention). Whenever I did find myself at rest, my imagination ran wild. I believed anything was possible, whether it was climbing the highest tree, scoring five goals in a hockey game, or capturing rabbits in my backyard with a milk crate.

Before John was born, we moved a mile down the street to Beers Ave, which became my home for the next twenty-two years. Built in the late 1950s, Beers Ave and its surrounding streets are mainly colonials, averaging roughly 1,600 square feet. Ours had three small bedrooms on the upper floor. The closets in each room were so tiny that my parents used all three of them to hold their wardrobes. Some houses had family rooms or enclosed porches attached to the main house, but nobody had garages, irrigation, or central air conditioning systems. I'm almost sure there were sidewalks along the streets, but nobody used them. Whether heading to the school bus stop, walking a dog, or pushing strollers, we just walked in the middle of the street.

Conservation land, including wetlands, tall forests, and natural waterways, surrounded Beers Ave. It was the center of my universe, and I took pride in knowing every worthy climbing tree, trail, and shortcut within a mile of my house. In one direction, I could ride my bike through the woods to my friend Tony's neighborhood; another path brought me to Washington Street, which shaved precious minutes off my trip to the baseball fields; and a few hundred yards from my driveway was Pork Chop Hill.

Pork Chop Hill was perhaps the most important monument of my childhood, but I never found out where the hill got its moniker. Someone must have envisioned the hill's shape to something akin to a pork chop, I guess, but I never once saw that image materialize in all my trips up and over the hill. The climb to the top wasn't easy, nor was the descent after a good dumping of snow. It was too steep and dangerous for sledding, but that didn't stop us from trying to conquer it.

I would be shocked if the current neighborhood kids even know Pork Chop Hill exists. To discover it would require unsupervised exploration, an elusive concept these days. They would have to forge pathways through the wild thorny brush, felled timber, wetlands, and poison ivy to find this beauty. They would likely return home dirty, bruised, and bloodied—or worse, with broken bones, as we did on occasion.

On the other side of Pork Chop Hill was a river, which fed directly into Jacobs Pond. The ponds seemed to freeze more often back in the '70s, and we took full advantage of the conditions. My dad taught me how to skate on that pond. With no helmet, just a hat and mittens, I pushed milk crates and metal folding chairs along the smooth surface for hours at a time. Even though I got a late start and didn't start skating until I was six, becoming a hockey player, like my dad, was a given. Not because he forced it upon me, but because *I wanted to be my dad*.

It was a ten-minute drive to Jacobs Pond by car—far too short to contain any life-lesson lectures from Dad, but indeed long enough for me to talk nonstop about learning how to skate and play hockey just like him.

When Dad wasn't driving me, I opted to use the river behind Pork Chop Hill to get to the pond. Getting from my front door on Beers Ave to the front shore of Jacobs Pond in under thirty minutes was invigorating. I never made the trip alone, though, which was a wise decision. On many occasions, the trek to the pond *was* the adventure, and no parent would have approved of this route had they known its dangers. We experienced far too many close calls on thin ice and unsafe conditions. The outskirts of the river were usually passable, but there were times I had to leap from frozen reed to frozen reed in my skates. I was undeterred, however—even when a foot or skate broke the ice and was briefly submerged.

Once we cleared the danger zone, it was smooth skating to the pond. The open ice in front of me seemed to stretch for miles, but I could cross it in only minutes at full speed—a little longer if I was pushing a puck and practicing my stickhandling. I remember the windburn on my face, the hundreds of pond hockey games played, and the rush to get back home from Pork Chop Hill before it got too dark.

But there are some memories I wish I could forget.

Having a skate go under the ice was scary, but what haunted me most were the torturous pranks carried out by the older guys after a skate. An unlucky kid would be grabbed by the arm and tossed onto the ice. Slowly, the boy would get dragged toward the center of the river, the part that was most definitely *not* frozen.

It happened to me twice and both times were horrific. My face burned from being dragged across the ice as I tried to crawl my way to safety. After exhausting every curse word I knew, I cried, screamed, and begged for my tormenter to stop. This abuse went on until an older brother ended it, but it was never fast enough.

How nobody went under was a miracle.

Pork Chop Hill is the tallest ridge in the area, but it wasn't imposing by any means. Regardless, reaching the top from Beers Ave involved risk, adventure, and a willingness to go beyond normal boundaries. The reward was worth it, and I'm not the only one who agrees. In recent years, a finished picnic table was placed atop the hill, as if someone—Norwell's Conservation Commission, presumably—recognized the beauty and peace Pork Chop Hill possesses.

Thrilling and terrifying, peaceful and tumultuous, memorable and nightmarish, and full of promise and fraught alike, Pork Chop Hill was the ultimate metaphor for my time on Beers Ave. Though just the beginning of my story, much of my time there went beyond normal boundaries, setting the tone for the rest of my life. It was only after my dad was diagnosed that I began to look at those years differently. Not only through my lens, but my dad's lens, as well.

Growing up in Norwell was a gift, but those years on Beers Ave were challenging for the Resnicks—beginning with the night my parents told us they were separating.

WORST NIGHT EVER

Home is where your story begins.

Stenciled on our kitchen wall for more than twelve years, I saw those six words every day. They were just words on the wall I hardly noticed—until my dad got Alzheimer's. Then, I couldn't stop thinking about them. They kept bringing me back to my childhood kitchen on Beers Ave, where my story began.

⌇ ⌇ ⌇

I was a happy kid all the time, but especially at dinnertime. Back then, the yellow wallpaper dotted with pears and oranges was crisp and bright, and the faux brick-patterned linoleum floors had yet to fade. It was tight but tidy, and my favorite room in the house.

One night, plopped in my usual seat—with my dad to my immediate left and older brother Bill to my right—I hogged the conversation as usual, gabbing about recess or lunch or a game we played after school. My mom dropped plates of food in front of us, and so began another typical dinner. Except on that night, it was anything but ordinary. My parents announced they were separating.

I didn't understand what that meant. Separating what? Or how? After my mom explained that she was moving out of the house forever, my brothers left the table, both crying. Why didn't I follow them upstairs, and why wasn't I crying? I stayed behind, too afraid to move. I pushed my food around the plate and kept my head down. I could swallow, but not speak. It was the first time words were hard to conjure. I was too young to understand the magnitude of their announcement yet was old enough to know something terrible had just happened.

My world, until that moment, consisted only of soccer games and Mrs. Epoch's classroom, in that order. Then came the rink, as I had just started playing hockey. Unlike Bill, I don't recall my parents arguing or growing distant from one another, or when my dad came through the front door, only to be bombarded by flying dinner plates. My mom hurled *actual* glass plates.

Still, even Bill couldn't have anticipated them splitting up, and no way in hell could he have imagined Mom moving out.

The days and weeks leading up to the moving truck's arrival were like a highly sensitive and confidential report, redacted to a mere sentence: *It happened, so let's turn the page and move on.* The separation meal is my only pre-divorce memory of the five of us; there's not another dinner, birthday party, holiday, or vacation I can recall before that night. I have a hazy recollection of the actual truck arriving, but the rest of that moment disappeared a long time ago. All I knew was she was with us, until she wasn't.

My mom moved to South Boston, back to her hometown. My parents decided we would alternate weekends between the city and Norwell, so basically, I had two homes growing up, though neither one felt like home. Being shuffled back and forth sounds crappy, but it wasn't really—at least, not initially.

Even after the divorce, our home on Beers Ave continued to host family gatherings, which provided some normalcy to our lives. Seeing my Grammy stationed at the kitchen table with a can of Miller Lite close by, keeping tabs on everyone as they passed, comforted me, as did my Uncle Jim, who was always the life of the party. He smoked his unfiltered Camels, drank his Crown Royal scotch, and told the best stories and jokes. He kept everything and everyone light, both before and after my parents divorced.

Our house was small, but it had a nice backyard. My cousins and I played on the jungle gym, climbed trees, or played tag; the adults played shuffleboard or drank beers on lawn chairs. The most impressive feature of the yard was the above-ground pool, but they emptied it after I nearly drowned. My dad ran into the house for a minute, which was enough time for me to jump in. I was facedown in the water when he came back out. I think I was three at the time. I say, *think*, because nobody talked about it—even though I can't imagine a more dramatic incident from my childhood.

It was like it never happened.

SOUTHIE

Located halfway between Boston and Cape Cod, Norwell is known for its schools, youth sports, pretty country roads, and idyllic neighborhoods. South Boston was pretty much the opposite: crowded double and triple-decker structures, sirens and cars honking at all hours, dirty concrete pavement, thick accents, and lots of walking to and from your destination. It was a brand-new world, of which I was equally terrified and enthralled.

Whether it was at Mom's apartment on Jenkins Street, off Dorchester Ave, or Glover Court near Broadway, Southie was an adventure. On weekends we dug for clams at Carson Beach for steaming, walked Castle Island with ice creams in hand, visited the stores on Broadway, played in Columbia Park, and explored the Old Colony Projects, where my grandmother lived.

Grammy's apartment was located at 1224 Columbia Road and faced the park. Like Jacobs Pond, I used to believe Columbia Park stretched for miles as a kid. It had lots of baseball fields, basketball courts, and swing sets. The football stadium was at the other end, but it would have been like an all-day trip to reach it. It seemed massive to me.

Many years later, my high school soccer team played a match in

Columbia Park. No longer a little boy, the park didn't overwhelm or fascinate me the same way as before. While warming up for the game, I looked around me and saw my grandmother's apartment, the beach, and the football stadium. In a few short years, I had grown up to the point where the entire park was in my field of vision instead of stretching endlessly in every direction. On that day, the park took on a whole new meaning for me when I glanced over to the sidelines and saw Grammy's face light up. Her smile was the only massive thing I saw.

Beyond the park, the JFK Presidential Library shone majestically. I didn't know what a Democrat or Republican was, or liberal or conservative, but it didn't matter; almost everyone in South Boston was *for* the Kennedys. I know my mom and grandmother were because they talked about them often and because I watched them wave, scream, and smile at anybody named Kennedy marching in Southie's annual St. Patrick's Day parade.

When I was old enough to form my own political opinions, some of which varied from the Kennedys' (and Grammy's), I always maintained a fondness for Ted Kennedy. It wasn't his distinct accent that I favored, nor did it have anything to do with our shared birthplace at St. Margaret's. It was his passion I admired, his palpable, almost contagious passion for standing up for the voiceless. It seemed genuine to me. His personal life may not have been perfect, but in the Senate, he was effective. He crossed the aisles to get things done; he could disagree with people, often vociferously, but remain likable at the same time.

When I met him at a small fundraiser in Boston, it was unlike meeting a movie star or professional athlete. There was no "nice to meet you"

———

line from him; it was always "nice to *see* you." In his presence, you were awed by a charisma born out of empathy, not practice. His first impression wasn't his best, but in the end, he won you over—and even though you may have disagreed with him, you understood his heart was in the right place.

It took years, but I realized Senator Kennedy and I had more in common than St. Margaret's, a dysfunctional family, and a passion to serve. For much of my professional life, I also struggled to make a good first impression. Before being diagnosed with ADHD, my words were often misconstrued; I was too direct, candid, and unapologetic for speaking my mind. In the end, however, you knew my heart was in the right place, and like Ted, I won you over.

South Boston is a special place. I was happy to call it *home*, but it took a while to get used to—especially Grammy's place in the projects. The burnt trash from the incinerators stung my eyes; loud voices erupted out of nowhere, both early in the morning and late at night, but its residents, who simultaneously held hearts of gold and an edginess that could rattle the Pope, grew on you over time. Even so, while I had always considered myself a tough kid growing up, I was not Southie tough. That was a whole different level of toughness.

Still, we adjusted and never said no to visiting Grammy. She made sure we held open the doors for others, said please and thank you, and helped around the apartment. She introduced me to blueberries soaked in milk, which became my favorite snack, and chocolate eclairs, my favorite dessert. Eventually, her neighbors accepted us, and we became part of the neighborhood. Chucky, the boy who lived upstairs and smoked butts, sat on the stoop and joked with us. He asked about hockey and colorfully shared his recent exploits.

Chucky was lovable and detestable at the same time. "Hey Mahhki, how many pipes did you break today?" he would say, insinuating that my weight caused me to crash through the concrete, bursting pipes underground as I fell.

"*Fuck* you, Chucky," I would reply, pretending to be tough but terrified he would punch me in the face.

Inside the apartment, I feared Grammy's two black cats. I hated them, and they *knew* it. I wanted to like them but couldn't. They had speckled green eyes and sharp claws. I hid under the covers at night so they wouldn't jump on the pullout couch and start purring in my face. I could hear their approach well in advance of their arrival. I silently begged them to leave me alone but to no avail. I swear they tormented me on purpose, for sport.

The cats made me uncomfortable, but they weren't the most challenging part about visiting Grammy. When I was five, my grandfather had a massive stroke, which left him unable to speak clearly. I tried my hardest to talk to him; I just couldn't understand what he was saying most of the time, which made him stammer more profusely. I was helpful to him in at least one way, though. I lost track of how many of his Marlboro cigarettes I lit. I used to think to myself: *Awesome! He's going to let me use a lighter!*

———

It took time for Grandpa and me to figure each other out, but we did. Maybe it was because we were both born with the same neurological condition called nystagmus. Nystagmus primarily impacts one's vision and causes continuous and involuntary movement of the eyes. My eyes move side to side nonstop, which causes my head to shake to compensate for the eye movement. From a visual standpoint, it's like being both nearsighted and farsighted, only it is not a correctable condition.

Having poor eyesight is a handicap I've dealt with my entire life. It impacted my hand-eye coordination, which made playing sports that much harder. It also brought unwanted attention. Teachers mistook my shaking head for disagreement, and kids asked embarrassing questions about it. They knew not to push me too far, though. Don't ask me how—they just knew.

The absolute worst day of every school year, by far, was vision screening day. It was even worse than the holiday and spring choral concerts. Putting aside the spectacle of elementary school concerts—getting dressed up and pretending to be excited to perform in front of the whole school and parents—the concerts were mainly a drag because I was tone-deaf and incapable of memorizing the lyrics. I'm not joking. The only song to which I knew every word was "Happy Birthday," something I'm afraid holds true to this day.

I'm just happy I never fainted before or during the performance, which seemed to happen at every concert. Besides, I had no trouble mouthing the words. Yet unlike the concerts, which were well announced weeks in advance, vision screening day always snuck up on me. By the time I realized it was *the day*, it was too late to do anything about it—like fake an illness so I would be sent home. It was dreadful how we lined up outside the nurse's office, waiting for our turn to look into an oversized 3D Viewmaster-type machine.

"Just read the third line, from left to right," the nurse said.

"Umm. I can't see any of the letters or numbers," I said.

"Are you sure?"

Yea, I'm pretty sure, just like I couldn't read them last year and the year before, I wanted to say but didn't.

I despised that machine. I went last and attempted to memorize the lines the students had said before me, but I couldn't. If only I had a note from Dad exempting me from taking it in the first place. I failed the vision test each and every year. Not only was I embarrassed, but I felt inferior to my classmates, at least on that particular day.

At least I passed the hearing test.

Not being able to speak with Grandpa about nystagmus—about anything—was brutal. It would have been fascinating to know him, especially to listen to his experiences as a soldier in World War II. I've seen photographs of him with his buddies but would love to know the stories behind them.

Beyond his military service, his family, the DiNatales, owned a flooring company. In my mind, they were famous, as they were the company that installed the parquet floor in the Old Boston Garden—which was both loved and hated by the home team and visitors alike.

The aging floor, with the Celtics' smiling leprechaun logo in the center, is also a surface on which bizarre things can happen. Move down the court, driving around the key, dribbling lightly. THOOMP, THOOMP, THOOMP, THOOMP. THUNK. When the ball hits one of the parquet's hidden dead spots, the ball dies about six inches off the floor instead of returning to the player's hand. The ball bounces like nowhere else in the NBA. A player can feel like he's lost his shorts when a dead spot strips him of the ball. (Chicago Tribune, June 07, 1987)

My grandfather watched TV and smoked his Marlboros. He shuffled to and from the bathroom or bedroom, slippers scraping the floor, coughing as he went—deep, phlegm-filled coughs. During high school and college, I stopped by as often as I could. It was never enough, and I felt guilty for not being more present. Before saying goodbye, Grammy would go to her bedroom and get some cash for me. Sometimes Grandpa did, too. I refused each time, but it was to no avail. You don't say no to grandparents.

In Southie, we spent most of our time in Mom's apartment. When we weren't tentatively exploring the neighborhood, we played a ridiculous amount of floor hockey inside. Without fail, our fighting, shouting, and goofing around followed us to Southie. We battled each other for hours. Bruins against the Canadians. Double overtime nail-biters. And that was before 10 a.m. We were intensely competitive, sometimes out of control.

South Boston and Norwell may have been opposite universes, but in the end, we handled both just fine. My parents were good about not overcompensating for the divorce. They didn't spoil us. (Well, Grammy tried to, but that was okay by all.) By the time we got Atari or another video game console, there were already two or three newer models on the market. We owned used bikes and hockey equipment. My mom did the clothes shopping before each new school year, but that was because my dad wouldn't, which was a blessing, in hindsight.

My dad didn't have many rules—or expectations, for that matter. I never asked permission to ride my bike to faraway neighborhoods, nor did I leave notes on the kitchen table saying I was building a fort or wandering the vast woods. We traveled to other neighborhoods to play street hockey and played flashlight tag long into the summer nights. I came home when the games ended or because other kids heard their parents shouting for them to come home.

For the most part, we knew which lines not to cross. Once, Dad washed my mouth with soap for swearing—at least he tried to. He made the mistake of wetting the gold Dial bar first, making it slippery and hard to control. I couldn't avoid complete contact with the bar, but it certainly didn't work as well as he intended. It certainly wasn't all good-natured hockey matches at Dad's. There were heated arguments, fights, and slammed doors aplenty; we shed tears behind closed doors, out of earshot. On many occasions, I screamed, "I hate you!" to both brothers, and remember saying it to my dad, too.

I enjoyed a freedom not experienced by my friends, which only made me love Beers Ave even more. Occasionally, I took advantage of the situation by hosting parties; fortunately, these were without the influence of cell phones and social media, which would have resulted in way too many out-of-control weekend nights. When they did exceed capacity, the Norwell cops were lenient with us. If the party wasn't on Beers Ave, it was still the meetup spot before heading out for the night.

For twenty-two years, I called Beers Ave my home. Although I vastly preferred it to Southie, and believed it was the ultimate place to grow up, I now see it for what it was: filled with moments, memories, and experiences that I both treasured and detested. I was nearly drowned twice by older kids but idolized them just the same. Our family room, filled with hockey trophies, medals, and memorabilia from successful tournaments and camps, was the coldest in the house, both literally and figuratively. Years after my mom moved out, the inside walls, cabinets, countertops, and floors begged for attention; the drawers got filled with useless junk or broken utensils; the outer shingles, doors, steps, and pavers experienced their own long, slow decline.

And I never seemed to notice.

Even our three dogs shared in the joy and misery of life on Beers Ave, having experienced both unconditional love and sorrow.

Fritzy was a purebred miniature schnauzer. His registered name with the American Kennel Club was Frederick Von Heinekin III. Don't ask me why. He was a miniature schnauzer, but if you asked my mom, she'd say there was nothing "mini" about him. He was the most treasured thing in my mom's life, other than her children. Sadly, he was tragically killed by a demented teenage boy when my mom was six months pregnant with John.

When he didn't come home that dreadful day, she refused to stop searching for him. She combed the woods for several weeks, desperately trying to find him. It was only after the kid's family moved away did she learn the truth, from witnesses. Fritzy was kicked in the head so hard by this evil boy that he was knocked under the partially frozen wetlands and drowned. The boys were too afraid of this psycho to tell my mom what had happened, so they waited to tell her until after he moved away. I have no recollection of the dog, but his demise still brings tears to my mother's eyes.

What kind of monster would do that to a dog?

Taffy was a gift to us from my grandmother. He came after Fritzy but stayed with us when my mom moved to Southie. Taffy was a mutt, but for the life of me, to this day, I could not identify his mix of breeds. I remember he was a caramel-colored dog of medium stature, more round than chiseled, and very calm. The dog seemed older than he was. I don't remember being attached to him the way most young kids are with their dogs.

Although not tragically killed like Fritzy, thank God, he was out of my life sooner than expected, as Taffy absconded with Mrs. Cushman, the elderly widow next door. For nearly a year, Taffy would be lured to her house, tempted with treats and food. One day, Mrs. Cushman appeared at our back door with Taffy in tow. She point-blank asked my dad if she could keep him. She explained that she had been sad and lonely since her husband passed, and Taffy brought her joy. My dad was speechless. I looked at Mrs. Cushman, then my dad, then at the dog. By this point, the dog had put on substantial weight. He wasn't just chubby; he was fat! My dad hemmed and hawed but gave in.

It wasn't long before Taffy died from a heart attack, but really, I tell my kids, he blew up from overeating.

———

Our third dog, Midnight, was a mess from the start. He was an adorable black lab puppy who unexpectedly arrived at our house one day. My mom brought him to us after Taffy's passing.

"All boys should have a dog," she said.

The fact that it pissed off my dad was just a bonus in her mind—and Midnight did piss him off. He took forever to train, liked to bite, never listened, and occasionally stole marinated steaks from the table, which earned him kicks from my dad.

Bill was either disinterested or didn't have the time to look after a dog, so Midnight's care fell on John and me. We were lousy at caring for Midnight. He charged after us every time we left the house and usually succeeded in slipping past us just as the door was closing. He was clever.

One day he started to follow the two of us as we rode our bikes to the baseball fields. I yelled at John to turn around and take Midnight home; he did the same to me. I was older, so there was no way I was turning around. We rode on. He ran after us, and then trailed off at some point.

We never saw Midnight again. He ran away and never returned.

For thirty years, I shouldered guilt because he ran off on my watch—until the truth came out. Midnight never did run away from home. It took him three decades, but Dad eventually told the truth about what happened to Midnight: Animal Control caught him and brought him to the dog pound, and when they called my dad to get him, he said no! It was Midnight's third visit to the pound, and Dad refused to get him. Just like that, Midnight was gone from our lives.

Like he never happened.

EASY-BAKE OVEN

Happy hour in the kitchen was the highlight of my mom's day while we were still a family. After a long day of work, she would gather us in the kitchen for five minutes, and we talked about our days. Then she started on dinner. I don't remember happy hour; I only know about it from her stories—nor do I remember what it was like to have a mom always around when growing up. I remember she took on some roles my dad either refused or was incapable of providing.

One of those roles included Christmas shopping. I'm not sure how old I was, but I circled the Easy-Bake Oven in the Sears Wish Book catalog while making my Christmas list one year. There were other items circled in the book: bikes, toys, race cars, trains, models, and of course, games, but I wanted the Oven as much as the toys.

Mom came through that year; it was hard to miss the Oven under the tree. I whipped up cakes, brownies, and cookies in those thin metal pans for the rest of school vacation. I didn't realize how tiny the treats were at the time, but their size didn't stop me from dreaming about opening a bakery one day.

Because of this fond memory, many years ago, I bought my daughter, Erin, her own Easy-Bake Oven. We were both surprised at how small the cookies were. The metal pans are now a thin plastic, and the cookies get "baked" with just a light bulb. Still, we made every one of the packets that came with the oven. When the supplies ran out, we stopped using the cheap crappy one and instead made actual cookies together in the range.

We baked together for a few years until she decided that she liked it better when I made the cookies myself, and all she had to do was eat them!

The Easy-Bake Oven was just a starting point for my cooking passion. The kitchen was my favorite room in the house, not only because I liked to eat, but because it was the only room where everyone had to gather at least once a day. Whether or not you wanted to eat or liked the meal Dad served, you still had to sit at the dinner table.

Before the Food Network and its countless cooking shows, I learned to cook in our tiny kitchen by watching my dad. I watched him fry chicken livers, marinate London broil steaks, mash potatoes and squash, and layer lasagna. My favorite cooking memories were in the backyard, though, working the grill. He taught me how to light the charcoals and cook wings, burgers, and steaks. Considering he had never cooked before my mom moved out, he became proficient at it pretty quickly.

There's also a good chance my cooking ambitions heightened due to the lack of food choices when growing up alone on weekends. My mom stopped coming to stay with us on weekends when I was in high school, and my dad was with his girlfriend on weekend nights. I got by on pasta, cereal, canned SpaghettiOs, and frozen microwave meals. Perhaps I was whipping up gourmet meals in my mind while eating a frozen dinner?

Either way, it was on Beers Ave that I discovered my passion for baking. I can't recall when I first wanted to own a bakery, but it was my first real ambition in life.

⌣⌣⌣

If I wasn't home, I was at Sean Fogarty's house—which I always preferred. The two of us and his brothers destroyed their kitchen pantry. Our appetites were never satisfied, and I loved how they had so many good treats: Hostess apple pies, Ring Dings, Devil Dogs, cupcakes, sugary cereals, and Drake's Coffee Cakes. Our absolute favorite thing to eat was Betty Crocker's Date Bar Mix—warm, just out of the oven. We ate them every weekend in high school. It didn't matter if it was 1 p.m. or 1 a.m., those Date Bars hit the spot. Betty Crocker stopped selling the mix shortly after I graduated from college, but you can bet I'll have a replica date bar in my bakery.

My mom stopped coming to Norwell right before I entered high school. It was a turning point in our relationship, though I didn't know it at the time. In her mind, it wasn't worth coming if we weren't going to be home most of the weekend. It was true; there were plenty of weekends where I slept in my bed but was otherwise absent. I admit our time together wasn't high quality, between sports, seeing friends, or just being a teenager alone in my room. But I *never* wanted her to stop coming.

I want to say that I understood her decision to stop coming, and I probably did. But that wasn't how I felt at the time. Whether I was physically home with her or not, she was my mom. Didn't she want to be part of our lives, even if it was on our schedule? Wasn't that how it was for most parents of teenagers?

I felt bad for John, who was two years younger than me. As lonely as I was as a teenager, it was ten times worse for him. We never discussed it, but I believe it to be true. For him, my mom's decision was the beginning of the end of a normal relationship between them. I think he knew this right away.

Her decision to stop spending weekends with us was the first of many choices that left an indelible mark on my life.

It Started With Mrs. Blake

I spent seven years at Grace Farrar Cole Elementary School, longer than any other school I attended. I remember my teachers' names from every grade, but not the principal, even though I spent many hours in his office with my friend, Marty Delany.

Marty moved to Norwell in the fourth grade, and we were inseparable. He was one of two kids, like me, with divorced parents. I don't know if that's why we ended up as best friends, but we were tight from the minute he moved to Norwell until he left. He lived with his mom about a mile from my house, and we wreaked all sorts of havoc together.

Right away, you had the feeling that Marty was raised far away from Norwell. He didn't play organized sports, but he was big, strong, and athletic. He was easily the toughest kid I knew. He wasn't Southie tough, but he was close. We were like brothers from the start.

At recess, I wouldn't label us as bullies—because we weren't. Yet we did cause a fair amount of trouble for ourselves, and yes, we did cross the line at times. Like when we accidentally broke Lee's arm. I can't remember if I was the one who got on my hands and knees behind Lee or

---

the one who pushed him over, but we landed in the principal's office, and Lee landed at the hospital. It was a stupid prank, and we felt awful about it.

I spent a lot of time with Marty growing up, watching wrestling, playing football in the yard, swapping stories about our divorced parents, and eating junk food. His mom could not have been nicer to me. I remember she took us to the Boston Garden to see our Saturday morning heroes and villains from the World Wrestling Federation. It was one thing to watch them on TV, but to see them in person was unreal. Jimmy Superfly Snuka, Ted Dibiasi, the Iron Sheik, Roddy Rowdy Piper, Andre the Giant, and Hulk Hogan were all there. Andre the Giant was seven feet, four inches tall and weighed 500 pounds!

My friendship with Marty changed in middle school, as I enlarged my circle of friends, but we stayed close until he moved to Pembroke in ninth grade.

I had a crush on my first-grade teacher, Mrs. McCann. She was the nicest teacher I had at Cole. In hindsight, she was likely only so nice to me because I showed up the first day with a cast on my left arm. I had fallen out of a neighbor's tree the week before school started and broke it. She was my all-time favorite teacher at Cole.

There was a pond behind the school, which provided science teachers an opportunity to take us on field trips. It's now called Hatch Pond. Surrounding the pond today are several well-maintained walking trails and an outdoor classroom, complete with wooden benches and a podium for the teacher. It's very Pilgrimesque. I noticed on my recent visit that what was visibly missing from the pond was the giant log that connected two former trails. I assumed that was because of me.

On one of our second-grade field trips, I was walking over a log when I fell off and splashed into the dirty water. There's a chance I was fooling around—maybe showing off—but honestly, I'm pretty sure I was just clumsy and fell. My mom always said I was clumsy as a kid. But I was embarrassed. I was probably the only kid in school history to have fallen into the pond. I didn't even get to change my clothes, as nobody was around to drop them off. I went back to class dirty and wet, and stayed dirty and wet all day.

I don't remember Hatch Pond being pretty, but on a recent visit, I was struck by its beauty. It looked clean, too, like you could swim in it. It was a far cry from how I remembered the pond, but on that day, standing on a well-built dock, I immediately deemed it worthy of rod and reel. As I looked around, something to my left caught my eye. That's when I saw it: *the log*. No longer in one piece and clearly out of place from when I was a student, it was two-thirds above the water. It's bark was faded and somewhat battered, but it was definitely the log. I saw it with my own two eyes.

Yes, I am sure; I will never forget that log.

The highlight of elementary school was the sixth-grade overnight class trip to Camp Wing in Duxbury. Boys in one cabin and girls in another. Scary stories, toasted marshmallows, and holding hands with the prettiest girl in the grade, Carolyn DeCoste! She was my first "girlfriend," though every time she and her friend Kristen rode their bikes through my neighborhood, I would climb a tree to avoid talking to them. Oh, I liked her; I was just too shy for my own good.

Yet, as cool as Camp Wing was, and as traumatic as falling into Hatch Pond was, they weren't my most significant elementary school memories. That honor belongs to Mrs. Blake, my fifth-grade English teacher, and her kind words during a parent-teacher conference with my dad. She told him I was a talented writer and should consider writing outside my required classwork. When Mrs. Blake shared their conversation with me the following day, I was instantly hooked on writing. I also wondered, *Why didn't my dad tell me?*

I'm not sure if it was because of her kindness and encouragement or something else, but writing, especially creative writing, *meant* something to me. Whether it was for my high school newspaper or just my personal journal, I was never happier than when I was attempting to transfer stories or poems in my head to paper. That summer, I subscribed to *Writer's Digest* and enrolled in a home-based writing course, though unfortunately, I didn't have the discipline to complete it.

If it weren't for Mrs. Blake, I never would have started journaling, which was the only way I knew how to process my emotions growing up. When things got hard for me in high school, I turned to my journal. Since I didn't feel like I could talk with my parents or siblings, my journal took the brunt of my venting. It gave me the chance to share my feelings and emotions, which I desperately needed to do, even if it was only on paper.

My experience at Cole—despite falling into the pond—was positive, happy, and fun. Many of my closest Norwell friends are Cole alums, including my oldest friend, Tony McLaughlin. Our dads coached youth hockey together, so we began skating around the same time. His early growth spurts put him on the basketball path instead of hockey, and he would go on to play college basketball.

Looking back, I can see that my teachers looked out for the Resnick boys. Perhaps they felt bad for us, but whatever the reason, they were kind and supportive. Some of my teachers I only knew briefly, like Mrs. Blake, and yet her comments to my dad launched a lifelong passion for writing.

Whenever I drive through Beers Ave today, which I do at least once a year, I am stunned by the smallness of it all—the homes, trees I used to climb, and my yard. When we weren't playing street hockey out front, we were playing football, capture-the-flag, or whiffle ball in the backyard. If you hit a ball deep to the fence on the opposite side, you were assured a home run. After all, a ball to the fence was a *bomb*!

Or was it?

I guess it was like the brownies I made in my Easy-Bake Oven—they seemed huge at the time, but were actually minuscule. Funny how that works: remembering your past one way, only to realize it was much different later in life.

Even the great Pork Chop Hill looks much smaller today.

Yet despite the smallness of Beers Ave and the surrounding streets, it's not lost on me that my first two life ambitions, baking and writing, are still with me today. Unlike my dad, I wanted to do the cooking in my household. It was a choice I was happy to make. Since my dad's Alzheimer's and COVID-19, these passions are stronger than ever.

I may never follow through on my dream to open that bakery, but as you can see, I have finally taken my writing passion to the next level.

PART TWO:

BUILDING CHARACTER

WORST PAPERBOY EVER

When I was twelve, my friend Jay got us jobs at Push Cart Farm in Hingham. Other than my paper route, it was my first real job. The commute from Beers Ave to the farm was a tad over two miles each way. Looking back, that seems like a long distance to travel for a summer job, especially on a secondhand, and often unreliable, used bike. That's just how it was, though. I didn't think much about the logistics or reality of biking to another town to pick vegetables in the ninety-degree heat. And neither did my dad.

I was already hot and tired from the bike ride most mornings, but it was vital to arrive on time. Being late meant less pay, since you had to wait for the truck to come back from the fields to get you, and you only got paid if you were working. Picking string beans, though monotonous, was my favorite. The farmers gave me a large bucket, assigned me a row, and then I picked beans for hours at a time. I never minded the task or the solitude that came with it. I was used to spending time alone.

Push Cart Farm was my first summer job, but I doubt another teenager in Norwell had more jobs than me. I spent two summers working at the farm before realizing I could get paid more for doing other jobs. Most of them involved sweating and dirty uniforms, whether bussing tables at the Ground Round, scooping ice cream, washing cars, landscaping, or house painting.

I worked in my local supermarket's bakery, which was tolerable, though anything but glamorous. For someone who wanted to own a bakery, you'd think this would have been a dream job. It wasn't. I never witnessed any baking. I worked nights, and most of the time I spent my shift in the oversized walk-in freezer, transferring frozen dough onto trays and then letting them sit overnight for the *real* baker to do her magic in the morning. I did manage to eat more than a reasonable amount of pastry and baked goods during my shifts, so it wasn't all that bad.

My first sales job was selling kitchen knives for Cutco, a direct-to-consumer cutlery company. The blades were American-made and guaranteed forever. All I had to do, they said, was let the knives do the work. The cutlery certainly did its part in my demonstrations, effortlessly slicing through fresh fruit, rope, and even copper pennies. I just sucked at my part: closing the sale. The successful kids were those with wealthy parents who had rich friends. They crushed it, while stiffs like me barely met their quota. I sold some knives, but only because my friends' parents felt obligated to buy at least one item from me. The set used in my presentations was still in the drawers of my dad's kitchen, thirty-plus years later.

The most challenging job in my youth was delivering *The Boston Globe*, which I did for more than three years. Although it earned me a $5,000 college scholarship, it was a miserable experience. Mornings were dark and quiet, winters were long and wet, and summers were hot and humid. I didn't like delivering newspapers, and I wasn't good at it. There were many days I didn't even finish my route because I was running late, and it was either finish my route or catch the bus to school.

I was the worst paperboy ever.

Need more proof? If I was subpar at delivering the papers, I was worse with the accounting aspect of the job. The paperboy also had to collect the money from his customers. I would make the rounds with my ledger, knock on every door, and collect the right amount of money each week. But I was always behind in my collections, which annoyed my customers, as they preferred to pay weekly rather than piling up debt. The labor of delivering papers was tolerable; the financial part was torture.

To qualify for the scholarship, you had to deliver the paper for three years, which was a long time. The scholarship helped reduce my college student loan total, so I was grateful, but let's be clear: *The Boston Globe* got their money's worth, as it was nearly impossible to keep paperboys longer than a year. Once the Christmas season ended and kids cashed in their holiday tips, it was time to move on. But not me. I was determined to earn that scholarship, no matter what I had to do.

I was a kid who wanted to work. I stumbled into the farm job because of my friend, but sought out the paper route myself. My dad strongly encouraged us to find jobs in high school, and required them while we were in college, but as a kid, there was no pressure or expectation to have a job. I fell in love with Saturday morning trips to the bank with my dad. I have no idea what sort of banking he was doing, but filling out the deposit slip and depositing $10, $15, or $20 into my account was so satisfying.

Today, when I pick tomatoes from my garden or shuck corn in the kitchen, I am often transported back to the farm. I see myself in the back of the dust-riddled and bouncy truck, eating raw corn in the middle of the fields, filling my bucket with green beans, stringing tomatoes (and cursing the stains left behind on my hands), and of course, enjoying payday.

The paper route was painful in every way imaginable, but the farm was almost fun. Yes, the bike ride sucked, especially when the chain would fall off my bike and I would arrive out of breath with grease-stained hands, but it sure did teach me the concept of grit and resilience.

CRUSHED

I might be the only person alive who loved middle school. While typically an awkward phase for most kids because of growth spurts, braces, hormones, shaving, school dances, dating, and general teenage attitudes, it wasn't for me. Not because I was special, but because I was clueless. I didn't have someone to discuss puberty and hormones, the importance of making good choices, or how to behave around girls. These conversations were nonexistent in our household.

Compared to my peers, I was generally unaware of fashion trends, rites of passage, or the appropriate social cues because I was on my own. You could say I lucked out in this regard, as it made these middle school years less stressful. I never overestimated the probability of bad things happening to me. Sure, I got upset if something didn't go my way, but I didn't take the outcomes to extremes. It bothered me but didn't paralyze me from continuing, whether with girls, hockey, or grades.

Bridget, one of the prettier popular girls, agreed to be my girlfriend, but she broke up with me because I was too shy. She dumped me right after I skipped the first school dance. I *wanted* to go, but I chickened out. I didn't know what to wear, how to dance, or how to kiss a girl.

During the day, I was hyper and happy, a joker and quasi class clown. I played sports at a high level with a fair amount of confidence. Yet with regard to girls, it was different. In my view, my clothes were crappy, my shoes were crappy, and my self-confidence was crappy.

Being afraid to kiss girls didn't prevent me from chasing after them, though. I was the guy who fell for girls who only wanted to be my friend. I wasn't the only one chasing the popular, pretty, and cool girls, but I seemed to be the only one who became their best friend instead of a boyfriend.

One particular seventh-grader had the biggest crush on me. Her name was Cindy, and she was cute in that awkward seventh-grade kind of way. Cindy was smart and funny, but I wasn't interested in dating her, mainly because I was busy chasing my crush. The irony was rich; *she* was chasing *me*, and *I* was chasing *someone else*. I used the "I like you, too, but as a friend" line, and the girl I had a crush on was using the same line on me!

A couple of years later, Cindy went from awkwardly cute to drop-dead gorgeous. And believe it or not, I was then the one chasing her. Only this time around, it was her turn to use the "friendship" line.

The eighth grade dance was a big deal at Norwell Junior High. After spending the last year and a half chasing the wrong girls, I finally found the right one. Her name was Anne. We knew each other but weren't friends, so I never imagined we would go to the dance together. That was the beauty of our relationship from the beginning.

The courtship began with a few timid phone calls during the week, smiles in the hallway, a locker visit here and there before school started, and, occasionally, a shared lunch in the school cafeteria. But once we got to know each other, we became very close—so close that I didn't stop loving her until my senior year of high school, even though we stopped dating in tenth grade.

It wasn't puppy love; it was puppy love on steroids—my first big crush. I loved the way her hair smelled, the way she smiled back at me, her large brown eyes, curly hair, and her handwritten notes. She came to my hockey games, which only made me fall for her even more. The eighth grade dance was the icing on the cake, the perfect end to middle school.

There's a difference between your first love and true love, and my feelings for Anne were the former. Yet the relationship satisfied me emotionally in ways that were sorely missing at home. Don't get me wrong, I know my parents loved me—they just didn't express that love effectively. My dad wasn't able to express his love through feelings or verbal communication. My mom simply wasn't present enough to give me what I needed.

It was hard to let go of my feelings for Anne because I was afraid I would never experience them again. It was naïve to think this way, but can you blame me?

My relationship with Anne was only part of the reason why I loved junior high so much. The main reason was because it was the last time I went to school with my Norwell friends. The town didn't have a high school hockey team, so attending Norwell High wasn't an option.

Going to a different school wasn't a big deal, but leaving my friends behind was. From elementary to middle school, I went to my friends first—for everything. Even their parents were like second parents to me. I was just a teenager, oblivious to my surroundings, but I received a different kind of love from the other adults in my life. They always had my back, perhaps knowing, somehow, that I needed their support to keep moving forward—either that, or their own parenting instincts knew that I wasn't getting the full range of emotional support at home.

ON MY OWN

My transition from public middle school to Catholic high school was smooth, and my first year at Xaverian exceeded expectations on every level but one: the one-hour commute to Xaverian, each way. While some kids struggled to adjust to a new and larger school, especially one with all boys, I had no trouble. I was used to figuring things out on my own, and although this didn't mean I was immune to anxiety or stress, it was just a smaller dose for me.

Unlike the prior two years at Norwell Junior High, I worked hard at Xaverian. The absence of girls minimized distractions and improved my focus in the classroom. But the main reason I worked so hard was because of my dad's sacrifice to send me there. Private school tuition wasn't as out of control as it is now, but it was still a large expense for our family. My older brother attended Norwell High, so I was the first to attend a school with tuition attached to it. I realized even then how lucky I was to have that opportunity, and there was no way I was going to let my dad down.

That first summer back home with my old Norwell friends was a blast, so returning to campus for my sophomore year was harder than I thought it would be. Instead of being excited for varsity soccer tryouts,

I watched them from the sidelines due to a back injury. It was my first time experiencing back strain, and it frustrated me. To the coach's credit, he offered me a chance to try out with the team after they cleared me to play, but I inexplicably declined and opted to play another year for the JV team.

It wasn't a wrong decision, but I wasn't proud of it, either. I took the easy route for the first time in my life, and I couldn't explain why.

I liked soccer and was a good player, but my true passion was ice hockey. I had an excellent chance of making the varsity team, which was difficult for sophomores in the vaunted Catholic Conference. But as fate would have it, I was unable to try out for that team either.

Immediately after the soccer season ended, I became ill with intense stomach pain and fatigue. I tried to settle my stomach with tea and crackers in the morning, but my appetite was nonexistent. I tried not to show that I was in pain, and even as my symptoms intensified, I remained silent. I did what was familiar to me—I dealt with it alone.

My initial concern about my stomach wasn't the pain I experienced; it was whether or not it would stop me from playing hockey. My youth hockey team, the South Shore Seahawks, was scheduled to play in Lake Placid, New York, over Thanksgiving weekend. My dad was the coach, and although we had been there before, there was no better hockey experience for a kid than Lake Placid. Just being in the same locker rooms as Mike Eruzione, Jack O'Callaghan, and Jim Craig was enough to give you goosebumps, but when you step on the ice and skate those warmup laps, it's downright electric!

———

Unfortunately, I would not be making the trip to Lake Placid. A few days before school broke for the holiday, I was in the Xaverian bathroom, and my urine was red. Not slightly pink, but a deep shade of red. Something was indeed wrong. I tried to stay calm but knew I had to tell my dad.

We went to our primary care doctor in Pembroke the next day and had my blood tested. When the results came back, they were shocked. Well, the doctor was. The test showed I had Hepatitis C, which he explained was typically transmitted through sexual intercourse or drug use. My dad didn't have much of a reaction. Whether he was just as confused as I was about the severity of Hepatitis or didn't know how to react, I'm not sure.

"It's okay, Mark, you can tell us if you have used drugs or are sexually active," the doctor said.

The doctor kept urging me to come clean with some sort of admission, but there was nothing to admit, for I had neither used drugs nor had sex before. Finally, after much consternation, it was assumed I contracted the disease from working that summer at our local nursing home. I was a janitor and probably made contact with a dirty needle while taking out the trash, which I did every day.

Missing the hockey trip was disappointing, but not trying out for the varsity team was almost unbearable. It took five additional weeks of rest before they cleared me to go back to school and hockey. Although I missed tryouts, the coaches were keen on having me play varsity at some point during the season. They decided I would skate with the freshman team, then JV, and eventually work my way up to varsity.

After a week of practice with the freshman team, I was ready for my first game. I scored a goal, and we won. The next game, however, was a much different result. We were playing our biggest rival, BC High. Halfway through the second period, I collided with one of their players and broke my right wrist. It wasn't a brutal hit, but my body had not fully recovered from the illness.

My season ended with a trip to the emergency room to set my right wrist.

It was also the end of my relationship with my girlfriend Anne. Less than twenty-four hours after my wrist broke, she came to visit me at my house. My wrist throbbed, and I couldn't get comfortable in any position. When I heard that she was coming to see me, I pushed the pain aside and sat up in my bed. I was excited to see her! Unfortunately, she wasn't there just to check on me; she was there to break up with me. I was devastated.

Writing about it sounds so sophomoric, but the pain was real, both physically and emotionally. I couldn't let go of her—giving up on us wasn't an option. There was always a chance we might get back together, *wasn't there?* After the breakup, we remained best friends, which made it even harder to let go.

Nothing went right my sophomore year. It was one major disappointment after another. I was in and out of school with injury, illness, and injury again.

I missed the Xaverian hockey season, but my youth hockey team qualified for the state tournament in March. We ended up in the championship game. It was the first state tournament final for my dad and me, but I was on the bench with a cast on, helplessly watching.

We lost the game to a stubborn South Boston team, 4 to 2. More heartache.

Unlike my feelings for my ex-girlfriend, the wrist healed—but it would break again in another game shortly after they cleared me to resume playing. This time my dad and I were at the Quincy hockey rink. I had just come off the ice after a long shift, but my replacement didn't jump on. Nobody did. So I hopped back onto the ice for a double shift.

The shift ended with another broken wrist.

On the drive to South Shore Hospital, with half my hockey equipment still on, I was angry. I was swearing at everyone and nobody.

"I hate hockey—I quit!"

"Mark, calm down," my dad finally managed to say after listening to me curse and spit for nearly ten minutes.

If there was ever a time in my life that I needed a mom nearby to console me, to make me feel better, to listen to my bitching—it was now. Dad was with me in the room when my wrist was set, but he wasn't holding my hand or reassuring me that everything would be fine. He wasn't that person. It's not that he didn't care or feel bad for me, but expressing or communicating empathy wasn't his strength and never had been.

At least this time, the doctor couldn't trick me when resetting the wrist. When he started his count, "One, two," I knew what was coming before "three" would arrive—*crack, scream, throb, tears.*

The year was a disaster, and I was desperate for some emotional support.

BEST YEAR EVER

That support never came, yet surprisingly, my sophomore year at Xaverian ended up being the best year of my life.

In the spring of 1988, with a cast still on my wrist from the second break, I applied for a scholarship to the Hugh O'Brian Youth Leadership Conference, or HOBY for short. Each year HOBY invites high schools in the United States to select a student to attend a state HOBY Leadership Seminar. The committee looks for sophomores who demonstrate outstanding leadership potential and other vital skills, including written and verbal communication, problem-solving, and my favorite, "having the courage to challenge authority."

I competed against five classmates for the scholarship. There was a written application, followed by an interview with a faculty committee. Their decision took a week, and despite my struggles that year, I held out hope that they would select me. I don't recall what I wrote, but I do remember Mr. Dalton, the chairperson of the HOBY committee, explaining why they chose me.

"All of you have the characteristics needed to qualify for the program, but we're choosing you, Mark, because we feel you have the most potential as a leader and would benefit the most from the HOBY program."

———

To hundreds of thousands of students, Hugh O'Brian was the founder of HOBY. To millions of adults, he was a television and movie star. In the summer of 1958, at the peak of his career as the lead in ABC's television series, *The Life and Legend of Wyatt Earp*, Mr. O'Brian visited Dr. Albert Schweitzer's famed medical mission in Africa. He spent nine days volunteering at the hospital, and the experience changed his life. Mr. O'Brian and Dr. Schweitzer, a 1952 Nobel Peace Prize recipient, talked about education, volunteerism, and leadership.

On his flight back to the United States, Mr. O'Brian couldn't stop thinking about his trip and Dr. Schweitzer's statement regarding education, in which he said, "*The most important part of education is teaching young people to think for themselves.*"

Soon after returning to the States, Mr. O'Brian created the Hugh O'Brian Youth Leadership organization, which was founded "to inspire and develop our global community of youth and volunteers to a life dedicated to leadership, service, and innovation."

Almost 500,000 high school sophomores have attended a HOBY conference, and I am proud to be one of them.

Granted, I was only fifteen years old, but the months leading up to the HOBY scholarship were the lowest points of my life so far. My sophomore year was emotionally, physically, and mentally draining. That is, until the HOBY decision. All of a sudden, the previous ten months seemed irrelevant. And while I had no idea what to expect that June at Boston College, the site of the 11th Annual Hugh O'Brian Youth Leadership Seminar, I can tell you that the experience changed my life forever.

Alongside hundreds of total strangers from across the state of Massachusetts, I spent four days at my HOBY conference at Boston College. I was equally nervous and excited about the conference because I was trying to figure out who I was—and who I wanted to be. I knew I was passionate about sports, but there had always been a part of me that wanted to excel off the ice, too.

Whatever I was searching for at HOBY—I found it. With ice breakers galore, group chants and competitions, and serious out-of-your-comfort-zone and on-the-spot speaking roles, the conference ignited something fierce within me. Over four days, I bonded, shared passions and interests with new friends, and listened to intriguing and successful leaders from Boston and beyond. But more than developing us as leaders, the HOBY team challenged us to serve our communities and the world around us.

I returned from HOBY energized, motivated, optimistic, and confident. The experience wasn't just a springboard for volunteerism within my community; it inspired me to serve others for the remainder of my life. By the time my junior year started at Xaverian, I was a changed young man.

⌣⸍ ⌣⸍ ⌣⸍

Hockey remained the most important part of my life, but after HOBY, it had serious competition during my final two years at Xaverian. I became a tour guide for Admissions, started writing for the newspaper, ran for student government vice president, and started volunteering at soup kitchens. In the spring of my junior year, I stepped up my game with six other classmates by volunteering to serve the homeless in Boston. The program was called Xaverian Community Experiences Life, or XCEL.

Neither my dad nor my friends understood why I wanted to be part of this program. Some of my classmates mocked me. Only my teachers praised my decision and encouraged me to enjoy the experience. It was anything but enjoyable, but I know what they meant.

Working at a soup kitchen in the suburbs was nothing like serving the homeless in Boston. I found this out firsthand when I lived at Haley House in Boston for five nights. Haley House staffed a live-in community of volunteers committed to living and working at their soup kitchen, usually for six months to a year. My classmates and I stayed with them above the kitchen and worked alongside them each day and night.

Every day was intense. And scary. On the second-to-last day of our program, my classmates and I were intentionally separated in downtown Boston. Our group leaders gave us each $1 *for lunch* and told us to meet back at the Boston Public Library two hours later. Then we were on our own.

I wandered for thirty minutes. I didn't know the streets of Boston well, so everywhere I went was unfamiliar. I remember sitting in the sun outside the Christian Science Monitor building. People walked by and stared at me or avoided making eye contact altogether. It was my fourth day in Boston, wearing the same clothes and beat-up sneakers. Toothbrushes and showers were not allowed (though deodorant was), so you can imagine how I looked.

I don't believe I've ever felt as lonely and isolated as I did that day. I was hungry, cold, and tired from all the walking. I wanted to ask these

strangers in their nice suits and skirts for money to eat but couldn't—
just another dollar for a candy bar and bottle of water?

By the time I left that part of Boston, I was disgusted by the looks
of shame I received, but continued walking, through affluent parts and
poor. I thought the two hours would go by quickly, but they didn't. It
was like time didn't exist. I began to notice things about the city that I
never had before, like the many narrow alleys on side streets, sometimes
with people tucked away in eves, sleeping, or covered in cardboard or
sleeping bags. The city was jammed with white-collar workers bustling
to and fro, oblivious to the underserved and abandoned homeless pop-
ulation.

I never did manage to spend that dollar.

On the last night of our stay, our group leaders woke us up at 4 a.m.
for a surprise morning walk. They told us to pack our possessions—basically a sleeping bag, jacket, and notebook—and then we left Haley
House in the dark. It was April, which meant it was cold.

We had no idea what was happening but began walking the streets of
Boston. To Copley Plaza, through Boston Common, into the Combat
Zone, to City Hospital, then to the Pine Street Inn, a homeless shel-
ter. It was eerily calm, quiet, and peaceful. We passed homeless men and
women in the shadows, and Rick (the adult volunteer with me) nodded
silently to them.

When we arrived at the Inn, one of the adult staff members spotted
me from across the room. She rushed over, pulled me aside, and started asking me questions. Rick was nowhere to be found. Her rapid-fire
questions seemed to stretch for minutes but were over in ten seconds.

———

"What are you doing here? Why are you on the streets? Do you have any family that can help you? How old are you?"

Before I could say a word, Rick finally showed up and steered her away from me. To explain the situation, I presumed.

I couldn't wait to get back to safety at Haley House.

When I returned from XCEL, I found it difficult to process what I had witnessed: the people I met, emotions I battled, and lessons learned. More than thirty years later, I can still vividly recall the experience.

I recently received Pine Street Inn's annual fundraising appeal letter.

Dear Mr. Resnick,

Imagine how it would feel to be homeless on a dark city street tonight . . . cold, hungry, and alone.

I don't have to imagine it because I saw it, albeit only briefly. Each time I pass a person holding a sign begging for money, I am emotionally torn. I want to unload the change or cash from my pockets but also feel my contribution is better served by donating directly to organizations like the Pine Street Inn.

The raw emotions generated from witnessing the homeless, both past and present, serves as a not-so-gentle reminder to give more—whether that be time or money—whenever possible.

At its core, HOBY's goal is to develop leadership potential. They did this by engaging us with community leaders, whether political, civic, corporate, educational, or artistic. It was basically a four-day TED Talk conference before that was such a thing.

Politics became an early passion of mine right after middle school, between reading the headlines of *The Boston Globe* on my paper route, following Tip O'Neill in his role as Speaker of the House of Representatives, and listening to talk radio while driving home from Xaverian with my dad. The dream of running for office one day was fueled by HOBY, which led to my desire to attend a different kind of conference called Close Up. According to its website, its mission was:

> *. . . built on the idea that young people from all backgrounds need a better understanding of the democratic process and their responsibility as citizens. The concept was simple: give students the opportunity to directly engage with the people, organizations, and institutions that represent our democracy, and they will develop the skills and attitudes they need for a lifetime of active citizenship. ("Close Up Foundation," closeup.org)*

It was a weeklong trip, yet unlike HOBY, this one had a cost associated with it. Xaverian provided partial scholarships to interested students, but my dad had to come up with the rest.

My younger brother John was now also at Xaverian, so with two tuitions to cover, plus ongoing hockey costs, this was an unexpected expense for my dad. But we made a deal: he would cover the balance of the trip and I would pay him back over the summer through one of my many jobs. I was off to the nation's capital for another larger-than-life experience.

It was my first time in Washington, D.C., and I absorbed it all. The history, power, influence, monuments, museums, and institutions that define our system of government and identity as a nation. I engaged in deep discussions with students from around the country, debated pressing issues through a Mock Congress event, sat in Congressional committee meetings, listened to the House of Representatives discuss an active bill that was up for debate, and met with ambassadors, lobbyists, and staffers from all three branches of government.

I was hooked—and began dreaming of my return as a United States Congressman.

Ironically, my first "run" for office, for junior class vice president, was underway when I was on the trip. My opponent was Jamie M., an outgoing personality and member of the football team. Both of us were allowed to put up signs around the school but only had one "debate," which consisted of a speech to our classmates in the auditorium.

In my defense, the day we were scheduled to make our speeches, I was in Washington, D.C. Unable to speak in person, my only choice was to record a message for my classmates. Jamie was riling up my peers in the auditorium, and I was in the Gallery, listening to members of the United States Congress rile up their peers. While Jamie promised free lunches on Fridays, I witnessed the inner workings of our government *up close*.

It would be the only election I would lose from that day forward.

So much changed in this time of my life—from missing out on Lake Placid and varsity hockey tryouts to receiving a recruitment letter from Notre Dame's hockey coach. From two trips to the emergency room to set my broken wrists to HOBY and Close Up. From being served fruit while sleeping half the day during my hepatitis illness to serving homeless men and women in Boston. From getting dumped to, well, still being dumped! You can't win them all!

It was an incredible turnaround—mentally, physically, and spiritually.

Throughout this part of my journey, a few things remained constant. My Norwell friends and I grew closer, as we anticipated our senior years of high school and the coveted perks that came along with it. Parties on Beers Ave picked up momentum as well. Hanging out at my house, Solo cups in hand, was a sanctuary of sorts from the everyday routines of our lives. Nobody was a jock or nerd or performer or stoner—it was just a bunch of kids having fun.

Yet, despite the positive turnaround in my life, there was still sadness—loneliness even. When the house was empty or late at night when I was grinding out a paper because I had procrastinated to no end, I felt it creeping toward me, lurking in the shadows of my room. It was difficult to push aside at times, and to be honest, I didn't always understand why it was there either.

Sure, the prior year was dramatic and challenging, but hadn't I successfully overcome those challenges? Wasn't my life moving in the right direction?

Moving at full speed on so many levels kept me from thinking about *why* I felt the sadness and loneliness, but it was the sudden and stark realization that I was on my own that made me recognize it during those alone times. Nobody I knew attended HOBY or Close Up. Only five other kids were with me at Haley House in Boston. My dad allowed me to participate in these programs (not that he had much choice), but we didn't talk about them—ever.

If I needed something from my teachers, coaches, friends, or my dad, I would get whatever it is that I needed. Except for emotional support. I was very much on my own in that regard.

GOODBYE, MY FRIEND

As much as I loved growing up with my dad and brothers on Beers Ave, I now recognize that I experienced a loneliness and emptiness that remains within me to this day. My dad was going in many directions, and so were we, between time spent in hockey rinks, friend's houses, commuting to Xaverian, summer jobs, working out, and more. There were some traumatic moments I had to experience by myself that went far beyond my rough sophomore year.

The most challenging part of high school occurred during my senior year when three people within my circle committed suicide. One was a classmate and former hockey teammate; another was a Xaverian teacher; and the third was my former best friend, Marty Delaney.

I wasn't close with Marty when he died, but we were once the closest of friends. We drifted apart in high school when he moved to Pembroke and I attended Xaverian. Of course, I regretted not keeping in touch with him, but without cell phones and social media, it was hard to stay connected. I was in the Norwell Public Library researching a paper when a friend from elementary school told me about Marty's suicide. I was in shock, which turned to anger, which morphed into depression.

I cried for what seemed like weeks. My outward appearance looked fine, but inside, I was devastated. It was the loneliest and saddest point in my life. I didn't have anybody with whom to talk or cry. My guidance counselor at school tried to get me to open up, but I just couldn't. Not with him. Not with anyone.

I questioned whether or not Marty would still be alive had we stayed friends.

I wish I had one person I could rely on, someone to lean on and get me through the ordeal. I never considered asking for help. It just wasn't an option that entered my mind. When things happened on Beers Ave, we figured them out by ourselves. We were alone, left confined to our bedroom that was no larger than a college dorm room—or prison cell. At least that's how it felt when things were hard to handle.

Dealing with Marty's suicide led to depression. I never had thoughts of hurting myself, just sadness, fatigue, and despondency. I lost interest in eating, playing hockey, school, and hanging with my friends. It didn't last longer than a few months, but it lasted long enough for me to remember, to this day, what depression feels like.

Neither of my parents recognized my depression. Perhaps I never allowed them to see it? More likely, they just didn't notice my mood swings, lack of energy and focus, or outright withdrawal during those few months. I mean, Mom wasn't around enough, and I certainly didn't reach out to her. It never crossed my mind to seek her counsel.

I remember telling my dad that Marty passed away, but I don't remember his reaction. He didn't attend the wake or funeral. Either way, there was no outward emotional response or level of support. That just wasn't who he was—or would ever be.

———

Thank God I had my journal.

It wasn't my father or family who were baking cakes and singing Happy Birthday to me while in high school; it was my friends. I was on my own for many important markers or milestones while living on Beers Ave. I signed myself up for driver's education and SAT prep courses and was responsible for most of my transportation to high school hockey games and practices. When it was time to apply to college, I managed the process myself—my initial list of schools to consider extended from Maine to San Diego.

I took a Greyhound bus to visit my brother Bill, who attended North Adams State College. The bus stopped in Williamstown first, and I scheduled a tour of Williams College. It was my top choice, and nothing was going to stop me from applying there. My mom met us there a couple of days later, and when we went back to Williams, I gave her a self-guided tour of the campus. I was eager to show her the sleeping bunks located inside the library. I thought those were the coolest things ever.

After the breakup with Anne, I deliberately avoided dating girls for the rest of my high school years. I maintained my feelings for her with the hopes that I would win her back, even though it was ridiculous. I put her on a pedestal; she could do no wrong. Even though she dated another guy in high school, we remained close friends. She continued to go to my hockey games, and we talked on the phone and hung out. I liked other girls along the way, fluctuating between a new one each month, but always pushed my potential feelings aside because I only wanted to be with Anne.

It was an unhealthy state of mind for a teenager, but by the time I was a senior in high school, I had lived with my dad and two brothers for nearly eleven years. When my mom stopped coming to Norwell on weekends, she was essentially out of our lives. Yes, we saw her on holidays and sporadically during the year, but she was not present enough to provide support to us—especially not emotional support. There were no women's products, clothing, or conversations about women within the house. Absent any maternal influence whatsoever, I clung to every feel-good emotion my relationship with Anne provided, no matter how unhealthy or one-sided it was.

We were not a family who shared feelings, and our communication was limited in its volume and substance. Most weekday nights it was John, my dad, and me eating dinner together; Bill was hardly home. He was either working at Kentucky Fried Chicken or—I'm not exactly sure where he was. I mainly saw Bill on Friday nights, when he decided to have people over for a late-night party, knowing my dad would be home within an hour or two.

I'm pretty sure Bill did this with the intention of getting caught, as he seemed to be looking for my dad's attention, even if it was in a negative way. Besides throwing parties, Bill hung out with some guys who always seemed to find themselves in trouble, or at least they relished crossing lines. Unfortunately, Bill wasn't going to get what he wanted. Even though my dad had to have known that a party had recently happened, he never said a word to Bill.

———

It wasn't his way—and never would be.

There was only one thing that would change how I felt about Anne: finding someone else.

It wasn't that girls were lining up to date me, or that I had some ultra ego, but once I opened myself up to the possibility of finding someone else, I did. She was right in front of me the entire time, and I never noticed.

I was at her friend Jessica's house, sitting in her living room, surrounded by a handful of girls. Just girls—I was the only guy there, which wasn't unusual when I was with this particular group of friends. It was no secret that I had spent the last two years trying to get Anne back. It seemed like the whole town of Norwell knew. Yet on that night, I somehow let it slip to one of them—Jessica, I believe—that I was starting to like someone else.

It was big news, and she immediately wanted to know who it was. I hesitated and tried to change the subject but had no such luck. I was reluctant to share the news because the person of my affection was in the room, which would have created a very awkward moment for the two of us. I had no clue if this person liked me, or could like me. I never bothered to find out—I just knew that I was starting to like her as more than a friend.

When I told Jessica (*what, you didn't really believe I could hold something like this back, did you?*) I thought she was going to slap me. I think she assumed I was playing a practical joke on her, as her reaction seemed to ignite the house on fire. I wasn't sure what to do next. I wasn't driving that night, so it's not like I could just leave. Nope, I had to face this head-on.

To my immense relief, Eleanor, the person I was falling for, did indeed have similar feelings toward me as well. She drove me home that night, and we had the chance to talk about our feelings. Then we kissed for the first time in my driveway on Beers Ave.

Eleanor was the nicest person I had ever met. For real. Friends with *everyone*, she lent her ear to whomever needed it, went out of her way to make people smile and laugh, was voted the most likely to succeed, and lit up a room with her smile. It was impossible not to like her.

If there was a consistent pattern to how I lived my life to this point, it was act, *then* think. In a few months, both of us were headed to different colleges, so why would either one of us want to begin a new relationship? The timing wasn't ideal, but we made the most of our time together, going to the beach, movies, parties, or just hanging out. It was the first serious dating relationship for both of us, and it felt good to be the ones doing couple things rather than listening to our friends talk about them.

We dated for a little more than two years, but ultimately, our relationship would not survive the time and distance away from one another. Years ago, I came across this quote by Dr. Miriam Kirmayer, a well-known clinical psychologist and relationship expert: "People come into our lives for a reason or season." I believe Eleanor came into my life for a reason. She helped me realize that I was deserving of love—and capable of loving someone back.

It was Eleanor, not my parents, siblings, or friends, who listened to my hopes and dreams for college and beyond. For the first time in my life, I could envision myself getting married. Not necessarily to Eleanor, but until we met, I had every intention of avoiding marriage. I never wanted to think about marrying a person because I didn't want there to be a chance it would not work out—and there was no way in hell I was going to do what my parents did to me.

After I spent two years of high school chasing someone who didn't make me feel loved, I was with someone who *only* made me feel loved. She taught me how to play tennis, went to my hockey games, helped me shop for new clothes—all of which made me a more confident person, both with girls and my life as a whole.

My dad liked her right away.

If it wasn't for Eleanor's kindness and compassion, I'm not sure how long it would have taken me to love someone —which is why it was deeply unsettling for me in college, not *wanting* to let go of my relationship with Eleanor, but *wanting* to be with another girl simultaneously. That happened during my junior year at Fairfield University, when I fell in love with my best friend.

BLINDED BY FEAR

My high school grades were good but not spectacular enough to apply to elite colleges. Yet I did anyway. Williams, Colby, and Hamilton were my top three choices, followed by Holy Cross and Connecticut College. Fairfield University was one of my safety schools. Although I knew I didn't have the grades or SAT scores to secure acceptance to my top schools, I held out hope that a hockey coach was going to pull some strings on my behalf.

That never materialized, and one rejection after another arrived in the mail to Beers Ave.

I applied to Fairfield sight unseen. The brochures highlighted its magnificent campus, and several teachers encouraged me to consider it. I'm glad they did. Not only did the oversized acceptance letter arrive in the mail, but along with it came a generous scholarship offer. I also knew that Fairfield's hockey coach, Doc McCarthy, had attended a few of my Xaverian games and seemed intent on getting me to play there.

People love to say that things happen for a reason, that things are either meant to be or not meant to be. It's hard to argue with this logic, so I won't; everything worked out better than I could have imagined when I enrolled at Fairfield. On my very first day, moments after moving into my dorm room, Coach McCarthy found me and gave me my new schedule.

"I got you out of Professor Petri's history class. He's a tough son of a bitch. Here's a copy of your new schedule," he said.

"Thanks, Doc," I replied with a massive grin on my face.

I *loved* my time at Fairfield University. I studied politics and English, the two subjects for which I was most passionate. In total, I took more than twenty-two courses between the two majors, with professors who had written novels and ran for political office. I became a better writer and more interested in pursuing a legal career and running for office one day.

In my first year on the hockey team, I was able to work my way up to the top line, which boosted my confidence to a whole new level. Academically, I suffered the usual first-semester lapse, but it wasn't because of excess partying. Adjusting to the schedule and rigor of college athletics took some time. Because Fairfield didn't have a rink on campus, we played twenty minutes away in Bridgeport. Practice start times ranged from 8 to 10 p.m. and lasted up to two hours. My senior year, we went the opposite route and were on the ice by 6:30 a.m. It was a grind.

I played hockey all four years but took advantage of other opportunities, too. My roommate and I had a radio show one year on the college's AM station, I played intramural soccer, I participated in community service, and I had campus jobs each year. Outside of hockey and the classroom, I spent most of my free time as a member of the Fairfield University Student Association (FUSA), the governing body responsible for the majority of campus programming and policy changes. I would eventually be elected to serve as its president my senior year. It was my proudest accomplishment and most valuable experience at Fairfield.

The most important Fairfield event, however, was meeting my future wife, Coleen Campbell.

Coleen was from Long Island, though you would not know it. She had no accent and, equally as important, no passionate allegiance to any of New York's professional sports teams. That was an unexpected bonus. Her ever-present and enormous smile, easy-going demeanor, and quick wit were more than enough for me to take notice of her when we met during the last week of freshman year.

We spent our sophomore year as best friends, eating, studying, and hanging out, but we wouldn't begin dating until October the following year. From then on, we were inseparable. We became more involved with FUSA together, and I was appointed to head their Student Entertainment Committee, which was responsible for planning concerts on campus. I booked an up-and-coming band called the Spin Doctors, and we sold out within four hours. It was the first time in years that FUSA had a sold-out concert.

I hadn't planned on running for FUSA president, but my predecessor, Steve Shannon, encouraged me to do so after the success of our concert. Playing on the hockey team gave me some name recognition, and of course, I took advantage of my nickname, Rez, by blasting the campus with "Rez for Prez" signs and stickers. I also had a brilliant campaign manager.

We won the election. I'm pretty sure it was our "Rez for Prez" slogan that secured the victory.

———

The position allowed me to work on behalf of 3,000 undergrad students and directly with university vice presidents, faculty and staff, trustees, and alumni. It was a prestigious role on campus but required enormous time, energy, and commitment.

I poured every moment of my free time into the job. Outside of the rink or classroom, I was in the FUSA office. Our team spent thousands of hours planning and running events, revamping academic policies, expanding cultural and diversity programming, and increasing attendance at athletic games. We put up and took down more than 10,000 chairs, posted thousands of flyers, and attended events almost every night of the week. FUSA was a full-time job for me.

My biggest accomplishment was successfully lobbying the Board of Trustees to build a new on-campus pub and coffeehouse called The Levee. The 3,500-square-foot facility was to be the centerpiece for student gatherings, while at the same time offering an alternative to the local bar scene. Unanimously supported by students and approved by the Board of Trustees in March of my senior year, The Levee became the largest student-led initiative in Fairfield's history.

I say *my* accomplishment merely because it was under my direction, and I played a crucial role in making it happen. But I must give proper credit and gratitude to my two amazing co-chairs, Alycen (my campaign manager) and Karen (who was only a freshman at the time). They worked tirelessly to complete the research, survey our students, and write the report. It was a team effort, but they deserve equal, if not *more*, credit for bringing the project to reality. There is simply no way this project would have become a reality without them, and I am beyond grateful for their dedication and commitment.

The Levee has gone through multiple iterations since it opened in the fall of 1995, though it is still used for smaller student events, and continues to serve beer, wine, and food. My daughter, Erin, eats there once a week—and I'm pretty sure she has told her friends that I played a role in its creation. One of these days, I'm going to petition the school to buy it back. In my view, it was never given a chance to be what it was intended to be—a premier hangout that offered an atmosphere unlike any other space on campus. For the students, run by students, with options for drinkers and non-drinkers alike. The potential is there!

I used to tell my family that being FUSA president was like being the CEO of a small business and that I learned more during that one year than I did in four years of classroom work. This wasn't a slight on my professors, though, as without their support, I would not have succeeded. Most of them were tuned into campus life and were quick to offer support and encouragement. And I needed it.

Despite our successes, there were setbacks, too. There were times I struggled mightily, especially to lead with confidence, delegate effectively, ask for help, and accept criticism. It was the first time I was the subject of targeted criticism, and it was not easy to look past it at times.

I remember a classmate of mine, who wrote for the school newspaper, taking my words out of context for a story he wrote. It was a few days after a laser-light-music show we booked at the Regina A. Quick Center for the Arts. Attendance was lighter than usual, and when asked about it, I said something like, "I don't care if 50 or 5,000 people show up, our role is to provide a wide variety of programming for Fairfield students." Instead, he wrote, "Resnick admitted he didn't care [that nobody attended]." I was careful with my words after that embarrassing (yet misconstrued) statement.

Of course, working closely with the *actual* president of Fairfield, Fr. Aloysius P. Kelley, S.J., is also something I treasure today. I always looked forward to our meetings in his magnificent office in Bellarmine Hall. Without fail, our twenty-minute allotted time extended to an hour and usually longer. Beyond discussing the inner workings of the University, local community, and student issues, Fr. Kelley was an incredible listener, a skill I would come to depend on when taking care of my dad.

Sometimes Fr. Kelley would randomly stop by my office in the basement of the Campus Center, usually around dinnertime when most people were eating or studying. I also enjoyed regular dinners at his home, both as a student and alumnus. Fr. Kelley would ultimately preside over my marriage to Coleen and baptize our three children: Campbell, Erin, and Sean. We remain in touch today, and I am grateful for everything he did for me during *and* after my time at Fairfield University.

My daughter, Erin, is currently a freshman at Fairfield, and I joke with her that she could become the first legacy FUSA president. She rolls her eyes at me, but I secretly think she digs the idea.

⌣ ⌣ ⌣

My FUSA experience was extraordinary. I always believed it was an essential part of my college experience. But it wasn't the most impactful one. That belongs to my mission volunteer trip to Jamaica. It was yet another life-altering experience and one on which I would come to rely when taking care of my dad.

Fairfield's mission volunteer program included trips to Ecuador, Haiti, or Jamaica. After a thorough vetting process, I was chosen to attend the Jamaica trip with nine other students. None of us stayed together during the trip; each of my classmates was assigned a host family. I stayed with the Anderson family just outside the Kingston city limits in what would be called a "lower middle class" home. Marlon Anderson was a year older than me and was my guide for the duration of the trip, which meant he escorted me everywhere I went, primarily for safety reasons.

My friend Jeff and I were assigned to work at Mother Teresa's Home for the Dying in downtown Kingston. It was more or less hospice care for homeless men and women. Within five minutes of our arrival at the home (the sisters didn't waste any time with their recruits), Jeff and I met Mr. Davis. He was picked up a few hours earlier from the streets of Kingston. The nuns told us to cut his long, dirty, matted dreadlocks, then strip him naked, bathe him, and dress him.

I can feel the raw emotion, uncertainty, and outright fear every time I think about our first encounter with Mr. Davis. The grime on his body, the matted dreadlocks, body odor, and those eyes—those dark, empty eyes. They haunted me far worse than the poverty I witnessed on the bus ride to the nursing home, the sewage lining the street, the burning trash, and rodents scurrying along sidewalks. The daily sights to and from the Home for the Dying were also far more jarring than anything I witnessed while serving the homeless in Boston. I never imagined I would see poverty and suffering like I did on this trip.

Mr. Davis was blind, but I am sure he could feel the tension and terror in our hearts. For the first time in my life, I was truly rattled and could not take the first steps in complying with the sisters' requests. And I didn't.

It was Jeff who acted first. He said something to me that would forever be tattooed in my mind: "What if this was our fathers who needed our help? Just think of them as we do this, and we'll get through this."

We spent ten days at the Home for the Dying in Kingston, and although we had many responsibilities, Jeff and I made sure to spend time with Mr. Davis each day. His features softened after a few days, and occasionally we would get a smile or slight grin, but very few words came out of his mouth.

It didn't matter that we didn't get any praise from the sisters during our time there, or even a thank you from Mr. Davis. Seeing Mr. Davis cleaned up and properly cared for was the only reward we needed. Instead of dying alone on the streets of Kingston, he now had a home in which to rest without fear. He was fed, bathed, and sleeping on a mattress.

I should have thanked Mr. Davis, not the other way around, for he gave me the strength, courage, and grace required to take care of my dad when he was most vulnerable as well. The circumstances with which Mr. Davis and my father found themselves were vastly different—but without question, the fortitude required to help them was not.

Jeff and I don't mention Mr. Davis when we get together nowadays, but he's with us just the same. I am eternally grateful to Jeff for his courage, strength, and wisdom during our time in Jamaica.

———

In hindsight, it's hard for me to believe it was a coincidence that I was chosen to work at this specific location nearly thirty years ago. You might be thinking there is no way that my time with Mr. Davis in Jamaica could be connected to taking care of my dad during his greatest time of need, but each time I had to help my dad undress and shower, shave his beard, clip his nails, and feed him—I thought of Mr. Davis.

I never knew my dad's story until he got Alzheimer's. I never made the connection to some of our shared experiences: being raised by single parents, our reliance on friends over family, an emotional disconnect at home, and overcoming loneliness and regret.

My dad had some flaws, many of which stemmed from his heartbreaking relationship with *his* father. Now that I know his story better, it's easier to understand why his communication, empathy, and affection for us fell short of what we needed—and, conversely, why I struggled to show similar qualities with my own family.

Discovering certain truths about him was hard to accept, like why his marriage to my mom failed, and his battles with addiction, loneliness, and his own unfulfilled emotional needs. But the dad I knew demonstrated a gentleness, selfless sacrifice, and quiet resolve to do the best for his boys, even if he wasn't always sure what that meant. It wasn't as if I overlooked his flaws, demons, and weaknesses all these years; I just didn't know they existed until his Alzheimer's disease gave us the chance to share our stories.

I only wish it hadn't taken a terminal disease to get started.

THE SHIRT OFF MY BACK

On the first day of student orientation, with 750 first-year students sitting side by side in the Quick Center, I listened to Fr. Kelley, president of Fairfield University, welcome us.

"As you embark upon your four years at Fairfield, I want you to remember two things. First, remember that the best four years of your life are always ahead of you. You will undoubtedly experience four exceptional, fun-filled, challenging, and exciting years. People often say that college was the best four years of their lives. But they are not. Nor should they be. The best four years of your life are always in front of you."

What he said next caught me off guard.

"Now, I want you to take a moment to look around you. Look to your left, look to your right, behind you, and ahead of you. There's a good chance that you are looking at someone with whom you will spend the rest of your life."

Fr. Kelley was right on both accounts. I had four tremendous years as a student, yet the foundation for my happiness ultimately came from a person at Fairfield, not the place itself.

A serendipitous encounter with Coleen Campbell the last week of our freshman year would be the turning point in my life. Our friendship the following year set the stage for a relationship that counteracted nearly every emotion and feeling that was missing up to that point: unhindered love, support, trust, and belief in who I was, and more importantly, who I was capable of becoming.

Two years after graduating from Fairfield, Coleen and I were married at St. Barnabas Parish in Bellmore, New York. We were twenty-four years old. There was discussion about getting married in Fairfield University's chapel, yet it was Coleen's dream to get married at St. Barnabas from the time she was a young girl. And St. Barnabas is as pretty as it gets during Christmas. I love the hundreds of red poinsettias scattered throughout the church and around the altar.

When I was deciding how to propose to Coleen the year before, around Christmas, Fr. Kelley helped create the plan. He offered his private dining room in Bellarmine, the grand mansion on campus, and suggested that I tell Coleen that he was inviting us to a dinner party with university vice presidents. It was a believable story, and she bought it. Coleen's mom was in on it and baked one of her famous Irish soda breads for the occasion. Let's just say Coleen was stunned to find the two of us alone in his dining room.

We got married on December 28, 1996. Coleen was so stunningly beautiful. I was an emotional wreck. When she was walking down the aisle toward the altar, with her huge smile, it was the first time I had experienced what they call "weak knees." It truly is a wonder I made it through the ceremony—or the reception, for that matter.

For one thing, I yawn when I am nervous—a lot! I must have yawned a thousand times leading up to her walking down the aisle to meet me.

———

Truthfully, though, I'm not sure who was more nervous, my brother John, who was my best man, or me. What a sight the two of us must have been; we were probably the first two people in the church to start crying.

Some people remember every detail about their wedding day, but I'm not one of them. There's plenty I do remember (like the uncontrollable yawning before the ceremony), and I certainly remember the homily given by Fr. Kelley. It was more like a fantastic roast of Coleen and me, and Fr. Kelley was hysterical; we loved it.

Things settled into the familiar wedding routine after our introduction as a married couple and our first dance. There was plenty of food, an open bar, and lots of dancing. Toward the end of the night, however, Coleen and I received a surprise. Before we knew it, my mom was on the stage, grabbing the microphone. She wanted to say a few words.

Oh, shit.

My mom did not appreciate Fr. Kelley's homily at the church and felt the need to offer a rebuttal. I remember storming out of the room barely a minute into her taking the microphone.

The one line I heard was something like, "Mark would do anything for his friends or family—he would give you the shirt off his back without question." The guests were just as surprised as Coleen and I were, but when I left the room, Coleen was stuck standing alone in the middle of the dance floor. The rest of the guests fled to safety to avoid the shit-storm that was taking place.

I was furious at my mom. Most guests understood the relationship we enjoyed with Fr. Kelley and were not offended by his homily. But she was. Or she didn't feel his comments were appropriate. Or maybe she was jealous of our relationship. All three, I assume. I never asked her.

Her impromptu speech at the wedding reception was just one example of how her absence in my life played out in real time. She was not in touch with my world and the relationships within it.

But should I have been embarrassed by my mom trying to say nice things about me? Despite the inappropriate timing of her comments, she was trying to compliment me, wasn't she?

Even as I write these words, my internal wiring is frizzing out. The middle child protector of peace and fairness within wants me to defend my mom, to give her the benefit of the doubt by saying her intentions were noble. But then, like always, I'm missing the larger point: if she was more a part of my life, she would have known how special our relationship was with Fr. Kelley and laughed along with the rest of our guests.

My mom and I have a complicated relationship. I can't say we're close; certainly not like Coleen is with her mom. I never felt she was *all in* with our relationship. After the divorce and those first few years after, I was still very unclear what a mom was supposed to do, meaning how involved she should have been in my life. I doubt she watched me play hockey more than a dozen times. Considering hockey was such an essential part of my life, you would think she would have attended lots of games. But she didn't.

Why wasn't she at my parent-teacher conferences, prom nights, or when I broke my wrist the first (or second) time? Where was she when I dealt with Marty's suicide?

If my kids didn't have Coleen in their lives, they, too, would be adversely affected in ways that are beyond comprehension. Think about all the jobs moms *usually* manage for their kids: holiday and birthday celebrations, report card conversations, school projects, back-to-school shopping, haircut styles, vacation planning, and dating advice. Then there are the *life-moment* discussions—dreams, plans, fears, and wishes. And don't forget the venting and consoling—caring, sharing, screaming, crying, reminding, asking, hugging, and helping.

Coleen is always asking the kids, *how can I help you*. Nobody ever asked me that. Not having my mom around during my formative years impacted me in ways I'm only now realizing. For example, sometimes, when I'm trying to help my daughter, Erin, figure something out or work through an issue, I'll say "all the wrong things." I guess saying, "Sometimes you have to deal with it and move on. Suck it up," isn't the most empathetic way to help your daughter deal with an issue she is having!

At the end of Erin's first semester at Fairfield, when the omicron variant of the COVID virus was spiking, many of her friends were sent home early because they tested positive. We had this conversation:

"I want to come home," she said. "None of my friends are here. Nobody is on campus. I'm afraid to leave my room because I don't want to get sick."

"Erin, it's going to be fine," I replied. "You're not going to get sick—and if you do—there's nothing we can do about it. It's out of your control."

"You don't understand! I'm all alone and haven't eaten and can't focus on my paper because I'm worried about getting COVID."

———

"You're right," I admitted. "I don't understand. I never went to school during a pandemic. But I do have experience with overcoming challenges—and I know that focusing on your worries is not going to help."

"But what if I get sick?" She still wasn't convinced.

"Then we'll come get you and take you home. In the meantime, try not to worry so much about what *could* happen, and focus on things that are in your control."

A few years ago, I would have said something less compassionate, like, "Erin, would you stop worrying? You're fine; and besides, there's nothing you can do about it. Forget about it and move on."

Still not perfect, but I'm working on it.

REUNITED WITH DAD

My passion for politics began organically, beginning with my paper route. Delivering *The Boston Globe* for three years turned me into an avid reader of the paper. Sometimes it was just the sports pages, but more often than not, I was reading most of the newspaper by the time I was fourteen. Then there were the annual St. Patrick's Day parades in South Boston. My mom brought me to them every year, and I was fascinated by the local political leaders smiling and waving to the crowds of people along the parade route.

Running for student body president in college wasn't something I ever envisioned or intended to do, but once elected, I was all in. I decided Washington, D.C., would be my next destination after Fairfield. I applied to the prestigious White House Internship Program, but my chances were the same as when I had applied to those elite colleges: practically zero. Fr. Kelley wrote my letter of recommendation, but it wasn't enough, and the program rejected me.

That wasn't going to stop me from heading to D.C., however. After graduation, I worked in New York City for my friend's father's construction company. I spent five months in New York City mixing cement, laying brick, making coffee runs, cleaning job sites, and talking sports, politics, and girls with a great bunch of guys. It was backbreaking work and yet extremely "rewarding," meaning, I don't regret it, but I'm glad I'm no longer doing it.

The next chapter in my story landed me in Arlington, Virginia, where I rented a room from a friend named Eddie. He was single and a homeowner, so it was an ideal arrangement, and I am grateful to Eddie for helping me follow my dream of finding a political job in and around Capitol Hill. Unfortunately, it only lasted six months before I packed up and returned home to Norwell.

I want to tell you that I worked my tail off to land my dream job, but I simply can't. Oh, I worked my tail off, but most of it was working at Bennigans, waiting on tables. To pay my rent, buy food and gas, and live in Virginia, I needed income. I worked afternoons and nights at the restaurant and then spent the mornings on resumes and cover letters. I sent hundreds of letters and went on many job interviews, but after months of grinding it out, it became abundantly clear that to find the type of job I wanted, I had to have an "in." And I most certainly didn't have one of those in Washington, D.C.

I contemplated graduate school and began studying for the exam but ultimately decided it was time to come home and regroup. Fortunately for me, as soon as I got home, Fairfield called to offer me an internship. After all, I did have an "in"—it just wasn't in D.C.; it was with the president of Fairfield University, Fr. Kelley, and his vice president of advancement, George Diffley.

In my role as FUSA president, I worked closely with Fr. Kelley and George. Both were mentors and friends, and they were only happy to

———

introduce me to what is known as institutional advancement—more commonly known as fundraising and alumni relations. I kept saying to Coleen that I wished there was a career that combined the best of the business world with the best of the nonprofit world. It turns out, there is, and it's called institutional advancement.

It took about a week on the job to realize that this was my calling. I was raising money for Fairfield, the place that meant everything to me. It was the perfect balance between sales and marketing and allowed me to build relationships with some incredible people. George took me under his wing, as did Janet Canepa from the alumni office, and together we plotted my future career in advancement.

I didn't have to go far, as Fairfield Prep, the Jesuit high school on the campus of the university, hired me as their director of alumni relations. Living and working in Fairfield was almost perfect. All was going according to plan, until one day, nearly three years on the job, the headmaster of Xaverian Brothers High School, my alma mater, was in my office offering me the chance to come home and work for him. Brother Dan was on campus chairing Fairfield Prep's re-accreditation process. I was unprepared for his offer but excited at the same time.

Coleen and I had been married a little over two years when Brother Dan offered me the job. This was a big decision for us. Fairfield was our ideal town in which to live, work, and raise children one day. But it was hard for me to turn away an opportunity to give back to Xaverian, a place that had given me so much. And it was a smart career move.

I took the job with Coleen's blessing, although it was challenging for her. She had left her comfort zone and a promising career to allow me to pursue my dream and passion. She resigned from her publishing job and started a new career at Boston University, also in advancement. She was a natural from the beginning. But what was once a day trip, a short trip home to see her parents, was now close to a four-hour car ride, each way.

It felt amazing to be back at Xaverian, my first home-away-from-home. At first, I felt a little odd calling former teachers by their first names, but that didn't last long. Neither did my time at Xaverian. Leaving Fairfield to move home to Massachusetts wasn't the last time I would have to ask Coleen to give something up.

A little under two years on the job at Xaverian, my dad invited me to lunch and dropped a bombshell on me. He wanted to know if I would leave Xaverian to start a business with him.

"You're leaving your company to sell printing on your own?" I asked.

"It's a franchise called Proforma. They support you on the back end, but we would own the franchise. Couple of guys in my office have already left to join them."

"And you want me to join you?"

"Why not? You're already selling my products part-time on the side—besides, I don't know how to use a computer!"

Another difficult decision about our future had to be made, which also made me realize what Coleen must have been feeling when I asked her to leave behind a career she truly enjoyed to start anew. Raising money for schools was a dream job, especially for my alma maters, Fairfield and Xaverian. My experiences at both schools were enriching, and mainly for the same reasons. Having grown up the way I did, with my dad raising my brothers and me, and in the absence of a maternal figure, these places were my actual "homes."

The opportunity to work alongside my dad was unexpected, but somewhat well timed. Less than six months into my tenure at Xaverian, my boss, the director of advancement, left to work for another nonprofit organization. I was promoted to acting director and stayed in that position for nearly a year. I fully expected to get the job on a permanent basis, but never did. My former boss, not liking his current new job, left that position and was rehired back as the director of advancement at Xaverian.

"I have good news," Brother Dan said as he walked into my office and sat opposite me.

"Great, what is it?" I asked, thinking we had secured a large fundraising gift.

"Larry's coming back. To Xaverian."

"Oh?"

"Isn't that great news?"

"Umm . . . yeah . . . sure."

He had to have seen the color drain from my face, felt the energy evaporate from the room, and heard the silent screams in my head, but he ignored them. It was clear he didn't want to extend the conversation—or have a difficult one with me—because he knew I was disappointed. A year as acting director and now I was demoted back to my former role. There's no way he didn't know I was anything but crushed.

I loved my job and working at Xaverian. I got along well with my former boss, too. But once you've been elevated to the top position, it's hard to accept a—was it a demotion? Not really. At least I don't know if you would call it a demotion in the traditional sense. Yet the news of my former boss's return was anything but great in my mind, so the timing of my dad's request to start a business with him was perfect.

He was sixty-two and I was twenty-seven years old when we formed Proforma Printing & Promotion.

For the next fourteen years, from 1999 until I left the family business in 2013, I spent a significant amount of time with my dad. The first several years, we had lunch or saw each other two to three times a week and talked multiple times a day. We were close. A few years into our business, we invited Bill and John to join us. Not only did I never dream of working with my dad—never in a million years did I envision, or even think about, working with Bill and John either. But we did, for almost fourteen years.

Yet, in late 2012, things changed for me, my family, and our business. My oldest child, Campbell, was in sixth grade at Blessed Sacrament School in Walpole, a Catholic elementary school. A few months into the school year, Campbell's first signs of anxiety appeared.

Frequent trips to the nurse meant time out of class, which led to special accommodations to allow him to leave class whenever his anxiety built up to the point where he could not control it. Shortness of breath, sometimes dizziness, loss of appetite, but always a pounding in his chest from the worry. Whatever the cause, his anxiety worsened as the year progressed. My office was 500 yards from his school, which allowed me to leave work to take care of him when required, which was *every day*.

For Coleen and me, it was the most challenging time of our young parenting lives. Erin was a superstar who stepped in at home to play with Sean and keep him company when we needed to be with Campbell.

Dealing with my own pain and suffering is one thing; it's quite another to deal with a child's. And Campbell did suffer. The panic attacks were especially frightening.

At the beginning of his anxiety battle, I had trouble understanding it. I was familiar with depression, as I live with it, and although the two often go hand in hand, I never experienced clinical anxiety. Growing up surrounded by other guys, it was always, "Suck it up; you're fine." That is, if you even bothered to tell someone about your problems.

I couldn't relate to what Campbell was going through, even though I was the one helping him during the day. But after watching him suffer on a near-daily basis, I came as close to understanding as one could. I dropped him off at school, went to my office and waited for the call from the nurse each day. I knew it was coming, just not when. Coleen and I couldn't even talk to one another on the phone, or we would break down and cry. We relied on texting to communicate about his status.

Professionally, it was hard to focus on anything but Campbell. Naturally. But it also brought pre-existing tensions among my brothers and me into focus. The biggest area of disagreement was the right path forward to take our already successful business to the next level. In the last few years, we had become one of Proforma's top franchises, but we knew the potential for growth was much higher.

———

I grew frustrated with our compensation model, as it didn't reward sales; we got paid the same regardless of one's sales. My motivation was at an all-time low when my brothers and I met in late December to finalize our 2013 sales and marketing plan.

Dad wasn't at the meeting, which wasn't unusual. He left these types of decisions up to us, as he was heading toward semi-retirement. A routine business meeting turned into something much more. An hour into it, all three of us were emotionally spent, as a large portion of the meeting was spent talking openly about each other's strengths and weaknesses, our personal and professional relationships with one another, and how to work better together.

It was one of our best meetings in years—until things took an unexpected turn.

A clear path for continued growth had emerged. The problem, however, was that we lacked unanimous buy-in for each of our newly proposed roles. Meaning on paper and in reality, our best chance for growth called for having two people focus on sales and one person focus on supporting the salesmen. In the past, all three of us sold and supported our own sales, but it wasn't the best use of our talents or resources. Having a more focused approach to selling *and* supporting our customers was the right solution.

Suddenly, our best meeting went cold, and I was fighting to save the company I started with my dad.

A month later, when we returned from Hawaii, I made the final decision to leave the family business. Even though I had started it with my dad, I thought I should walk away from the company to save my relationships and the Resnick family. I didn't see any other way to move forward together, and I didn't have the heart to force anybody out. I didn't want to go, but I also couldn't stay.

My decision to leave my dad and our business was agony. I remember going to my basement to bawl my eyes out quite frequently. I buried my face on the couch and cried, desperate to hide my feelings and tears from the rest of my family. And while it is easy to regret the decision in hindsight, it was the right decision for me at the time. I needed a fresh start, away from my family business.

I broke the news to my dad while having lunch at the 99 Restaurant, one of New England's homegrown franchise restaurants (and one of his favorite places to eat). The lunch brought me right back to the time when my dad invited me to join him in business—only now, I was the one with a shocking announcement.

It was quintessential Dad—very little reaction—but I could see on his face that he was crushed. We both were, as we had such a great run working together, and the decision had nothing to do with our relationship. Dad and I were almost always on the same page. He supported me when I had to build my book of business, and I supported him when his sales were on the downside. It was fourteen beautiful years working with my dad and best friend.

Bill and John were genuinely surprised. Despite the difficult months prior to the heated December meeting and inability to decide on our growth strategy, neither one expected I would walk away from the business. In hindsight, I don't regret leaving the company, but I have regrets over the process, both in telling my dad and brothers and post-announcement planning. I should have spent more time discussing my options with them, and even more time planning for what the breakup of our company would mean for our relationships.

My new job allowed me to run a new promotional products division for a local printing company owned by my friend. On paper, it was a good fit for both of us, and by March, I was working for someone else for the first time in fourteen years.

If there was any good news, it was that I was back to working for myself, which gave me the flexibility to be present for my dad. This allowed me to see him nearly every day. Only this time, it would be at Whitney Place in Sharon. I was back working with Dad, just in a different role. Someone was looking out for us.

BEERS AVE

I don't know how nearly thirty years have passed since I left Beers Ave. Drifting off to sleep some nights, I think of it.

I see myself hanging from the branch in the Kearnses' tree. I grip the tree with only my right hand, presumably to show off my strength. There is no fear of letting go and falling to the ground, but when I finally let go, I land hard on my left arm. There's no loud thump or cracking bone upon impact. I barely register the pain, though I know it is there. I continue playing with my friends. Later that evening, my parents take me to the hospital to get it examined.

"It's broken, all right, but the good news is that we don't have to set it," says the doctor on duty.

On a late summer night, I am hiding in my neighbor's overgrown bushes during a massive flashlight tag game. I'm alone. I prefer to hide by myself because I don't trust the other kids to keep quiet; they always give themselves up by laughing or whispering too loudly. I'm practically holding my breath so as not to give away my position. I haven't been caught once so far, which I am pretty proud of.

One of the older kids tosses sticks left and right to divide everyone into teams on the street in front of my house, waiting for the street hockey game to start. Young kids, old kids—everyone is ready. I come out of the house in full goalie gear—pads, helmet, gloves, and stick—and I am nervous. Some of the kids are six years older than me and have wicked slapshots. There's a mix of wood and plastic hitting the pavement, pucks are bouncing, and pre-game taunts are tossed back and forth.

I triumphantly steal the flag and free my teammates, using my speed to outrun the slower kids. It was an intense capture the flag game on Brant-wood Road. There must be thirty kids playing. The other team had made its bold run to capture our flag, but I was faster today.

Twigs and dried leaves crunch under my bike tires as they ride the worn path to Tony's house, a slight trepidation in my soul as the woods darken and crowd me. It's quiet—too quiet for my liking.

My pulse quickens as I watch Anne and her friends play softball after school at the fields. The bike ride through the woods was uneventful, though I'm still somewhat bothered by leaving Midnight behind.

My thigh muscles tighten and my throat burns from rollerblading as fast as I can across town to Sean's house. It's dark, but the roads are empty.

A bee stings my arm while sleeping in our unfinished basement in the middle of the night. My attempt at having my own room fails and it's off to plan B. The family room?

Dust mites swirl and float under my bed as I hide and wait for my dad to wake up, finish his exercises, shower, eat, then leave for work—another successful day of school skipped on my part.

My brothers and I jam into my dad's air-conditioned bedroom and litter the floor with sleeping bags as we escape the heat and humidity on another summer night.

A line of kids patiently await their turn at the keg on a Saturday night, Solo cups in hand. Later that night, mosquitoes buzz and float near my head after a night of open doors and windows.

Midnight steals a marinated steak off the kitchen counter . . . Dad falls asleep after a long day and a couple of martinis . . . Mom takes me to the emergency room to treat my third-degree burns after spilling boiling water on myself while making tea late one night . . . my wrist is snapped back into place . . . the shingles on the side of the house crack and slip out of place from neglect . . . the scrap wood from taking down the pool and deck remain piled in the back of the yard . . . the shed nearly burns down while I play with matches . . . I sneak Mom's cigarettes and almost choke on the disgusting smoke . . . a hard-boiled egg isn't boiled, and the yolk leaks all over my brown Easter suit . . . Dad forgets to give me money to buy something at the Scholastic Book Fair . . . Marty and I disrupt Mr. O'Keefe's history class, again . . . I fail another eye vision test . . . I perform miserably on the drums during a fifth-grade concert . . . my partner dissects the frog for me . . . I borrow Rachel's Whitney Houston report in music class . . . I turn away from the group when I kiss a girl for the first time at Sean's party . . . tears drip down my cheeks as I cry myself to sleep upon learning of Marty's suicide.

I don't want to forget these memories, even the painful or embarrassing ones. After all, it was just a father and his three boys, trying to figure things out as they went.

I never battled my brothers for attention, though we did battle with fists and hurtful words. But those weren't the kind of fights that gave way to shame, guilt, or regret. No, the battles that hurt the most were the unseen ones: loneliness, low self-esteem, the feeling of not being loved. I fought those battles every day.

Twenty-five years after leaving Beers Ave and forty years after my parents split, I'm still not sure why my mom was the one who moved out. It just doesn't seem believable that my mom would *choose* to move out, leaving her boys on Beers Ave.

And yet, still, Beers Ave is not only where my story began—it's where I dreamed of becoming a professional baker, best-selling author, and United States Congressman.

Part Three:

DAD'S STORY

Boys From Brighton

During my dad's Alzheimer's battle, especially the last two years, I spent more time with him than I did during the previous twenty years combined. I discovered that we had many things in common, from being raised by single parents to our fondness for our hometowns. Before his sickness, Dad said very little about his childhood and the challenges he faced as the man-of-the-house, older brother, and dedicated son.

To tell his story, I leaned on old conversations and memories from our talks these past two years, plus, car rides to and from Xaverian and hockey rinks, our time together in the backyard working on the garden or barbecuing, business and casino trips, some of his friends, and snippets from my mom.

My dad's story began in Brighton, Massachusetts, a neighborhood of Boston just off the shores of the Charles River.

He lived in an apartment with his mom and sister on Beacon Street, one of Boston's iconic streets, passing through neighborhoods like Beacon Hill, Back Bay, Kenmore, and Chestnut Hill. The apartment complex actually sat on the border of Brighton and Brookline. He told me there were kids in the same building who attended Brookline High School. Living a few doors down the hall would have undoubtedly changed the trajectory of their lives, as Brookline High was superior to Brighton, with better quality of education, physical space, and growth opportunities.

His father, William Resnick, owned a jewelry store in Boston's diamond district. The store was moderately successful, and they lived a comfortable life. Unfortunately, my grandfather had a gambling and drinking addiction. His gambling debts nearly destroyed the business and, quite definitively, ruined their family. Whether he was kicked out by my grandmother or he intentionally abandoned them, I do not know, but once he was gone, he was gone for good.

My grandmother Shirley raised my dad and his sister. She took over her husband's jewelry business and kept it going for many years. She was intelligent and hardworking, a pioneer in many ways. Not only did Shirley hold her own in a male-dominated industry, but she also went to college and graduated from Boston University. People were impressed every time I told them my dad *and* grandmother both attended BU.

After her husband left, Shirley remarried, but that, too, ended in divorce. She died from breast cancer when I was two, so I never knew her.

My father was an average student but an above-average hockey player. He played varsity hockey each year at Brighton High, and after the

Navy, he would play a year for Boston University. Despite the freedoms he had as a teenager and young adult growing up in the city, my dad was a responsible young man. He always contributed financially to the household, was not prone to finding trouble, and worked hard.

His best friends were Kevin Morris and Jerry Sullivan, who lived around the corner from him in Brighton, and Kenny Riccioli, who was from Revere.

"Everyone loved your father. We respected and looked up to him. He seemed always to have his shit together, which wasn't easy with the guys we hung out with," said Kenny.

When Kenny found out my dad's Alzheimer's was advancing, he booked a flight from Naples, FL, to spend time with his friend. We went out to dinner with him, my dad, and my two brothers and I listened to him spin one story after another. The stories about my dad made him sound like a tough guy.

"One night we found ourselves in a bit of trouble," said Kenny. "It was one of those dark Boston alleys outside a bar. Four of them and three of us. Didn't look good for us—they seemed itching for a fight. Your dad, he's not very tall, but he was imposing. So he starts rolling up his sleeves as if to say, 'Let's do this.' And that's all it took. The other guys looked at each other and walked away."

According to Kenny, my dad was pretty quiet in the locker room, even when he was a captain. Instead, he led by example on the ice with his grit and hustle. Kenny had the gift of gab and liked to embellish the truth, but one thing you didn't have to take with a grain of salt was his love of my dad. He openly cried, talking about how great a man my dad was and the fantastic job he did raising us. Kenny called him the toughest man he knew. I would come to believe this myself, soon enough.

My dad didn't share generational cliché stories like walking two miles to school, uphill both ways, with no shoes. On occasion, however, he shared stories about sneaking into the old Boston Garden and Fenway Park, which you could do back then. Then there was the story of his only boxing match inside an actual ring, in which he secured a first-round knockout. He worked for a beer manufacturer, which allowed him to buy beers at $0.05 apiece, and briefly for the postal service. The details were scarce, but his enthusiasm for sharing them was not.

My father's oldest friend, Kevin, was always my "Uncle Kevin." He was my Godfather. Every Super Bowl Sunday, we went to Uncle Kevin's house for a party. What was unique about him was the story of how he lost his leg when he was twelve years old, playing a game of "chicken" with an oncoming train. He lost the game, and his leg, which resulted in him living with a plastic leg from the thigh down for the rest of his life. Despite this, he still managed to play ice hockey, not only for Brighton High but also for Boston College. He was a goalie, which made sense, given his propensity to take on fast-moving objects.

Dad and Kevin were prone to playing practical jokes on the younger kids at the rink. After practice, the kids used to volunteer to untie the skates of the older guys. Sometimes they got spare change for the service, as a tip, and sometimes they experienced the shock of a lifetime. Kevin used to loosen up his fake leg enough so that if you pulled hard enough, it would unattach.

When a kid would be struggling to pull the loosened skate off, Kevin would say, "It's okay, kid, just pull harder. A little harder. Almost there . . ."

———

The kid would eventually pull so hard that his leg would come right off. The poor kids used to scream and freak out while holding his plastic leg!

Other than Kenny Riccioli, there were no other friends I could talk to about my father's teen or young adult years. However, his sister Linda, who was his best friend, was my other Godparent and had some stories to share.

"I think you were in the fourth grade when you held your first sleepover party."

"I remember. It was my birthday party, right?" I asked.

"That's right. Unfortunately, days before the party, your father's gout flared up something wicked. He was in so much pain but didn't want to ask you to cancel the party. He hobbled around, serving pizza and cake. I know he wasn't a man of many words, but he tried his best to give you a normal childhood."

Linda and her husband, Jim, were city-dwellers, but not of the Southie kind. You weren't going to swindle those two, but at the same time, they didn't have the rough edges like residents in South Boston. Jim was a handyman and owned a tow truck company. He worked all the time, smoked two packs of cigarettes a day, and drank hard. Not a violent drunk, but he did get a little nasty with his words.

Linda owned a thrift store in Brighton Center, so she was constantly buying and selling very old items, including collectibles. Her store was a fascinating place to visit, not just for the items on the shelves. Her customers were every bit as interesting. I only recall seeing older adults in the store, as in *old* people, but that was likely due to the time of day I visited.

———

Boston University was one of my first customers after starting Proforma. After visiting customers on BU's campus, I would drive a mile up the street to Linda's Brighton store. I would get a big kiss on the cheek, which always left a bright red or pink lipstick stain. She was incredibly loving, generous, and funny, but she gave me that Jewish guilt every time I saw her—always about not visiting or calling her enough. And she was right.

Linda and my dad were both diagnosed with terminal illnesses in 2014. Hers was lung cancer, and Dad's was Alzheimer's. She ultimately lost her battle with lung cancer in 2017. She and my father were close, and even though he didn't talk about her death, you could tell he was devastated by it.

A man of few words and a giant heart. That was my dad.

DOC RESNICK

Besides being raised by single parents and loving our hometowns, hockey was the most significant experience my dad and I shared. Ice hockey was a savior for the Resnick men. It kept us in shape, for one thing, but more importantly, it kept us out of trouble. Unfortunately for me, I also shared my dad's handles (stick handling skills). Neither one of us excelled at stickhandling, but damn, we could skate like the wind. Speed was our game. His skating skills were good enough to allow him to play for Boston University, even after a two-year break while he was in the Navy.

After graduating from Brighton High, he went right to the Navy. I never got a clear answer from Dad as to why he joined the Navy so soon after graduating. Perhaps he wasn't ready for college, either academically, mentally, or financially? I asked him several times, but never got the complete story. I also asked my mom and brothers about it, but we came up empty.

From what we could gather about his time in the Navy, he was first stationed at the Naval Training Center in Bainbridge, Maryland for bootcamp in the 4th regiment, company 69. Located on the Susquehanna River, Bainbridge was thirty-five miles northeast of Baltimore. It was only in operation for thirty-four years.

———

After bootcamp, he attended dental school for three months and was then assigned to the USS Vulcan as a Navy dental technician. Dad spent the bulk of his service time on the Vulcan, which was based out of Norfolk, Virginia. I googled the ship once and showed it to my dad; his face lit up with recognition, but no other words or conversation followed. That was toward the end of his stay in assisted living.

During his time in the Navy, I know he visited Puerto Rico and Cuba, but mainly the ship was docked in Norfolk, Virginia. He was, in fact, a dental technician. He loved to share the story of how he performed actual dental work on a sailor. The dentist was not on board the ship for whatever reason when this man came looking for my dad.

"Doc, doc, you have to help me. This one tooth is killing me."

And my dad helped him. With drill in hand, he cleaned out the rotten tooth, mixed the cavity filling, and filled the hole. He never told the sailor he wasn't a doctor. He figured he had watched the dentist do it enough times that he would give it a shot. The next day, the patient found him.

"Doc, thanks for taking care of that tooth. I feel much better!"

That was the only Navy story we got from him. Even his tattoo was without a backstory. Inked on his left shoulder, it was the size of a hockey puck. It featured a wreath of some sort with a ship in the center. Below it were the initials "U," "S," and "N." I never found one like it during my research online, though it wasn't nearly as colorful or detailed as most I saw.

After his honorable discharge from the Navy in 1957, my dad returned to Brighton. He enrolled at Boston University and studied business management. Once on campus, he convinced the hockey coaches to let him try out for the team, which they did. He had brought his hockey equipment to the Navy and managed to get in some skating at the local rinks, which would prove to be a wise move. He made the freshman team as a twenty-year-old. The coaches loved his speed, believing he would vie for a spot on the varsity team the following year.

My father never made it onto the varsity team. He quit the team after his first year, citing the need to work to pay for his tuition. Tuition was $400 a semester or $800 for the year. He received money from the G.I. Bill, which, along with a part-time job, paid the full amount of his college tuition. He was proud to say he didn't have to burden his mom financially to get through college, yet the decision to quit hockey was one that caused him regret later in his life. I could see it in his eyes every time we attended a Boston University hockey game with my kids.

After graduating from Boston University with a degree in business administration, my dad took his first professional job with Standard Register. This company primarily sold business forms, labels, and envelopes. For the rest of his professional career, he remained in this industry and only worked for a handful of different companies. Like many of his generation, he didn't consider switching jobs. He was well trained and moderately successful in sales. He never got rich but was always able to pay the bills, including tuition bills.

In the mid-1960s, early in his career with Standard Register, my dad ran into his father for the last time. The story gave me goosebumps the few times he shared it.

Elevators move from floor to floor, stopping, opening, and then closing again. That's what they do. People enter and exit on their way to meetings, events, or maybe just a social visit to an old acquaintance. However, what elevators don't usually do is bring you face to face with your estranged father.

That's what this one did, though.

As a young salesman, fresh off his rigorous corporate sales training program and eager for his next appointment, my dad was doing what most of us do in the elevator: staring at the numbers moving up or down, anticipating his final destination. When the door opened, an older man walked in and shuffled next to him. They exchanged glances and courteous nods. My father then looked back over at the man and fixed an incredulous gaze upon him. *Nothing*. No sideways glance, no uncomfortable sensation of being stared at with laser intensity.

"You don't know who I am, do you?" asked my father.

"No. Do we know each other?" replied the elderly man.

"I *used* to be your son."

On cue, the elevator did what it was supposed to do and opened. My dad exited and never looked back. It was the last time he saw his father until he passed away. Reluctantly, he did attend his father's funeral. It is the only story my dad shared with me regarding his father.

Joining the Navy right out of high school wasn't exactly extreme, and I can see why he might have needed some time away from home to figure things out, but I have a nagging feeling there was more to the story—and it upsets me that I missed out on the opportunity to learn it.

I've shared as many stories as my kids will listen to about my life. It has always baffled me that my dad never shared more about his life with me. The reason he didn't, I think, is twofold.

The first explanation for the lack of detail surrounding his life, even when prodded, was that he could not recall it. Perhaps his Alzheimer's began long before 2014. It's hard for me to imagine that someone wouldn't be able to remember a significant moment or experience in one's life, such as joining the Navy right after high school, quitting the BU hockey team, or giving up on a marriage.

Second, I'm willing to bet that some of his memories were blocked out or pushed aside intentionally. Whether it was his father's complete abdication or why he could not—or would not—effectively communicate with my mom, part of me feels like he wanted to forget those moments intentionally. As if the regret or burden was too much to carry.

Gambling On Love

My parents met at a bar called Herbies, located on Atlantic Avenue in Boston. Herbie Schwartz owned the place, and supposedly, the food was good and drinks were cheap. Herbie was a former Marine, so the dingy bar was decked in Marine and patriotic décor. It was a popular bar for those who worked along Atlantic Ave, which included my parents, who worked in the same building. My dad was with a printing company, and Mom was working for the Sheraton.

For their first date, he took my mom to the Suffolk Downs Racetrack in East Boston. I guess he figured that if he didn't like her, at least he would have a good time betting on the horses.

I always knew my dad enjoyed gambling. I would see him fill out his weekly NFL gambling sheets or read the racing forms at home as a kid. He took us to the Marshfield Fair each summer, which featured horse racing most days. As he got older, his hobby wasn't golf or fishing; he went to Las Vegas or Mohegan Sun instead.

His annual Las Vegas trips began in his early sixties. My brothers and I hated that his idea of a great vacation was going to Las Vegas. Eventually, we stopped complaining about it, though we never condoned it. He often tried to convince me that it would make a great family vacation.

"But Dad, Vegas centers around gambling, smoking, drinking, and inappropriate behavior everywhere you look. How is that good for young children?"

He argued passionately about the entertainment value: the lions at MGM, the roller coaster, aquarium, water and laser shows, shopping, and great pools. It was a hopeless discussion. Gambling conversations, in general, were uncomfortable. His trip to Las Vegas was the highlight of his year—so much so that he occasionally made two trips in a year. He never wanted to use an ATM while in Las Vegas, so he brought thousands of dollars in cash with him during each trip, usually hidden away in his money belt.

I never once thought to myself that he had a *problem*, though. Incredibly, I didn't make the connection to *his* father's gambling habit sooner.

I made several trips with him to Vegas. He always stayed at the Flamingo hotel, which was one of the older properties on the strip. He had his routines and habits, some of which annoyed me. For example, he was a notoriously slow player at the tables, whether it was blackjack or Let it Ride. Part of it was intentional; to slow the dealer down meant, in his mind, taking away some of the casino's advantage. Mostly, though, I think he just wanted to relax and enjoy every minute at the table.

He was a generous tipper at the casino, and within the hotel in general. He never looked past people—not the hostess, pit manager, coat check attendant, waitress, or housekeeper. It was one of his qualities I admired the most, and one in which I had adopted from a young age without knowing from where it came. The more I witnessed him up close on these trips, the more grateful I became for his kindness and compassion. To never put yourself above others is a lesson I strive to teach my children at every opportunity.

As I mentioned earlier, it was my mother who moved out of the house when they separated. *How is that even possible?* Today, kids of divorced parents shuffle from one parent's home to the other's; one week on and one week off, but back then, the father moved out—end of the story. Not for us.

Either way, my brothers and I certainly didn't realize how different we were due to being raised by a single parent, never mind a dad. Things like checking homework, looking into our friends, talking to teachers when we struggled, helping with college applications, and just listening to our problems didn't occur regularly.

The lack of maternal care, compassion, and empathy took its toll on all of us over time. Regardless of how well our father did with the rest of his responsibilities, we suffered mightily from not having a mom around. We didn't receive much positive reinforcement or reassurances from either of them. Because we didn't have iPhones, laptops, or other devices to entertain or educate us, we had to figure things out for ourselves, which in many ways worked to my advantage later in life. I was less dependent on others to solve problems, I could advocate for myself, and I knew how to take the initiative in exploring new opportunities.

TEN COMMANDMENTS OF HOCKEY

Ice hockey was part of my life the moment I was born. As soon as my parents moved to Norwell in 1970, my dad began coaching for the South Shore Seahawks, the youth hockey program for the towns of Norwell, Scituate, and Cohasset. By the time I started playing games, the program added Hull and Marshfield as well. There were always sticks, pucks, and skates in the house as a toddler, only they were my dad's. He was coaching teams long before we laced up our skates for the first time, building a name for himself within the local hockey community.

When his boys were old enough to play on teams, we finally got the chance to have him as our coach. I loved it. I can say from experience that not every player who is the son (or daughter) of a coach enjoys the experience, but I truly did. There was never special treatment—quite the opposite, in fact. He pushed me harder and seemed to go out of his way to avoid favoritism. This never bothered me.

Coach Resnick experienced tremendous success as a youth hockey coach, capturing prestigious league and tournament championships. He coached dozens and dozens of kids who went on to play college hockey.

A few were drafted by professional teams and played in the NHL. One of them was Jamie Kelley from Scituate, a standout player and Boston Bruins draft pick.

> *I joined the Seahawks Peewees when I was in seventh grade. My first coach was Barry Resnick, a Norwell guy. I learned the fundamentals of hockey from Coach Resnick. He was a good teacher, and I absorbed a lot of hockey knowledge from him. It was my first exposure to real team hockey, and I loved it. ("Jamie Kelly Profile, A Hockey History of Scituate MA," hockeyscituate.com)*

Other than my dad's full salt-and-pepper beard, his former players would remember him well by his Ten Commandments of Hockey. If you played for Coach Resnick, you knew about his hockey commandments.

They were legendary.

I believe my dad got the original hockey commandments from Dick Devereux, a coach from Scituate. He refined them, adding some of his own, then asked his players to recite them before every game. There were twenty-nine in total, divided into three sections: TEN COMMANDMENTS, RULES OF PASSING, AND MAN-DATORIES. Players were supposed to be fully dressed and ready to recite the hockey commandments fifteen minutes before game time.

You never wanted to walk in during the reading of the commandments; not only would you be embarrassed, but it was also likely to impact your playing time.

I once tried to replicate the concept when I coached youth soccer and failed miserably. I couldn't get the kids to focus on them for more than a minute. It was a humbling experience. But my dad got buy-in from every one of his teams. We got dressed, passed out the sheets, then one kid was selected by my dad to lead the group.

"I WILL SKATE MY LANE!" the kid shouted.

"*I WILL SKATE MY LANE!*" fourteen other players shouted after him.

"I WILL KEEP TWO HANDS ON MY STICK AND MY STICK ON THE ICE!"

"*I WILL KEEP TWO HANDS ON MY STICK AND MY STICK ON THE ICE!*" we shouted back.

Reciting them couldn't have taken more than five minutes in total, but we said them before every game. *Parents must have thought he was nuts.* His former players loved my dad (except those who got cut from his teams). Don't ask me why the Rules of Passing section only has nine commandments—I never noticed until the writing of this book that this was the case.

TEN COMMANDMENTS:

1. *I WILL skate my lane.*
2. *I WILL keep two hands on my stick and my stick on the ice.*
3. *I WILL NOT turn my back to the puck or to my opponent's goal.*
4. *I WILL NOT get a penalty when my team is behind.*
5. *I WILL NOT go backward in our zone except on a power play.*
6. *I WILL NOT go offside on a two-on-one, three-on-one, or three-on-two—straddle the blue line.*
7. *I WILL control my wing between the blue lines.*
8. *I WILL NOT hog the puck, except when I am left alone.*

9. *I WILL keep my body between the puck and the man.*

10. *IF I am in a shooting position, I WILL take the shot.*

RULES OF PASSING:

1. *I WILL NEVER pass to the man standing still.*

2. *I WILL NEVER pass the puck foolishly.*

3. *I WILL ALWAYS pass the puck to improve our offensive position.*

4. *I WILL keep my head up and never pass to the covered man.*

5. *I WILL headman the puck.*

6. *AFTER passing the puck, I WILL skate to get into position for a return pass.*

7. *I WILL NEVER pass diagonally in my own zone unless 100 percent sure of the pass.*

8. *I WILL NOT pass or carry the puck in front of my own net or throw it out blindly from behind the net.*

9. *I WILL pass the puck into the offensive zone—only if I have no skating room and no one to pass to.*

MAN-DATORIES:

1. *Skate to the puck.*

2. *I WILL take the man if I cannot get the puck.*

3. *I WILL backcheck and pick up the open man when the other team has the puck.*

4. *One on one, I WILL ALWAYS take the man.*

5. *I WILL check the man passing the puck.*

6. *First man in takes the puck carrier.*

———

7. *Second man in takes the puck.*

8. *Player in front of the net must face the puck and lean on his stick.*

9. *You must never allow the team to be outnumbered in its own zone.*

10. *Puck carrier is never the last man to leave the zone.*

My dad was the founder of high school hockey in Norwell, at least according to us. He was the first to create a club hockey team in the mid-'80s, scheduling games against other high school teams. I was only in middle school at the time but was allowed to play on the team. We competed against kids much older than me, so it was good preparation for high school hockey at Xaverian. Years later, long after I graduated from high school, they would formally make ice hockey a high school sport at Norwell High. Nice work, Coach Resnick.

My dad was a quiet man, meaning he preferred to keep to himself rather than socialize with other parents or be part of a crowd. I think he enjoyed the quiet time he got and wanted to focus on watching his kids playing hockey rather than chit chatting with parents. He was not anti-social, especially with friends and family, but never needed or wanted to draw unnecessary attention to himself. He was constantly balancing his responsibilities as a single father and his career: cooking, grocery shopping, laundry, yard work, shuffling us around, coaching, summer camps, boy scouts, swimming lessons, hockey, and soccer.

I will be the second to admit that my dad didn't have all the answers (he would be the first). My friends' parents would tell me how lucky we were to have such a great father in high school. Everything he did was for his boys. I don't think it is hyperbole to say that in many ways, he was the talk of the town for many years when the Resnicks were growing up; now, as a parent myself, I fully understand why. Nowadays, Coleen and I both work full-time, and not a day goes by when we don't complain about our complete schedules and tired bodies. I can't imagine doing this alone. Every time I think about how overwhelming that must have been for him, I want to hug my dad and thank him for his sacrifice and commitment to us.

Not only did Coach Resnick SKATE his lane—but as the puck carrier in our family, he was never the last man to leave the zone, either.

PAPA SMURF

I used to wonder if my dad felt he got screwed for having to raise three boys by himself. Whether he was left to raise us, volunteered to raise us, or just decided it was best if he (and not my mom) would raise his three boys, I'm still not sure. But as I continue to write, reflect, and grow as a person, I can say with certainty that he didn't get screwed.

Early in our Proforma business, selling promotional products, apparel, business forms, and printed collateral, Dad and I discussed overpricing for a specific customer of his.

"Aren't we screwing the customer by charging so much?" I asked.

"Not at all," he said. "First, this client is always changing his mind, which causes more work for us. Our meetings should take ten minutes, but he stretches them for hours. Second—and here's the important thing to remember: 'You're only getting screwed if you think you're getting screwed.'"

"I guess so."

"Trust me, he gets the best possible service from us. In his mind, he gets his money's worth. Nobody else is going to service him as we do."

Of course, my dad was right.

My friends affectionately called my dad Big D or Papa Smurf grow-ing up. I doubt my father reached the full five feet, six inches listed on his license, and there were times his weight topped 250 pounds. Those features, plus his salt and pepper—or mainly salty—beard, supported the Papa Smurf nickname, though we usually only referred to him as such outside of his presence.

When friends were over in the summer, Big D would routinely make his appearance, cooking on the grill or participating in the hot-pep-per-eating contests we had. We picked them directly from his crowded garden in the backyard. Dad's garden was a source of pride and included strawberries, peppers, tomatoes, cucumbers, squash, beans, and some-times carrots, potatoes, onions, and even corn.

None of my friends could beat Big D in a pepper-eating contest. He loved spicy foods, sauces, and dips. He was the only person I knew who slabbed on that hot brown mustard that Chinese restaurants serve, though I think my brother John has since followed suit.

After town soccer games, my Norwell friends shouted, "What's up, Big D!" Despite having three boys play youth sports, he tried his best to make all of our games. Not an easy feat, but he didn't seem to miss many soccer games. Hockey games were much harder because we played in rinks throughout the state of Massachusetts, from Pembroke, which was south of Norwell, to rinks north of Boston.

It wasn't until my dad got Alzheimer's that I truly grasped the total-ity of his sacrifices. Growing up, I didn't see it. I wanted to be loved and reassured, praised, comforted, and understood. I didn't get that from him in the traditional way. But I was imitating his other qualities, such as kindness, respect, generosity, selflessness, humility, humor, and willingness to improve by learning new skills, whether coaching drills, recipes, or cribbage strategies.

My father gave the most of himself to others, even when he didn't realize he could provide much. In my view, he always tried to do the right thing. Most importantly, he knew the difference between a reason and an excuse, and never made excuses for his actions.

There was a fundamental dichotomy between the happiness and loneliness we experienced as young boys, teenagers, and young adults while growing up with my dad. I truly enjoyed living on Beers Ave. *Or did I?* Growing up without a mom in the house was brutal. I am who I am because of it, and that cuts both ways. We were polite, respectful, and genuinely good kids, but we had real issues with emotions, affection, social cues, and, most importantly, confidence and trust.

In most cases, we didn't even help each other. I wasn't close to Bill with our three-year grade gap, which has impacted our relationship. I was then, and continue to be, much closer to John, as we were closer in age and seemed more dependent on each other. I believe I was helpful to him; I know I tried to include him whenever possible.

I used to believe my home on Beers Ave was this incredibly special place. All my life, actually. Of the four Resnick men, I'm probably the only one who clung to the perception of happiness and contentment on

Beers Ave. I never gave much thought to the negative connotations the house held—only the positive ones.

But how, exactly, is it possible for me to have such positive feelings about my home when there was so much sadness?

What I loved about living there was what came with it. The perks, so to speak: the neighborhood kids, my personal freedom and independence, the town of Norwell itself, and mostly, my friends. My years at Cole Elementary and Norwell Junior High were positive, even if they were not productive. I associate my learning how to skate, my hockey career, cooking, and writing passions to Beers Ave. And the street name is pretty cool.

Yet the painful memories far outweigh the good ones: that dreadful night my parents announced their separation; or going to bed Christmas Eve with only one parent in the house; hiding under my bed with the millions of dust mites until my dad went to work so I could skip school to finish a paper; cooking for myself on weekends; celebrating birthdays with friends instead of a family, or having nobody to talk to when an old friend committed suicide.

I now see that my brothers and my dad were happy to escape Beers Ave. Beyond the clutter and confusion inside the walls was a house filled with sadness. It was not a happy place for them, and I'm ashamed that I never realized it.

For me, Beers Ave was my identity—today it might be called a brand—and I never wanted to lose that. I can't help but hold a place in my heart for it. Perhaps it's my obstinance to let go of the past, regardless of the pain or suffering attached to it? Either way, I've come to accept it for what it was—only the beginning of my story.

———

The coldness, loneliness, and darkness I felt growing up have never completely gone away. The emotions can be masked, ignored, and shamed away, but they are always there, bubbling below the surface. To be honest, I never once considered that my dad was dealing with those same emotions his whole life, too.

I also never imagined that he would one day be relieved of them, only not by choice. His Alzheimer's took care of that for him, along with his memories, hopes, and dreams. Witnessing such a decline is something I wouldn't wish on my worst enemy.

———

CHASED BY DEMONS

It was always hard to decipher whether my dad craved familiarity and *the known* or just lacked the imagination and desire to want more out of life. In his mind, there was nothing wrong with visiting Las Vegas every year rather than trying new destinations.

"You like to visit Disney World, and I like Las Vegas," he said.

Given a choice, he would stay at the Flamingo over any other hotel on the Las Vegas strip. Yes, he built up loyalty points by staying there, but he could also use those same points to try different hotels, yet he never did. He was more comfortable eating at the 99 Restaurant than Legal Seafood, and for as long as I can remember, my father used doctors from the same Pembroke practice since I was a kid. Same office building, different doctors. He didn't care for his current primary care doctor but would not look for a new one. That's because he liked and was comfortable with his nurse practitioner.

Dad's Alzheimer's journey began on a routine visit to his doctor's office. He was seventy-seven years old. Forgetfulness was not something he was closely monitoring. *Then again, maybe his doctors were?*

It was customary for us to learn about his medical history on the fly—meaning, we picked up bits and pieces of it only because it came up in conversation. For example, I learned that his mom died from breast cancer only after telling him that Coleen's sister had cancer. When my youngest son, Sean, went to the doctor for a heart murmur when he was seven, I learned more about Dad's aortic stenosis. Dad's father was an alcoholic, which I knew, but I didn't know he had a gambling problem until many years later when Dad and I were in Vegas together. I vaguely recall him telling me that one of his relatives was a well-known psychologist at Harvard who had "gone mad" and killed himself. I don't even know if the story is true, but it got me thinking that maybe this relative had Lewy body dementia, which drove him to end his life—as Robin Williams did in 2014.

Forgetfulness is par for the course for those in their seventies, but something in that visit concerned his nurse practitioner enough to recommend further evaluation. She sent him to a psychiatrist to assess whether he was dealing with memory loss due to normal aging or something more serious, like dementia. She was right; he was in the early stages of Alzheimer's.

John broke the news to me. I didn't hear it directly from my dad.

"What are we talking about here, John, a year, a few years—fifteen?" I asked him, anxious, but not outright panicked.

"We don't really know—it's different for everybody. Some people live with it for a long time. We have no idea."

There was no need to ask about a cure, for I knew there wasn't one.

It would be two additional years before he would seek an appointment with a neurologist. In the meantime, things were pretty much status quo. My dad could drive, cook meals, attend functions, go shopping, and do just about anything else that he usually would. The only noticeable signs to us were his forgetting little memories or moments, some go-to jokes, and occasionally, names. He would eventually remember what he had forgotten.

"It's the sickness," he would say whenever he forgot the words or lost his train of thought. During his seven-year battle with Alzheimer's, I never once heard him use the term Alzheimer's or dementia.

By the time my dad had his psych evaluation nearly three years later, he was dealing with multiple aspects of the disease: short-term memory loss, trouble with directions and instructions, depression, and hallucinations. Despite the delay between the psychiatrist and neurologist appointments, the game clock for his Alzheimer's had officially started.

From my perspective, 2017 was the first *actual* year of his Alzheimer's. Even then, my dad was mainly on an even keel when we got together or talked on the phone. He was intentionally less talkative and somewhat less social than usual at family events, yet again, not so much that you knew something was wrong. Forgetful at times, but you wouldn't say he was sick unless told. Primarily, he was embarrassed about forgetting words and stories that used to come so quickly to him; thus, he shied away from talking whenever he was overwhelmed.

The first noticeable sign his disease was progressing was after he shared news of a car accident. Nobody other than my dad was involved. He told us he took a wrong turn onto a road under repair and hit a barricade. So the story went. He was fine, but the car needed some work. I knew it was only a matter of time before things got worse, but I had no idea those days were coming so quickly.

In July of that year, he turned eighty years old and was the recipient of a surprise party for the first time in his life. John put together an oversized framed collage of photos for him, which would become the single most important item in his possession.

"Hey, John, this is amazing, thanks," he said, as he pointed at the photos. "We took that one in Las Vegas, remember?" he added to everyone and no one in particular.

"Look at this one, Dad, with you and Jane. That was the night of my inauguration at Fairfield."

"Sure, I remember."

About twenty photos in total representing various shades of his beard, styles of his eyeglasses, and depictions of his weight, surrounded by his boys, Jane, sister Linda, and niece Sara. The photos and his reaction to them, along with the event itself, were a mental bookend for me, the last permanent memory of normalcy with my father.

I dreaded thinking about the day I would see the other end of the bookend.

Things slowly unraveled after his birthday. Because John lived one town over from my dad, he took the brunt of calls and routinely drove to the condo to settle him down or deal with immediate issues. Honestly, I couldn't see the decline the same way he did. It wasn't an "out of sight, out of mind" situation; I simply wasn't the person who was helping him get through his week like John was. My time was coming, but it was mainly John who navigated these early waters with my dad.

The following year, 2018, was an altogether different story. My dad was now routinely forgetting how to find his way to very well-known locations, like local hockey rinks. Even driving the few miles to John's house was becoming a struggle for him. Whenever he went to Sean's hockey games, I was always on the bench coaching, so I didn't talk to him until after. At the last game he would attend, he admitted that he wasn't sure which player was Sean on the ice. This admission caught me by surprise, as he had watched Sean play for many years, and he always wore number twenty-one in honor of Mike Eruzione from the 1980 Olympic Hockey Team.

Then, less than two weeks before my last Pembroke visit, my dad went out for a drive in mid-March, 2019, and ended up at South Shore Hospital. We believe he was driving to John's house but got lost. Thankfully, there was no accident or misfortune, but he was confused and had to pull over to flag down a police officer for assistance. The policeman called an ambulance and sent him to the hospital, which resulted in the suspension of his driver's license.

It was yet another "last time" for Dad. With his last strand of independence stripped away, my dad's new reality scared us all.

From that day on, my dad was dependent on us for just about everything. With no car, he couldn't go to the pharmacy to get his meds, the supermarket to get food, or to the local Dunkin' Donuts to get his daily cup of coffee. Even if he had lived in the city, within walking distance to each of these places, we couldn't trust that he wouldn't get lost—or worse—hit by a moving car, bus, or trolley.

Upon arriving at Dad's condo a few times each week, I would administer his pills and refill them if needed, before taking him out to eat.

"What do I do now?" he asked when we got back from the restaurant or supermarket.

"Just relax and take it easy. Jane will be up later."

"Great, thanks, Markus."

He read the paper, watched a lot of TV, and took naps, but mostly, he waited for us to show up each day to take him out of the house. Sometimes it was breakfast, other times lunch. We took turns visiting, but I was with him two to three times a week from that point on. John had been helping Dad for more than a year, taking him to doctor appointments, food shopping, paying the bills, and supporting him.

It was during this time that he experienced hallucinations. Before we realized it, they were becoming permanent fixtures in his life. He would see "things" or "little people" in the condo. In the basement, where my dad's office, treadmill, and TV were, Dad saw "them" sitting nearby on the furniture. They were innocent in the sense that they never threatened or spoke to him. But they silently stared at him. Months later, while scrolling through the photos on his phone, I saw that he was trying to take pictures of them. To show us, presumably. Just recalling the images he tried to take of his "guests" makes me want to cry.

We didn't know what to call these creatures, so we created the term "demons" to describe them. According to my dad, some of them were missing limbs and had menacing faces, and the more he tried not to see the demons, the more terrifying they became. But again, there was never any communication from the demons, nor did they attempt to harm Dad. The demons ultimately played a prominent role in our lives, too. Besides scaring my dad, they caused him to start calling us at 3:30, 4:00, or 5:00 in the morning.

"What should I do? *They are everywhere,*" he would say.

His neurologist prescribed anti-hallucination medication to deal with the demons and help him sleep. They were not working. And even though his Alzheimer's was still somewhat in the "mild" stage, it was slowly taking over his life for good. The phone calls to my brothers and me were frequent, and I made the forty-five-minute trip from Walpole to Pembroke several times a week to make sure he was taking his meds and eating at least one quality meal a day. The trips to his condo were not a burden or bother. I was happy to see him and provide some much-needed company and familiarity.

Neither of us expected what was to come next.

LAST DAY AT HOME

It was my second trip to see my dad that week, but I didn't mind. I usually spent the forty-five-minute drive to his Pembroke condo listening to podcasts or audiobooks, both of which provided temporary relief from worrying about my dad.

As I got closer to Pembroke, the next podcast in the queue started to play. It was Lewis Howes's *The School of Greatness*. Bubba Watson, the twelve-time PGA Tour winner, was Lewis's guest on the show, and he was sharing a story about his father's battle with throat cancer. At the 2010 Ryder Cup in Wales, Mr. Watson's doctors told the family that he only had a few months to live. After the last match finished, Bubba broke down and cried. Not because Europe reclaimed the Ryder Cup, but because he knew his father had just watched him play golf for the last time.

Once again, my day began with tears.

Just after 9 a.m., I pulled into the visitor parking spot in front of Dad's condo. I paused before entering through the unlocked sliding glass doors so I could inhale one last breath of fresh air. My dad's life partner (my "stepmom"), Jane, was a lifelong smoker, and once I stepped inside, I knew I would be overwhelmed with the acrid smell of stale cigarette smoke, which was baked into the walls, carpets, furniture, and fixtures.

It latched onto every fiber of your clothing and coated the back of your throat. It was simply inescapable.

But on that particular morning, something far worse than the stink of Jane's decades-old smoking habit hit me first. My dad was not watching TV, skimming the paper, or napping, as he usually was, passing time until someone visited. No, this time, I nearly walked into him. He was sitting, more like *slouching,* on a kitchen chair, directly in front of me. His glossy blue eyes met mine, and he nodded his head in acknowledgment. I briefly wondered how long he had been sitting there, but the thought came and went in seconds.

"Are you all right, Dad?" I asked, breaking the silence.

"Markus. Thank God you're here. *The demons are everywhere,*" he replied, snapping out of his transfixed state of mind.

My dad could no longer stay there; the dementia demons were too much. There was no time to make a plan or analyze the situation. I would worry about those things later.

"Time to go, Dad. Let's get your things."

Together we packed a bag of clothes and toiletries, and I left Jane a note on the table. Then we left his condo for the last time that morning and started what would be the beginning of ten days together—ten unforgettable days with Dad.

Of course, we will never know why or *how* all this happened to my dad. Dementia can take years to show signs, and even though he knew much sooner than we did about his condition, there's no way he could have mapped out a plan by himself. I say "by himself" because, for most of the day, my dad was alone.

My parents' divorce papers were signed, dried, and delivered before I entered third grade. My dad was already dating someone else—or maybe they were dating before the divorce was finalized?

The formal start to his relationship with Jane was never confirmed, but I believe it was 1979. They saw each other every weekend, with my dad going over to Jane's apartment in Weymouth after dinner on Friday nights, returning home to Norwell around midnight. On Saturday afternoon, he would head to Jane's and then spend the night there.

Although my dad and Jane never officially married, I have referred to Jane as my stepmom for a very long time.

They met at The Barnside, a well-known local tavern in Norwell, since torn down and replaced with a boutique strip mall. Jane taught in a local school system, primarily middle school English. She looked and dressed the part, with her readers permanently hung around her neck, flowery understated dresses, flat shoes, and oversized cotton canvas tote bag on her arm, overflowing with papers that needed to be graded.

For as long as I've known Jane, she has been a night owl. She used to stay up late to correct her student's papers and finish grading, then, on the weekends, would sleep in, often until late afternoon. She smoked cigarettes, drank cheap white wine, and was always sick.

Cold, flu, infection, strep throat, bronchitis, chronic fatigue, and the mother of all chronic illnesses: fibromyalgia, a disorder characterized by widespread musculoskeletal pain, fatigue, and sleep, memory, and mood issues. It would only get worse over time.

Dad went back and forth to Weymouth on weekends for seventeen years before they finally moved in with one another. They bought a condo in Pembroke, further south of Norwell but still fifteen minutes before Cape Cod. The sale of our home on Beers Ave was long overdue, but Dad wanted to wait until John was on his way to college before selling. So he said. I think that the real reason for the delay was to put off giving my mom $50,000 from the sale of the Norwell house, which was the arrangement they made at the time of their divorce.

When Jane retired from teaching, her late-night bedtime and late-afternoon wakeup routine continued. She was on the opposite schedule of my dad, who got up early, had coffee, read the paper, and started his day by 8 a.m. Unless she had an appointment or event, Jane would be just getting up around 3 p.m., which meant Dad was by himself most of the day for years.

Pre-Alzheimer's, his alone time wasn't a huge deal, although I believe he would have preferred a more compatible arrangement. Post-Alzheimer's diagnosis, this was the absolute worst scenario for him.

In the months leading up to my dad's last day in his Pembroke condo, the loneliness, depression, anxiety, and dementia took their toll. With no support system in place, things spun out of control. I was in shock at the sight of his condition that morning and upset with myself for letting it get to this point.

Why hadn't I moved him in with me sooner?

PART FOUR:

TEN DAYS WITH DAD

DAY ONE: LONDON BROIL

We were both a bit rattled. My dad had no idea he had just left his home for the last time. Packing a bag full of clothes and toiletries probably didn't mean much to him. I think he believed we were going away for the night, on a trip. For me, I had no idea what I was doing. There was no planning on my part; I saw a problem and reacted.

As was typical of late, he was hungry. Most days, my dad only had one meal a day, usually just a sandwich or leftovers from when we took him out. Once the doctor told him to stop drinking, he complied immediately and lost a fair amount of weight. But now that his regular eating habits had also changed, the weight loss made him look older than his eighty-one-year-old body.

We stopped at his favorite sandwich shop, Crossroads, and devoured sandwiches. At least he could still eat. The conversation in the car was quieter than usual. I had no idea what was going through his mind, but I was trying to figure out what to do next. I called Coleen and gave her a brief update, then Lynda, my business partner, to fill her in as well.

On the way back to Walpole, we stopped at a supermarket to get things for dinner. By the time we arrived at Shaw's Market, ninety minutes or so after we left Pembroke, Dad was much calmer. There were no more demons present or talk of them, and that was huge. His face had returned to its natural color, and for the first time in what seemed like a long time, I saw glimpses of the old Dad. When I asked him what he wanted for dinner, he surprised me with his answer: London broil steak with squash and potatoes, which he would often cook for us growing up in Norwell.

It was the first of many flashbacks for both of us during his stay with my family.

By the time a nice nap was behind him and dinner was ready, my dad was a completely different person. I am not kidding. It was amazing to see the transformation. It was the first home-cooked dinner he had had in quite some time, and Dad ate like a champ that night. The unease I felt about removing him from the condo was gone.

Over the next ten days with me, I made sure he ate very well, which meant my family ate very well. After my dad stopped drinking, he developed quite a sweet tooth. Lots of ice cream, but almost any kind of dessert worked for him. Although I cook dinner regularly for my family, we also ordered take-out a couple of times a week when things got busy. But with Dad here, I was back to cooking complete meals each night. More importantly, my dad was "back" to being himself.

Coleen was intimately aware of my dad's Alzheimer's and his day-to-day routines, but today was different. She, too, was taken aback by the day's events, understandably. We all were. All I knew was that he could not return to the condo; he had suffered there long enough. And while

———

improvising was nothing new to me, it was a big deal to have Papa stay with us for Coleen and the kids. Was he staying the night, a few nights, longer? Where was he sleeping?

Not only did I need time to work on a permanent solution for my dad, but I also wanted to understand what challenges he faced during the night. I decided the best course of action was to stay in a hotel the first couple of nights. I booked us at the Holiday Inn in Norwood, and after dessert, we headed there.

It seemed like the right thing to do. John and I were already trying to get my dad into an assisted living arrangement, but none of us knew how long that would take. Ten days turned out to be enough time to make it all happen, but night one was with me in the hotel. I *needed* to know what he was experiencing each night. Would the demons be present with us in Norwood? Was he having trouble sleeping? What time was he going to bed and waking up?

It didn't take long for me to experience his routines. After a very long day, we arrived at the hotel around 8 p.m. and were asleep by 9:30. I expected him to crash much sooner, but he wanted to stay up as late as he could before taking his nighttime medication, which in part, helped him sleep. He was used to waiting until 10 p.m. to take his meds, but that didn't happen. I can only imagine how exhausted he must have been. I could barely keep my eyes open.

He made six trips to the bathroom on his first night at the hotel and thought nothing of it the following morning. That resulted in six separate times I woke up in a panic that he would unlock the door and start wandering the hotel.

———

Dad didn't have much trouble getting back to bed, which was a huge relief. It helped that we were in a hotel room, and the distance between the mattress and bathroom was minimal. He talked in his sleep often, was prone to snoring, and seemed to have sleep apnea. But overall, it wasn't as bad as I expected it to be.

Day Two: Still No Plan

Day two started with a shower, nap, and breakfast. Although he seemed to sleep well, Dad was quick to "rest" after he showered. He fell asleep on the bed while I got ready. My dad would nap two or three times a day. Sometimes it was a quick twenty-minute rest, and other times, it was an hour on the couch.

The plan for our second day was, well . . . again, I didn't have one. It was a workday for me, so we went back to my home office in Walpole after breakfast. Fortunately, I was no longer working for someone else. My new job with American Solutions for Business gave me the support and resources to thrive once again.

While I attempted to catch up on emails, my dad watched TV, napped, or sometimes just sat nearby and watched me work. Though he retired less than two years ago, it seemed more like ten years; he didn't have the ability to recall that we were once partners in business (for almost fourteen years) or likely the type of products he sold throughout his career. He knew he was a salesman but could no longer describe the products he sold—business forms, stationery, business cards, and then eventually, promotional products.

There wouldn't be much normalcy for me during the next ten days. My assistant, Lynda, covered for me whenever I was taking care of my dad, but I still needed to handle some things personally. I was blessed to have such a fantastic support group, between Coleen at home and Lynda in the office. My kids were super understanding and also quite worried about their grandfather. And now that I was working for myself again, I had the flexibility needed to make this arrangement work. Had I not taken that job with American Solutions, my dad would have still been dealing with the demons alone in his condo.

During four years of commuting to Xaverian, my dad and I spent a lot of time in the car together. My friend Bill's dad drove us to school in the morning, and Dad drove us home in the afternoon. At least until we could drive ourselves.

After minimal catch-up on our days—i.e., "How was your day?"—most of our time in the car was spent listening to either sports radio or Rush Limbaugh's program. I would have more to say to my dad than the other way around, but considering how much time we actually spent with one another, it's unfortunate that we didn't have many substantive or serious conversations. I'm sure we had some, but they weren't numerous or extensive in nature.

There's nothing wrong with silence, don't get me wrong, but I'm always interested in hearing about my kids' days—especially now that they are older. I don't always get it, but I try to initiate the conversation. My dad wasn't good at initiating. He listened, or at least I think he was listening, but I missed out on having someone prod me for more information—news about friends or classes, college considerations, or upcoming games.

Besides listening to the radio, another ritual was our daily stop at the supermarket to purchase items for dinner. I never understood, as a kid, why we had to stop each day; why didn't he buy food for more than one meal at a time? After I became a parent, I somehow fell into that same pattern. No matter how hard I tried to plan meals for the week or cook in advance, it never worked well for my schedule.

And here we were again, years and years later, back at the supermarket together, buying food for that night's dinner. I picked out the dinner, and he picked out the dessert, only it would be me doing the cooking and him watching me cook, waiting patiently for it to be served.

Over the next ten days, we enjoyed a wide variety of meals: salmon, meatballs, chicken parmesan, burgers, and swordfish. Other than the London broil or some other grilled meat, there was very little similarity to the meals he made for us—chicken livers, Hamburger Helper, Shake 'N Bake chicken, beef stew, or lasagna and the ones I cooked. It didn't matter, though; it was such a joy to cook for him. That night's meal was cheeseburgers with cannolis and eclairs for dessert.

With two nights at the hotel under my belt, it was time to return home. It was my turn to be exhausted, but I pushed it aside to focus on being present with my dad, both in conversation and observation. Those caring for people with dementia genuinely suffer the most. They witness things that make them laugh, cry, and get angry, all within a few minutes of each other. Even though my dad was barely two days under my care, I had already experienced every possible emotion, including fascination. *Is that even an emotion?*

DAY THREE: TIME MACHINE

Every day was a new adventure. I asked him more about his childhood and life before he married but didn't glean much new information. We talked about his career, coaching experiences, and his time as a single father. Bits and pieces, coming at random times. Without many filters, conversations just happened. Thoughts came and went freely.

Sean was the lucky one who gave up his room for his Papa. My dad slept in Sean's bed, and I slept on a cot a few feet from him. I say I "slept," but similar to the hotel, it was difficult to get any meaningful sleep. The hotel was much easier because I could lock the door to the hall, but the stairs in my home were just feet from Sean's room. I was on edge each night worrying about my dad wandering or falling down the stairs. One wrong turn could spell disaster and bring a whole new level of stress and worry to the situation.

The nights were the hardest for all of us. The bathroom was a mere three feet from Sean's door, yet each time Dad woke to use the bathroom, I had to make sure he made it safely back to bed. Without fail, he could never find his way back to Sean's bed. He tried several times to enter Erin's and Campbell's rooms until I got up and walked him back to bed. He still woke up to use the bathroom at least five times a night—but perhaps that was entirely normal for him? I know Coleen had difficulty sleeping, too. Her main concern was him falling down the stairs; fortunately, he never tried to use them.

Finding your way back to bed after going to the bathroom sounds like a small thing, especially when it is directly across the hall. But for those with dementia, it can be anything but small. Short-term memories, even from thirty seconds ago, can vanish instantly. You wonder how that is even possible for a few days, then accept it and deal with it. Still, when a person with dementia is in your care, you understand all too well the endless possibilities of misery imposed upon them. And watching your mom or dad go through this is heartbreaking.

We had salmon on day three, but that wasn't the highlight of the night, at least not for my family.

The most challenging aspect of Alzheimer's—"the sickness," as he called it—was figuring out what was real and imaginary. His mind would float between worlds, which made sense when he told us about his time machine. Yes, you heard me correctly: a time machine.

The way he explained it, the time machine magically placed him in another location in an instant. One minute he's home watching TV, the next he's at the Boston Garden.

"It's cool. You get in and push a button and—bang—you're somewhere else. Just like that. It's really cool!"

"Sounds amazing, Dad. Where did you get it?"

"Get what?"

"The time machine?"

"Oh, I don't know. I've always had one."

I was so fascinated when he talked about it. It was the simplest way to describe what took place in his mind; he was literally moving between worlds—his past and present. The time machine allowed me to see where his brain took him, including the casino, trips to Arizona, or visiting old friends and events.

The trips in the time machine were not all pleasant, however. On occasion, he would be in Quincy with friends, anticipating a fight with another group of guys. "Gangs," he called them. At other times, he was at the casino, only he would be down thousands of dollars and was worried about how to pay the casino back.

I would constantly have to reassure him that it was just "the sickness" (sometimes I used the word dementia, but rarely Alzheimer's) playing tricks on his mind. He nodded thoughtfully and accepted my explanation.

Day Four: The Dog

Coleen and I never wanted a dog in the house. We were busy enough with three kids, so there was no way we were taking on the added responsibility of a dog. Besides, we were constantly traveling to see her parents at their home on Long Island, or their vacation home in Pennsylvania. The kids never fought hard enough for one, either, so it was never a serious consideration.

During dinner on the fourth night, chicken parm, my dad accidentally dropped a piece of bread on the floor. He leaned over the side of his chair to get it but was unsuccessful. He couldn't reach it.

"Just leave it, Dad. The dog will get it," I joked with him.

"Oh, right, good idea."

A few minutes later, the kids and I couldn't help but laugh when we saw him trying to feed the dog under the table.

"What are you doing, Dad?"

"Oh, I was just giving a little something to the dog."

"I was joking with you, Dad—we don't have a dog!"

"Ha, ha—you got me." He laughed.

Maintaining your sense of humor while caring for someone with Alzheimer's is essential. Sometimes we laughed with my dad—other times we laughed at what he said. He didn't know this, of course, but it was okay. All of us needed little breaks from the continuous state of worry that filled the house.

DAY FIVE:
WHITNEY PLACE

For the rest of that week, we settled into our routine: breakfast, nap, some work for me, trips to the supermarket, picking up the kids from school, another nap, cooking dinner, some TV, then back to bed.

We visited three assisted living homes that week and eventually selected Whitney Place in Sharon. It was the newest of the three and was clean, modern, and friendly. It had a memory care wing, traditional assisted, and independent living residents. Having all three types of residents was important to me, as I expected he would have the chance to socialize with non-dementia residents as well.

At this point, my dad was in the "mild" stage of dementia. He could carry on a conversation and recall the basics, like his career, education, and most big events in his life, and physically was in good shape. The past four days with us were getting his appetite and energy back on track for the next part of his journey. That night I made baked haddock with buttery Ritz cracker topping. Dessert was cheesecake again.

Personally, it was great to have him by my side for these past few days. I didn't know what lay ahead for him specifically, or our relationship, but some of the tremendous guilt I felt about taking him from his home was subsiding. It was getting real. My dad had already spent his last day in his condo, and with Jane, and didn't even know it. We talked about him moving to a new home often, and like usual, sometimes he seemed to understand; at other times, he seemed to think this was a vacation.

It was emotionally draining for my entire family. I wouldn't say *on edge* was the most accurate description we felt, but it was something akin to that. During the day it was just the two of us. In between work and getting the kids to and from school, my dad and I spent every minute of the day with one another. And it truly was wonderful, despite the complexities of dealing with someone with Alzheimer's.

Prior to my dad's Alzheimer's diagnosis, I knew very few people who had the disease and only witnessed it up close with one person. I'll call him Mr. D.

Mr. D. was a salesman like me. I never found out exactly what type of product he sold, but he was an amazing storyteller. Very funny with a large personality, Mr. D. was well liked by everyone. I only saw him one week a year during our annual Pennsylvania vacation in the Poconos, yet he was one of my favorites.

When I learned about Mr. D.'s Alzheimer's diagnosis, I was shocked. I'm sure there were visible signs to his family long before we were told, but because I only saw him in July, on vacation, it had been a full year since I last saw him. He looked great. He still smiled a lot. But the joking and storytelling were gone. We had pleasant conversations, just not deep and personal ones like years prior.

———

Fortunately for Mr. D., he was able to stay in his home with the assistance of family and outside professional care. My brothers and I briefly discussed the possibility of my dad moving in with one of us, but the talks weren't expansive. Before day one started, I was kicking myself for not making this decision years ago, but by day six, I realized we had made the right choice. Not because the house couldn't handle it, but because I don't believe *I* could have. At least not while maintaining a full-time job.

I was only my dad's caregiver for ten days. My heart goes out to those who have served in this role much longer, even years. The toll it takes on caregivers is enormous, and I was grateful that we had found an assisted living complex in Sharon, which was located in the next town over, or about ten minutes away.

Each day together brought uncertainty, surprise, frustration, panic, laughter, exhaustion, and heartbreak.

"One day at a time," Coleen reminded me.

"More like one minute at a time," I joked.

At that point, it had only been close to a week ago that I had rescued my dad from the demons. Since then, his demeanor, morale, and personality had returned to normal levels for this stage in his disease. It was remarkable to witness. In a few more days, our time living together would be over; he was moving on Saturday of that week. I was both relieved and saddened. Still, I was determined to make the best of our time left together under the same roof.

And there were more surprises in store for us.

DAY SIX: FLAMINGOS

Dinners were my favorite part of the day with Dad. The conversations were interesting, mainly because you never knew what was going to come out of his mouth. We learned about the time machine a few days earlier. On day six, while I was preparing a dinner of chicken marsala, he spotted flamingos across the street.

My dad wore glasses his entire life, which gave him twenty-twenty vision. His vision remained strong during his time with Alzheimer's. He had no trouble seeing street signs and even took pride in giving me directions on routes to familiar places, like his barbershop or dentist.

It was also his way of showing me that he was *normal*. He was past the point of understanding that his brain wasn't normal, but not so far past that he didn't have moments of recognition that something wasn't right with his health.

Despite his solid vision, my dad experienced hallucinations nearly every day. He could accurately read street signs from 100 yards away but couldn't decipher that the pink plastic flamingos in my neighbor's yard across the street were not real.

"That's cool," my dad said as he looked out the window.

"What's cool?"

"Your neighbor has flamingos in his front yard. Like ten of them. Come take a look."

People who aren't used to being around someone with Alzheimer's would probably try and correct them. They might say, "Those are just plastic figurines; they aren't real flamingos."

It wasn't my habit to correct him. Unless he was afraid of a hallucination, I simply went along with it. I never saw the point in making him feel different or abnormal. Plus, in his mind, they were 100 percent real.

"Yeah, pretty cool, Dad."

The demons from his Pembroke condo had disappeared, so seeing flamingos in the neighborhood was just fine with me.

DAY SEVEN:
PAIN IN THE ASS

During the week, my dad was bothered by hemorrhoids. You could see that he was uncomfortable, especially the last few days in Walpole.

It seems that those impacted with Alzheimer's tend to keep their main personality traits even after the diagnosis. In other words, if a person was funny and witty before their diagnosis, they usually retained those traits in the early to middle stages of their disease. If they were a person who always complained or was negative, they tended to stay that way—and often got more negative. This pattern proved accurate for my dad.

Despite the obvious pain and discomfort from his hemorrhoids, he never complained, which made it difficult to determine how bad they were. My dad was a formidable man in this regard. I know, lots of people think their fathers are tough. And maybe they are. I just didn't realize how tough mine was.

When we went to Whitney to sign the paperwork, Dad couldn't sit still. I thought he was nervous about the move, but really, he couldn't sit in the chair due to his discomfort from the hemorrhoids. We bolted for home once the paperwork was completed and signed so he could lie down.

Dad had no new hallucinations or inventions to share. It was a relatively quiet meal, with fried chicken tenders, and of course, he devoured his entire plate. Vanilla ice cream with chocolate sauce for dessert. His afternoon naps were getting longer, and his bottom was still causing him pain and discomfort.

We continued to give him stool softeners during his stay but, unfortunately, would soon regret that decision.

Day Eight: Mr. Frank

My dad had been going to the same barber in Quincy Center for almost forty years. His name was Mr. Frank.

Personally, I don't find getting my hair cut exciting, or something to look forward to—probably because it is a reminder of how little hair I have left. But Dad always seemed to enjoy his visits with Mr. Frank. That day was no exception.

Having lived in Quincy before moving to Norwell, and coaching enough games at the Quincy hockey rink, my dad knew the city quite well. He gave me turn-by-turn directions, which I patiently accepted. I had only been to the barbershop once, a few months ago, and was surprised to learn how old Mr. Frank was. Or looked, anyway. He had to have been in his late eighties.

I barely knew the man, but perhaps because I knew that day's visit was yet another *last* for my dad, there was a certain amount of respect for Mr. Frank. He had been cutting my dad's hair for forty years, and their relationship was about to end.

My dad was always a generous tipper but was steadfast in his belief that you don't tip the owner when he is the one cutting your hair. I disagreed with him but wasn't about to argue the point.

———

When Mr. Frank finished cutting his hair, and my dad was attempting to put on his jacket, I gave Mr. Frank $20. He hesitated but nodded and accepted it.

He knew it would be the last time he would see my dad.

Oh, and dinner was swordfish, steamed asparagus, and a baked potato. Chocolate ice cream for dessert. Only two days remained with my dad.

DAY NINE:
THE EMERGENCY ROOM

Dad slept more than usual the couple of days prior to day nine. He would wake up, eat his Raisin Bran, drink coffee, then be napping an hour later while I worked on the computer. He would take small naps throughout the day and usually a longer one in the afternoon.

Even with the most basic conversations or actions, he had become more aloof. For instance, getting out of the car—whenever I parked the car, I had to open his door for him. He would usually follow me with a prompt, but on this day, he just sat in the car. After spending more than a week with us, I started to get frustrated with him for the first time.

"C'mon, Dad. Let's go."

It was like he couldn't hear me. It was weird; something wasn't right. He was not his usual funny and pleasant self and could not follow simple requests or instructions. But it wasn't until dinner that evening that I realized something was really wrong.

At first glance, it seemed like my dad was not hungry. The plate of food was in front of him, yet I'm not sure he realized it was even there. I remember him picking up his drink and putting it down right in the center of the

———

plate. He was spaced out, quiet, and confused. At one point, he got up to use the bathroom. His balance was shaky, and he didn't know where to go, even though it was just feet away and we prompted him toward it. He just stood there—he couldn't communicate with words. Then he started to pull down his pants as if to go right there in the dining room.

"Dad, what are you doing!" I yelled as the kids looked on in horror. I quickly ushered him to the bathroom.

Turns out, he didn't even have to go.

With Dad still dazed and confused, we got him to the couch. That's when we noticed how flush he was and took his temperature. It was 101 degrees. My sister-in-law is a nurse, so I called her from my upstairs bathroom. I was panicked and upset and started crying on the phone. I could no longer keep my emotions in check. I tried to calm myself down enough to ask them what to do, but no words would come out. I was trying to stop the heaving, trying to breathe. Should I take him to the hospital the night before he moved to assisted living or give him Tylenol to lower the fever? There was a long pause on my part until I could re-gain partial composure.

We gave him Tylenol but decided to take him to the urgent care in Foxboro. *Just breathe. Focus on getting him in the car.* Coleen offered to drive, but I declined. I was starting to regain control.

He still had a low-grade fever when we saw the medical team at the urgent care, but at least it was trending in the right direction. I told them about his hemorrhoids and asked them to examine them, as I thought they might be related. I was surprised to learn that my dad didn't have hemorrhoids.

No, instead, they told me he had a pilonidal cyst on his buttocks. The cyst was infected, and that's what the pain was the entire week. Only they could not treat him, so we went to Newton-Wellesley Hospital.

The emergency room was quiet for a Friday night, and they admitted him rather quickly. Unfortunately, that would be the quickest part of the evening. A feeling of guilt overcame me for being so frustrated with my dad all afternoon and evening. The man probably had a fever most of the day, and I missed all the signs. It was a terrifying experience for the whole family. It also, surprisingly, turned out to be one of the best days with Dad.

My earlier panic subsided, but the exhaustion from the past nine days hit me hard, and I still had no idea what was coming next. Like you do in an emergency room, you wait. And wait. And wait some more. Dad was agitated, uneasy, and far from his usual demeanor. The nurses had difficulty finding a vein to draw blood. Nobody, myself included, had any luck getting him to pee into a container, which made him even more upset and unruly.

It was 10 p.m. when we arrived at Newton-Wellesley. The doctor saw him, ran some tests, and came back to discuss the "procedure" a while after midnight. I will spare you two hours' worth of time between the doctor's initial visit and diagnosis, as well as many more unsuccessful attempts to get an Alzheimer's patient to pee into a cup. The procedure involved cutting and then draining the cyst, which they did right in his room. Let's just say it wasn't pleasant for any of us, but after the doctor finished and cleaned up, my dad slowly began to return to his old self, just like that.

And you know what, the next two hours were two of the best of the past ten days. The fever was gone, as was most of the pain from the infection. He was also hydrated again from the IVs. My dad was himself again. He drifted off to sleep at times, but when his eyes were open, he and I were having some great conversations. We laughed and told stories to each other. Well, mainly, I asked questions and listened. And laughed. There were some moments I even forgot he had Alzheimer's—that's how good it was.

We chatted about my mom and Jane, his sister Linda, my brothers, Norwell, coaching and hockey, and his long career as a salesman. Then he really surprised me.

"Did I ever tell you the story about seeing my dad in the elevator?"

"No," I lied. "What happened?"

"Well, I hadn't seen him in a long time. I mean years. I wasn't sure if he was alive. Anyway, one day I was in the elevator—I don't know where—and in comes this guy. He has no idea who I am. So, I ask him—I say, 'Excuse me, do you know who I am?' He says nothing. Then the door opens, and I started to leave. But then I say, 'I was once your son,' or something like that. I never saw him again—until his funeral."

"You went to his funeral?"

"Yeah, I did. I didn't want to—but Linda made me go."

"What was that like, the funeral?"

"No idea—I don't remember."

We laughed at that.

Amazing, right, that this was the one story he shared with me in detail? Not in a million years would he be able to intentionally remember that story during his illness, but that's Alzheimer's for you: moments of total recall, then—poof—back in the vault.

The exhaustion was hitting me hard by that point, but when he was awake, I was awake. And when he rested, I rested, but not before putting my hand on his to reassure him I was right there with him. The machines softly hummed and beeped, the IV peacefully dripped along, and a wholesome relief coursed through my own body when I realized he was going to be okay.

Honestly, I have no idea what I made for dinner that night, his last with my family in Walpole.

Day Ten: Cleanup

After ten days with us, it was time for him to move into the memory care wing at Whitney. It would be, by far, our longest day together.

We got back from the hospital at 3 a.m. and managed to get six hours of sleep. I was wiped out. My dad seemed fine though, so there was no sense in complaining. It is impossible to know what someone with Alzheimer's is thinking at any particular moment. However, I am sure that my dad didn't think he was moving to an assisted living home full-time. We had talked about it for ten days, but it would take months for the permanence to be felt by us all. Because my dad had a fever the day before, I wondered if it was even appropriate for him to arrive that day. Then again, he wasn't going to school. We were renting an apartment—his apartment—and as such, whether or not he was feeling ill or uncomfortable would not be an issue.

Much to the relief of my family, especially Erin and Sean, who had seen how delirious he was the previous night, Dad was back to making jokes and looked much, much better. It was almost like it never happened: the fever, the trip to the emergency room, and the cyst itself. Unfortunately, I was brought back to reality when I realized I had to change his dressings.

I had almost forgotten about that part until I opened my eyes and saw the gauze practically hanging out of his underwear. *Oh no, here we go.* I immediately thought of Mr. Davis, the homeless man in Jamaica, and my friend Jeff's words nearly twenty-five years ago: "What if this was our fathers who needed our help? Just think of them as we do this, and we'll get through this."

It wouldn't be the last time I had to recite those words to myself over the coming year. Fortunately, things were healing much quicker than I anticipated. But it was still hard. I had to clean the area, pack it with new gauze, and tape it back up. Not long after I finished, we had another issue with cleaning up.

Remember those stool softeners we were giving my dad all week to treat his hemorrhoids? Well, those were still in his system, and he didn't make it to the bathroom. I had to clean up the carpet—then clean him up all over again. Gloves, wipes, gauze, tape, then repeat for two more days. Things settled down after that initial accident, though I felt horrible for Sean, as the carpet in his room was *spoiled*.

John and Kerri were at Whitney Place, setting up my dad's room. There wasn't much to do but wait until they called to tell us the room was ready. I was sad and nervous but also relieved at the same time. I had no idea what to expect in the hours and days to come, yet I understood that our ten unforgettable days together were a blessing. I sometimes receive stares of disbelief when I share this feeling, but it's the truth.

My ten days with dad were demanding and draining—there is no questioning that fact. But they were only just the beginning of incredible closeness, a bond that will endure forever—and a lasting solace in knowing that I was there for him when he needed it most. His years of selflessness and sacrifice for so many people, especially his boys, were over. It was now my turn to take care of him, and I would not disappoint him—or myself.

It was a long journey to get him there. I am grateful that I had help from Coleen and my family along the way. While I was moving my dad into his new home in Sharon, Coleen was cleaning Sean's rug and moving him back in. We struggled to deal with my dad's Alzheimer's during those ten days, but we struggled together.

One of the hidden blessings to come was that I was about to get to know my dad better than at any point in my life.

PART FIVE:

ASSISTED "LIVING"

FIRST NIGHT

Move-in day was Saturday, April 13, 2019. We arrived late afternoon after John and Kerri finished setting up the room. The highlight of the room was his framed collage of photos from his eightieth birthday party. My dad took great pride in showing every guest the images, and over time it became a barometer of his memory. Some of the names and faces would fade over the next few months, but until that time came, he cherished those photos. The rest of the room was minimalistic: bed, end tables, recliner, bureau, and television. It was more than enough for his needs.

We had two room choices before his arrival. One was at the end of the hall, which was farthest away from the dining room. It was a quieter part of the floor, except after breakfast, where they would gather for morning exercise and activities. I chose the one closest to the dining room, which was pretty much the center of the entire floor. My thought was, with three meals a day in the dining room, it would be easier to find his way back to the room. And it was easier, at least for his first few months at Whitney.

Whitney Place had three floors: the ground floor was home to the memory care residents, and the upper two floors hosted the independent living residents, plus an auditorium for events and movies, an informal dining area, and some recreation space (including a library, pool tables, and televisions). That night, my brothers and I took Dad to the main dining room for dinner, primarily used by the upper-floor residents but open to everyone. It was a full-service restaurant with a menu, whereas Dad's dining room had fixed menu choices to minimize decision-making anxiety.

We tried to talk casually, but it was apparent that we were anxious about saying goodbye. After dinner, Bill and John were first to do so, and I'm sure the rides home to Milton and Duxbury were tear-filled and sad. I know mine was.

I stayed with my dad for another couple of hours, as I wanted to be there for him when he turned off the lights on his first night alone at Whitney. We spent some time with other residents who were watching TV. Around 9 p.m., I helped him get ready for bed. It was the ultimate role reversal: tucking my dad in, chatting before the lights went off, and telling him everything would be okay. I took a photo of him on that first night, a smile on his face, then told him I loved him. The conversation that night, like it did most evenings after, went like this:

"See you in the morning for breakfast, Dad."

"Sounds good, my man."

"Night, Dad. I love you."

"I love you, too. Wait! One more thing, what time?"

"What time what?"

"What time is breakfast? Where should I meet you?"

"Oh. I think 8 o'clock. But don't worry, Dad. I'll find you. Okay?"

———

"All right. Thanks, Mark."

"See you tomorrow."

"Okay."

"Night, Dad."

"Night."

The drive home to Walpole was ten minutes. I was exhausted. It was a long day. It would be a long year ahead. I thanked God that he was close. I cried the whole way home.

And I prayed to God that He would take my dad peacefully in his sleep.

———

WHERE YOU BEEN, MARKUS?

The following morning, I showed up just before 8 a.m. Dad was fully dressed but napping on his bed. He was one of the early risers on the floor, and the aides attended to him first, getting him dressed and ready for the day. If he happened to be sleeping when I arrived, I would quietly lie down next to him. Sometimes I just sat and listened to him breathe or talk in his sleep; other times, I fell asleep next to him. I used to love those moments together. The most magical part of my day was the first time he saw me. His face would light up; he was so relieved to see me. That recognition was priceless.

"Oh, there you are. I was looking for you."

It was as if I had just left him five minutes ago, even though it had been twelve hours since we last saw each other.

This routine played out hundreds of times over the coming nine months and left me asking myself the same question: *how long would this go on?* Not just Alzheimer's—but his life. He had aortic stenosis, which meant one of his valves was narrowed to the point of reducing his blood flow to the body, making his heart work harder. His aortic ste-

---

nosis was severe, yet he didn't outwardly show symptoms, such as chest pain, fatigue, or shortness of breath. And even when he did start to experience them, he just plowed ahead.

On his second night at Whitney, I took him upstairs to watch the Celtics game. We had the place to ourselves, as most residents were in their rooms by 8 p.m. Of all the pro sports teams in Boston, he loved watching the Celtics the most. Years ago, Jane's cousin worked for the Celtics, which allowed my dad to attend games and Celtics' receptions.

During halftime, we played a game of pool. We were both terrible at it, but just watching my dad play pool made me happy. I took a video and sent it to my brothers; they were impressed, too. It was the only time we played pool together—another first and last for both of us.

Before Alzheimer's, watching TV at night was the mainstay of his nightly routine. It always was. He fell asleep on the couch after a couple of drinks each night while watching it. Many nights in Norwell, I would wake him up to go to bed. He was exhausted from his long days of working and taking care of us.

Unfortunately, by the time he moved to Whitney, he couldn't sit through an entire game anymore. That was tough to witness, as he enjoyed both the Celtics and TV. Neither could hold his attention in his new home.

For the first month or two, I saw my dad twice a day. I would eat breakfast with him and then swing by after dinner. After breakfast, the recreation staff took the residents down the hall for morning exercise, including physical and mental activities. Man, he hated the morning routine. He never warmed up to it and avoided the rec staff whenever he had the wherewithal to do so. I encouraged him to attend and would even sit with him for the beginning part. It was like dropping the kids off at daycare; sometimes, you had to stay behind with them until they got acclimated, then you would sneak out when they were preoccupied. Only I never snuck out on my dad.

I always said goodbye and "See you later."

After dinner, when I returned in the evening, he was usually aimlessly walking around or sitting with the residents at the far end of the building. They would watch TV or be playing bingo or some other game. He would see me approaching from twenty yards away and bounce up to meet me.

"Markus!"

"Hey, Dad!"

"Where have you been?"

He was so excited to see me, and frankly, to get away from whatever activity they were doing. Leaving him after my visit was always hard for both of us. He hated when I had to go, and I did as well. It was so sad, leaving him there. He never fully embraced the routines, whether it was morning exercise or post-dinner snack and TV time. But we talked a lot. I engaged him in conversation as much as possible. I would video his responses, and I'm glad I did that. I still look back and listen to them often. He would say the funniest things on camera. Sometimes he would ham it up. As time went on, he lost his ability to "turn it on" and would sometimes just stare blankly at me recording him.

Whitney had a lovely dining room for the independent-living residents, and we could take my dad there for any meal at any time. I tried to take him down at least twice a week for a change of pace, but mainly it was to let him be part of the "real world" again. The memory care wing at Whitney was beautiful, and at first glance, seemed to have a lot of room to roam. Yet, the reality is residents were locked into a confined space. For some, it was like a prison sentence. They had free rein to go anywhere they wanted, but there wasn't much real estate to visit.

The main dining room might as well have been another state to my dad. After one meal early on, one of the non-memory-care residents started a conversation with my dad.

"Where are you from?" he asked.

"Scituate," my dad replied.

When they finished chatting, we returned to his room.

"Dad, you lived in Norwell and Pembroke for the past forty-six years. Why did you tell that man you were from Scituate?"

"I don't know; it just sounded better."

He talked a lot about Scituate, Weymouth, and Quincy, mainly random incidents that popped into his mind. I would tell him about a Xaverian football game, and he would ask me how Weymouth did. Jane lived in Weymouth before moving to Pembroke with my dad, so I assume that was the connection in his brain. He never mentioned Norwell or Pembroke, which I found fascinating. I know the former wasn't a happy place for him, and the latter certainly wasn't toward the end of his time there.

For as long as I can remember, my father kept a savings jar in his bedroom closet. I'm not talking loose change, but dollar bills, as in ones, fives, or twenties. After work, he changed into comfortable clothes and made the daily deposit into the jar. The savings added up quickly, and over a year—or in between Vegas trips—he accumulated thousands of dollars when he got older. He never went to the bank for vacation money. He withdrew cash from the savings jar.

At Whitney, the topic of money was near constant his first few months. He insisted on carrying a wallet with cash in it. *Old habits die hard.*

"You're all set; I took care of all your debts, Dad. You are even with everyone."

"You did that for me? Thanks, Markus. I feel better. I'd still like to have some extra money in case I need it."

"Everything is included in your rent, Dad. It's like an all-inclusive resort here."

"What about tips?" he would ask.

"Those are included. In fact, you're not allowed to tip anybody. The staff can't accept tips."

"That sucks."

I made a point of adding some singles to his wallet every time I saw him. The director wasn't happy with me. She suggested I remove his wallet altogether. It was the first of many times I ignored her advice. The wallet was important to him. Besides, he had already given up enough things from his old life, and it wasn't hurting anyone. So what if, half the time, his wallet was left in a pair of pants and was washed along with the rest of his laundry? Sometimes I would walk into his room and dollar bills would be drying on his bureau.

He would give me frequent updates on his gaming luck if we weren't talking about his wallet and how much cash was in it. In his mind, he was regularly on vacation in Las Vegas.

"I'm down about a grand right now."

"What were you playing, blackjack or Let it Ride?"

"Little bit of both."

"Don't worry; you always get it back."

THERE'S SOMETHING ABOUT MARY

The staff warmed up to my dad right away. They appreciated his sense of humor and quick one-liners, even when he botched them! He was generous with his hellos and friendly to everyone. Even though I would describe my dad as a quiet man, he was chatty, outgoing, and funny when he was comfortable with you, and the staff got to see that every day.

I smiled a lot with my dad. So much so that he was constantly asking me about it.

"Why are you always smiling?" he asked.

"I'm just happy to be with you."

No matter how difficult a visit was or sad I was to leave, I made sure I was smiling when we were together. It was genuine. I was so happy to be with Dad—grateful to have that time together. I wanted to be fully present each visit, and for the most part, I was. The only time I sort of rushed our visits was on Sunday evenings when it was time to refill his medication. For the first four months, I saw him every day but Saturdays, and most of the time, I saw him more than once a day.

———

What my dad didn't realize was that he smiled a lot, too.

His Alzheimer's caused him to say hilarious and often outrageous things. After one appointment with his neurologist, he leaned in and whispered, "I got laid here last night." We were at South Shore Hospital, walking toward the exit.

"Really, with whom?"

"One of the nurses, but let's keep that between us girls, okay?"

Another time, in the front seat of my car on the way to Duxbury, he said something about Mary, his new friend at Whitney Place. She was more like his new girlfriend, at least in his mind, and we didn't stop him from believing that.

"What was that you just said, Dad?"

"Mary is pregnant, or at least that's what I heard."

Coleen and the kids were in the car and could not stop laughing about his Mary comment.

"She's pregnant?"

"Yep, that's what I heard."

I met Mary the week before Dad moved in. We stopped by for lunch one day so he could get familiar with the dining room. Mary was sitting across the room with three other women. When lunch was almost over, my dad overheard them discussing something about the city of Brighton, which was his hometown. To his credit, he got up and said, "I'll be right back," before proceeding to head over and join the conversation. It was an incredible sight to witness. A few minutes later, I went over and introduced myself.

I looked at Mary and said, "And who are you here visiting?"

"I'm not visiting anyone. I live here."

———

"Of course. Well, it's nice to see you, Mary."

She looked like she could have been visiting her mom. Her hair seemed styled, she wore makeup, and she was well dressed. She immediately took to my dad, probably because there were so few men living at Whitney—or at least, so few men who seemed somewhat put together. You often hear about nursing home romances, but I didn't believe that they existed. They do. I would get to know her better than any other resident.

"I'm part Portuguese and part Irish," Mary would say, with a wink, in her imitation Irish brogue.

Then in her next sentence, I learned that her father was a boxer. In fact, I learned a lot from her in one breakfast conversation.

"I dated Frank Sinatra when I lived in New York," she said with a wicked grin.

"Wow! That's a cool story. Tell me another."

"I also sold cars for Ernie Boch. I sued his ass and won. They paid me a lot of money."

All of her comments proved to be true. I got to know Mary's daughter, and she confirmed Mary's often-repeated backstory. From day one, Dad sat with Mary at every meal. He was by her side day and night. Mary was fond of my dad—she was a lifesaver.

To find someone like Mary so quickly in his time at Whitney was important. I recall reading a story about Justice Sandra Day O'Connor and how she dealt with her husband's Alzheimer's. On one visit, her husband introduced her to his girlfriend. She wasn't upset at all; she knew how vital companionship was in these places, and if he was happy, she was happy. With my dad, it made a *huge* difference.

———

Mary and my dad were inseparable for the first few months. I even got them on video dancing together. Mary was so good with my dad, but she was a tough woman and often got into fights with residents—about sitting in *her* chair, talking too loud, or just being nosy. She could be nasty at times, and it was awkward to witness. Even my dad would tell me about Mary's fights. Still, I will always be grateful to Mary for taking care of my dad early on at Whitney. I know my dad's transition would've been much more difficult without Mary in his life.

In addition to Mary, we sat with Elizabeth and Violet each morning for breakfast.

"Good morning, ladies! *It's nice to see you* today," was my standard greeting.

Violet was one of my favorites. She was in her early nineties and such a pleasant woman. You knew she was a kind, loving parent and wife; you could tell by sitting with her—patient, calm, and easy-going. We watched the birds flying in and out of the trees outside the windows, and I kept her coffee fresh and hot.

Elizabeth was a tea drinker. She enjoyed her daily crossword puzzle and took great pride in knowing the date and day of the week. (She was probably the only one who knew both each day.) Elizabeth was engaging during conversation. I wouldn't call her a know-it-all, as that sounds too negative, but she was confident, if not stubborn at times. She defended herself well when Mary was on the attack, though, making for some entertaining meals. Eventually, she would tire of Mary's antics and move to another table permanently. One day, Bobbie ("the girl with a guy's name," according to my dad) was sitting with Elizabeth and asked who my dad was.

———

"Oh, that's Barry," Elizabeth said. "He's senile!"

It became clear early on that most of them did not realize they, themselves, had dementia; many didn't know why they were living there. Ruth, another one of my favorites, would say to me almost every day, "I just don't feel good; I don't feel like myself today. I don't know what's wrong with me."

I often wondered why the staff didn't have more programming or discussions about their dementia. My dad, to his credit, wanted to talk about it and asked me why they never did.

"I just think it would be helpful, that's all," he said.

"I agree with you. I think it would be helpful."

Breakfast with Dad was a big hit for the other residents, too. Very rarely did another visitor stop in for breakfast. I felt like I was a bright spot in their days. I asked about their families, complimented their outfits, or answered questions. In short order, I would get to know all of them well. Seeing their faces light up when I walked into the dining room was pretty special.

After breakfast, Dad and I would take a walk around the building, which measured one-quarter of a mile. It was good for him to get some fresh air, as they spent most of their time indoors. This one-on-one time allowed him to tell me about his adventures at the casino tables ("I was down last night") or share another argument Mary got into with someone.

Being part of this Alzheimer's world was, at times, amazing to witness. I listened to their stories, complaints, and confusion. I poured them coffee and brought them breakfast when the staff needed help. The conversations I had with each of them were uplifting and sad at the same time. Many were once incredibly successful and talented moms and dads. Now, they were someone entirely different.

At any given time, fifty or so residents were living in the memory care wing at Whitney. All of them had some form of dementia. Most could no longer tell you why they were there, but regardless, most residents living in my dad's wing could carry on a conversation. That is, they could comment on the weather, watch TV, share a story about something from their past, or reply to basic questions. Many did not remember their conversations ten minutes later (and that is rather generous) but most could give you their essential background: where they grew up, what they did for a living, and how many children they had.

But my dad had a different form of dementia. His was a hybrid of Alzheimer's and Lewy body dementia. The primary difference was that Lewy body didn't just lead to memory loss; it also hampered a person's mood, behavior, thoughts, and actions. He had trouble getting the words to come out in the proper sequence and with language itself. He was the only resident I interacted with that had difficulty carrying on a conversation. He knew what he wanted to say, but what came out of his mouth sometimes didn't fit the conversation. I became adept at determining what my dad was saying and often translated his answers to those around him.

His hearing was fine. It was so good that he would hear questions from across the room and answer them.

———

"Do you want some more coffee, Ruth?" an aide would ask a woman across the room.

"No, I'm fine," Dad would reply.

Even though they were two tables away and not talking to him, he would often reply as if they were speaking to him. It was challenging at times, sometimes funny, and occasionally very frustrating. It would only worsen over time.

It was never a burden to show up each day to see Dad. It was exhausting but not burdensome. It was tough for him to be at Whitney. He put up a brave face but was lost without me by his side. He never felt comfortable or at peace in assisted living. It was stressful for him, trying to figure out what he should be doing all day long. And he was always worried that I wasn't coming back to see him. One Thursday night, I reminded him that Coleen and I would be going to Pennsylvania for the weekend to spend time with her family at their vacation home.

"I'll be back Monday though, okay?"

He looked at me with a shocked expression.

"That's terrible."

"What's terrible, Dad?"

"You are moving to Pennsylvania?"

"No, Dad, I'm just going for the weekend. I'll be back for breakfast Monday morning."

"Oh, thank God."

Fortunately for both of us, he still had Mary by his side.

-

PARANOID AND WEEPY

Owned by Salmon Health & Retirement, which operates six retirement communities, Whitney Place was relatively brand new. It opened its doors in October of 2017. That's one of the features we liked about the facility. It was a beautiful campus and well maintained. The reviews were good, and it seemed like a good fit for my dad.

Our overall experience at Whitney Place was positive and I'm grateful to Michelle at 2Sisters Senior Living Advisors for the referral. Like any new situation, however, there's a learning curve---especially for first-time sandwich parents like me.

After less than three weeks at Whitney, my dad reportedly had a fall. There were no witnesses to the fall, and by the time the night aides came to him, my dad was on his feet. They heard a loud noise and assumed he fell, but nobody at Whitney could tell us what had happened. The staff called an ambulance and Dad was sent to the hospital.

Anytime somebody with Alzheimer's or dementia is sent to the hospital, for any reason, they never come back the same. My dad had a great start at Whitney Place until the incident, which was a total disaster. He was sent to Norwood Hospital for a CT scan, which they provided, but was then sent to another hospital because Norwood didn't have a specialist on staff to read the test results.

From there, he went to St. Elizabeth's Hospital in Boston. Because the CT scan indicated blood in the brain, the medical staff there doubled, almost tripled, his anti-seizure medicine. The nurse on duty included my dad's full medical history and report, which indicated his Alzheimer's and current medications. Still, because the doctor could not tell if the blood was old or new, hospital protocol dictated that they prescribe anti-seizure medication to slow any bleeding in the brain.

That was probably the worst thing they could've done for my dad. Upon returning from the two-day hospital visit, he was banged up for the next few weeks. He just wasn't himself. His speech and movement had declined, and his hallucinations increased. He didn't see any demons—those disappeared once and for all when he left Pembroke—but he was seeing shapes, animals, and people who weren't there. The hallucinations were innocent, but his paranoia was scary.

Texting was my primary communication with my brothers on Dad's condition. Here are some messages John and I exchanged following his return from the hospital:

Rough start today. Paranoid about the workers hurting him. He didn't want me to leave. Will check on him later.

Saw Dad today. At first very normal. Then he started crying. Never seen him cry before. We had lunch. It was nice. Typical ramble but overall pretty good; super emotional. Hard to leave. I felt like I was locking him in.

Leaving now. He was good until I told him I was leaving. Started

freaking out and asking, "How am I getting home?" I had trouble getting
him to sit in his chair.

He was in bad shape this morning. Paranoid and weepy.

Everybody at Whitney noticed his rapid decline, from the aides and
nurses to the recreation staff and Mary. And there were other noticeable
changes. He now had significant depth perception issues while walking
and eating. He would pick up his coffee, take a sip, and put it down in
the middle of his plate. Steps were tricky; he often tripped over his own
feet walking down the hall. Lewy body dementia often comes with hallucinations, and sometimes violent behavior or action. The trip to the
hospital seemed to exasperate those symptoms.

The Whitney staff recommended around-the-clock care for him after he threatened to kill a worker with a machete. That was troubling on
many fronts, but as soon as we adjusted his Seroquel medication, he no
longer said anything remotely violent or threatening. A few weeks later,
he said to the staffer, with a huge smile on his face, "Hi Matthew. I used
to hate you but don't anymore."

The change in medication was critical, but there was something else
at play here: sleep—or lack of it. When my dad was staying with me, he
would nap two or three times a day. Yet, at Whitney, he wasn't taking
any naps. The hospital incident shed light on some concerns at Whitney
and allowed me to address them with the general manager and care director. I had questions and needed answers:

What was the actual communication policy for alerting families when there is an issue (who gets called and when)?

Can you clarify the policy on sending residents to the hospital?

Is the staff checking on my dad every hour at night like they are supposed to?

What time is he going to sleep at night? Waking up? Is he resting during the day? Can you provide a sleep chart for us?

How often is he taking a shower? Can you make sure he is showering every other day?

It was yet another role reversal for my dad and me. I had to look after his best interests and advocate for proper care. I felt like I was in a parent-teacher meeting. The same basic guidelines apply: if you don't speak up, your child (or, in this case, parent) can fall through the system-wide cracks. It's not like I knew how to do this going into the experience. The brochures are pretty, the building is clean, and the sales team says all the right things; so how would I know that we needed to stay on top of his daily care?

To their credit, the team at Whitney Place responded promptly. From the director on down, the staff was diligent about making sure my dad was properly supported in his new home. Although it took an incident to confirm certain internal policies, my dad's care not only got better because of it, but his Alzheimer's leveled off for the next couple of months.

You take what you can get, knowing that things can decline at any point.

PERSPECTIVE

Three months into Dad's stay at Whitney, things had settled down quite a bit. It took him nearly a month to recover from his hospital trip, but gradually, he did recover. Physically, he looked terrific. When people asked how my dad was doing, I told them he was doing great. At times, this puzzled my brothers, as his Alzheimer's was always *bad* to them. They did not see Dad every day, so his condition seemed to get much worse with each visit. They often just saw him struggling with his words or speaking gibberish, depending on the time of day—and he did both, often.

However, when you see someone with Alzheimer's every day, your perspective changes. You see good days and bad, whether it relates to their mood, speech, movement, memory, appetite, or energy level. I was there six days a week, talking to my dad and other residents, so naturally, my viewpoint on how Dad was doing would be different.

I was incredibly proud of how he battled back from his hospital visit and was pleased to see that his medication adjustment had drastically reduced his paranoia. But there's no question his dementia worsened. I should have expected a decline at some point, yet it was still hard to accept. Compared to his peers, he had a more challenging time communicating. In fairness to my dad, he worked hard to engage in conversation.

I constantly asked him questions to keep the conversation moving, increasing his chances of saying the wrong words. While his friends could handle basic conversations better, I certainly was not asking them the kind of questions I posed to my dad. Such as: *What's on your mind today? Tell me about your dreams. How is everything going with Mary? Are you meeting new people? Have you used the time machine lately?*

Assuming it wasn't lost or buried in one of the bureau drawers, Dad still carried his wallet with him each day. However, unlike the first few months, his near-constant worries faded about having enough money in his wallet. Unfortunately, that was a metaphor for other lifestyle changes as well. Television, for example. Like his wallet, the TV remote often went missing, and even when it was around, he could no longer figure out how to use it. He couldn't turn on the TV or change the channels. A few times a week, when we passed Glen, the head of facilities, he would ask him to come to the room later to fix his TV (translation: help him use the remote). That lasted about four months until my dad started noticing that his TV was no longer in need of fixing.

That's because it was always on.

The overnight television issue drove me nuts. I was constantly reminding the night staff to make sure his TV was off after he fell asleep. They were required to check on him hourly, so why didn't they ever turn the TV off? I understood that these situations are routine for staff members, and are likely not worth sharing with family members, but for us newbies, these things matter, especially when you're writing large checks out to them each month.

It was easy to get lulled into a false sense of security when Dad's Alzheimer's leveled out for a month, two, or six months without any noticeable change to his behavior, speech, or gait. The hard truth, the reality that never fully sank in, was that things were guaranteed to get worse for my dad. I knew they would but didn't want to acknowledge it.

The summer months of July and August were level months for him. Physically, he looked good. His walking, besides his usual depth perception issues with stairs and steps, was excellent. He often complained about his chronic lower back and hip pain, but we continued our post-breakfast walks, and our talks remained productive.

He would often ask me, "How's my talking today?" He was very conscious of losing the ability to communicate well. I could understand most of what he said, even if the words didn't always match his intentions. If I didn't know what he was trying to communicate, I just rolled with it, but usually, I knew. I was his "interpreter," so to speak.

In July, we went to John and Kerri's house to celebrate his birthday. He was great. Somehow, he managed to keep it together whenever he had to, such as a celebration or doctor's appointment.

Spending time outside with him during the summer months was my favorite. Just sitting by the main entrance, relaxing in the sunshine and warm weather, greeting people as they came and went. I continued to video him each time I visited and captured some more funny lines from him. I wasn't recording for that purpose but rather to document his digression.

"Dad, give me some words of wisdom or advice."

"Try not shaving for a week."

The conversations about money were essentially over. His newest concern was whether he had enough food in the room: milk, soda, snacks.

"You said you were going to send me some more."

"You don't need any more cash, Dad."

"Take a look in there; it's all soft drinks."

"Oh . . . food. You need more food?"

"I don't want it to be all sweets either. Maybe some nice cookies or something."

"Well, cookies are sort of sweet, aren't they?"

"What I want is something I can go two or three nights and not get all screwed up."

"Like maybe peanut butter crackers?"

"I've got some peanut butter, from three weeks ago or four, whatever I got there, uh, and I don't know if I screwed them up or something. I was doing fine with them. I guess you can't really keep them in a . . . there must be some treatment for them in the doctors."

Translation: He would like more snacks, and not just soda.

I had already bought bread, peanut butter, and jelly because he asked for them, but it was almost impossible for him to make a sandwich himself, and it was all likely tossed. I think I threw out the bread myself because it was getting old. I did tell him I would take him food shopping, and he was calling me out nicely!

"We can go shopping after the doctor's," I told him.

"That would be nice. I am not trying to burst . . . to push you away. I say this is crazy; I can't just live on soda water . . . and, you know, money comes out when you're putting $15 or $20 a month, something like that. You just get drained. I know you say you don't need it [money]— not need it like you would at a third game of a world series, you know, but otherwise it's a necessary evil. And that's all I can say about that."

Translation: "I'm not trying to be a pain in the ass."

He also acknowledged that he didn't need money at Whitney, which I had been telling him for the past four months. I understood what he was talking about; we were on the same page, even though some of the words were jumbled or *out there*, such as "*not need it like you would at a third game of a world series.*" So, when my brothers asked me how he was doing, I thought he was doing great, to be honest.

It was all a matter of perspective.

THE BREAKUP

The struggle to get the right words out of his mouth became more pronounced in the fall. The other noticeable changes I witnessed were his difficulty finding his room and his declining spatial awareness. It was no longer automatic that he could find his way back to his room after a meal or activity. He would walk right up to it and stare at it; it's like he could sense that it was the right place but wasn't sure. Even seeing the shadow box next to the door that contained memories from his past wasn't enough to assure him that he had the correct room. That was tough to witness. Though, to be fair, he was not the only one who could not find his room.

By "declining spatial awareness," I mean, if you walked a few steps behind him, you might as well have disappeared. Walking down the hall to get coffee, if I stopped to talk with someone, I was gone, as if I went somewhere in his time machine. Then, when I caught up with him again and walked beside him, he would say, "Oh, there you are."

Yet despite the changes, our daily conversations continued, which meant my videos continued. As I expected, the responses were up and down; some were funny, others heartfelt, and some were surprising, at least in terms of how much information Dad could recall on a good day.

———

"How are you today, Dad?"

"I'm doing great, man. As long as I can meet people in this rat trap. Sorry about that. Can't help it."

"Are you happy?"

"No," he said a little too quickly, and we both laughed out loud. "Little bit, maybe," he added quickly.

He still had the wits about him to comment on how "this place is like a prison" almost five months in. And even though I prompted him to say things about Bill and John, I never told him what to say.

For my brother Bill's fiftieth birthday message, he said, "Hi Bill, just telling to say, good birthday to me, because, you know, you're worth it. Talk to you later. No, wait . . . I'm going as we come, so I am really winging it. I love you and will be glad to see ya."

At the end of September, we were having lunch in the main dining room, and he shared a story about the Seahawks, the youth hockey program in which we belonged, and he coached. He described a big come-from-behind win his team had against Natick.

"So, ah, we were really up for it, because these are the one, two [number one and two ranked teams]. We get out, bang, puck in the net. Bang, puck in the net. Bang, puck in the net. 3-5 is the score."

"Are you winning or losing?" I asked.

"Losing. But then it was bang, 4-5. Bang, 5-5. Then at the end of the second . . . [period] we got five goals and tied. It ended up being 7-6. They couldn't believe it, the Natick kids. Couldn't believe it [that we came back and beat them]. That's the best team we played all year."

He goes on to talk about a Lake Placid tournament game against a team from Michigan. We always referred to them as the Compuware team because that's who the team's sponsor was; their uniforms were plastered with Compuware logos.

"We were down a couple of goals to them, and they were one of the best teams in the country. What helped us, though, was that our team could hit in games. The Michigan kids weren't allowed to hit yet, but here, everyone could. We dumped the puck in and kept using the body. We checked them all over the ice. They didn't know what to do. They were the best team—but we beat them."

"Great story. I love hearing that one."

"The only big game we didn't win was the States . . . we lost to Southie. That was really exciting."

He was referring to my South Shore Seahawks team and the state championship game against South Boston, the one in which I could not play because of my broken wrist.

It was our most extended recorded conversation. No surprise it was about hockey. The actual words that came out might have been out of order, but the detail was excellent. The Compuware game took place in 1980—forty years ago. My dad wasn't one to brag, but he enjoyed sharing the Compuware story before he got sick. It was the most memorable coaching win of his career. You could say that the win over Compuware was like their Miracle on Ice, which was ironic, as the actual Miracle game took place in the same rink two months prior.

The last few months of my dad's time at Whitney were *bumpy*. He was forgetting people in his life permanently, including my stepmom, Jane, his partner of almost forty years. The staff dressed, bathed, and changed him; he could no longer take care of himself without major prompts and assistance. He had issues with his bowel movement timing, which led to accidents, and he was still occasionally urinating in the trash can.

There were also long stretches of silence when he was standing in front of his photo collage and it was understood, by me at least, that the days of asking him about the people and places on that collage were over. Once the pride and joy of his possessions, it was now hardly noticed or understood by my dad. I had no choice but to push those feelings of sorrow aside because I was not included among the forgotten.

For the time being.

Because I saw him daily, his face continued to light up with recognition when he saw me enter the room. I made a promise to myself that I would continue visiting him for as long as he remembered me. Not a day went by that he didn't recognize me, and in fact, the visits became longer over time. It became more difficult to leave him there, for even though there were other residents and staff present, he was increasingly feeling more alone. He could not communicate that to me, but I saw it on his face and in his body language. I felt it.

The emotional weight I felt with each visit was getting heavier. Conversations were harder to manage, as Dad began to have difficulty hearing or understanding the words I was using.

"Dad, would you like me to leave your water on the table?"

"What's a PC?"

I would repeat the question. Then repeat it again. And he still didn't understand.

I tried to stay calm, and managed to, but I would often leave him more upset than usual. Was it Alzheimer's, his hearing, or a combination of both? There was no way for any of us to know it, but his health was declining rapidly—and not because of his Alzheimer's.

In the late fall, the big news in my dad's life was that he and Mary had broken up. Mary could be tough to deal with, but as I said, she was a Godsend for my dad. She literally saved his life in the first few months. Had she not taken to my dad within days of his arrival, he would have been utterly lost without her. The saddest part was that just prior to their "breakup," Mary had suffered a mild stroke. She was gone for a few weeks, and she was a different person when she came back. They always are.

Even my dad knew that Mary wasn't the same person she was before, and I was sad for him. Somehow, he knew, or at least believed, that they were officially over as a couple.

The following month, we were able to get Dad to Duxbury for Thanksgiving. Once again, he was able to come across as doing better than he was. It was a fine showing for my dad, and we all enjoyed his presence. Unfortunately, it would be the last time he would see the extended family together.

It also marked the beginning of his darkest days at Whitney Place.

Your Father Needs Help

By Christmas, Dad's Alzheimer's was taking over, or so we assumed. His energy level was low, and his gibberish was intensifying. He was beginning to eat less and was far spacier than ever before.

Coleen and I were planning to host Christmas at our house so that Dad could be with us. Unfortunately, a stomach bug went through Whitney right before Christmas. It lasted nearly two weeks, and we postponed hosting the families because of it.

On Christmas Day, I headed over to have lunch with him. There was no meaningful recognition on his part that it was Christmas, yet I felt fortunate to be able to see him, nonetheless. And I was relieved that he was no longer experiencing symptoms from the illness that went through the building. It wasn't our finest two hours together, as my mind was elsewhere. We were getting ready to travel to Pennsylvania to be with Coleen's family. I was sad to leave him behind—sad he would be alone for Christmas and terrified that something terrible would happen while I was away.

January 2020 would be the roughest month at Whitney for Dad. Each morning I saw him for breakfast, Ruth, his ninety-year-old friend and someone I had spent many hours getting to know, would call me over to her table.

"Your father needs help. He's not right. Something is wrong with him. He's wandering the halls. He needs help."

And she was 100 percent right. I knew he needed help but didn't know how to help him. It was a terrible feeling when a dementia resident was pointing out that my father needed help. I know the aides could see that he needed more assistance, too, but seeing an older man wander in the halls or have trouble talking or eating was par for the course at Whitney. It didn't stick out to them as it did to me.

Some meals, Dad couldn't even feed himself properly. He was unsteady on his feet, so they tried to keep him confined to his room more than they usually would. As tired as he was, I'm sure he was trying to get up and walk around; he never wanted to feel left out or alone. That's just who he was. I was already with him two hours a day and couldn't always get back a second time to see him.

On the afternoon of January 17, I went to visit Dad. The aides had said he was pale and weak and that they couldn't get him out of his recliner. They were not wrong.

He was a disaster. Something was wrong. He could not feed himself, so I ordered him a sandwich, and we ate in his room. He had a few bites, so that was a good sign. He felt warm, but the nurses were not allowed to take his temperature, which I thought was insane. They reminded me that this wasn't a healthcare facility, like a nursing home.

———

I called Coleen to bring a thermometer to me, and sure enough, he had a fever. Another trip to the hospital for my dad and me.

The ER in January was the last place you wanted to be. It was jammed with sick people, some wearing masks, due to the large volume of flu cases. We checked in around 8 p.m. at South Shore Hospital and waited. Every sniff, cough, and sneeze made me cringe, yet neither of us wore masks. It seems crazy in hindsight, but mask-wearing had yet to be the norm. It was still two months before the COVID-19 pandemic hit.

The ER staff treated my dad in the hallway because all the emergency rooms were full—they usually were at this hospital. The nurse could not find any reliable veins from which to draw blood. This problem wasn't entirely unusual; the last few times he required blood to be drawn, a similar result occurred. Even a more experienced nurse had difficulty tapping a vein. The pricking and prodding only agitated my dad further. He angrily snapped at them and pulled away, which is something I hadn't seen in quite some time. After many unsuccessful attempts in both arms, they managed to get enough blood to the labs for analysis.

The results didn't just shock me—they shocked his entire medical team. His hemoglobin blood counts were dangerously low. While a normal range is eleven to eighteen, his was a five! He needed a blood transfusion right away to bring those numbers up. But why were his numbers so low? That was the next question we had.

By 9:30 the following morning, he was on his fourth bag of blood. For the next two days, the family took turns staying with Dad in his room. By Sunday, he was more alert and talkative. It was still largely gibberish, but at least he was communicating more. In many ways, this hospital visit was similar to the night before he moved into Whitney—only this time, I was much less optimistic about his future.

It wasn't his Alzheimer's or aortic stenosis that caused him to lose so much blood. It was colon cancer.

FALLING

His doctor gave us four options regarding the cancer: chemotherapy through an IV at the clinic, oral chemotherapy, iron IV and blood transfusions as required, or do absolutely nothing. The colon cancer itself wasn't in danger of killing him in the short term; the doctor said Dad would likely not see serious complications for two years, if left untreated. But honestly, his overall condition was terrible. He wasn't going to be able to get to the clinic or handle any chemo. Surgery wasn't a viable option due to his heart condition, and the anesthesia medication required would substantially worsen his Alzheimer's.

My brothers and I decided we were not going to treat his colon cancer.

The two weeks following his discharge were difficult. His new Alzheimer's baseline was rough. It was hard for him to communicate and eat; it was almost like he had a minor stroke. We knew his time at Whitney was coming to an end when the staff talked about him needing twenty-four-hour care at a rate of $28 per hour, which was three times the amount of our current spending for his care. His dramatic decline further ignited my emotional distress, which was not easy to reconcile.

Since my dad moved to Whitney, I had been recording him almost daily. Sometimes fifteen seconds, and other times a few minutes. But it was a video from John, sent to me on February 1, the day I arrived in Texas for a business trip, that almost did me in. There were no words on the recording, just my dad staring at a patch of wall in his room. *His face was inches from the wall, and he was just staring at it.* The staring went on for ten minutes, mesmerized by something and yet nothing. I only got a snippet of the nearly ten-minute-long episode, but it was more than enough for me to lose it that morning in my hotel room.

When I took Dad from Pembroke for the last time, ten months ago, it was by choice. His last day at Whitney would not be. The day John took that video was his last day there. After John said goodbye and was driving home, he received a call from Whitney saying Dad had fallen and was not responding; he was conscious and unhurt, just not responding to their prompts to sit up or move. Protocol required them to call an ambulance, and he was on his way to another hospital. John returned to Whitney and followed the ambulance to Good Samaritan Hospital in Brockton. It was the start of another grueling week.

The medical staff at Good Samaritan found nothing wrong with my dad. They were ready to send him back to Whitney, but fortunately, John convinced them to admit him for the night. He argued that he could not safely go back to Whitney, and they agreed. One night became three, which became seven, which was precisely the amount of time we needed to get him into a nursing home for full-time, around-the-clock care.

Dad slept nearly the entire seven days he was in Good Samaritan. I returned from Texas with a nasty cold, so it took me a few days to see him at the hospital. When I did see him, he could barely open his eyes. The situation was so dire that John said his goodbyes to him, just in case.

John believed my dad would last a week, or less, at the nursing home. I don't recall thinking along those lines. I didn't have high expectations or hopes that he would make another rebound, but I intentionally didn't say goodbye to him. I can't explain why, but it didn't feel to me that it was that time yet. He had rebounded so many times in the past; why couldn't he do it again?

Because I was in Texas during most of my dad's stay, John worked directly with 2Sisters Senior Living Advisors to locate a nursing home. They were the ones who found Whitney Place for us and were super helpful once again. It was a relief to have them jump on this right away and we were, again, grateful to Michelle and her team.

However, of the four places they identified, based on location and reviews, only one could take him immediately: Newfield House, located in Plymouth. It was a private nursing home about fifty minutes from Walpole but only twelve minutes from John's house in Duxbury.

While my dad lived at Whitney Place in Sharon, I could be in his room or by his side in under ten minutes for the past ten months. We hadn't been this close to one another since I lived with him in Norwell twenty-five years ago. It was an absolute gift, a blessing, one of many I experienced during his battle with Alzheimer's.

Whether Dad would last a few days, months, or longer at his new home at Newfield, I was relieved that one of his boys would continue to

———

be close. I would not have admitted it at the time, but I was exhausted. Essentially, it was ten months and ten days of constant worry, stress, and responsibility for him while still maintaining full-time duties with my own family, like making dinner each night, getting the kids to school, and coaching hockey. I had every intention of seeing him multiple times a week, but just not every day like I had been doing. It was time to pass the torch on to John.

"The place is old and dated," John told me, "but it's clean, and the care seems really good."

He was tempering our expectations because Whitney Place was so bright, clean, and relatively new. I trusted his judgment completely and was not worried.

After seven nights at Good Samaritan, Dad was discharged and prepped for his next and final destination. I followed his ambulance to Newfield to get him settled. He left the hospital in a stretcher, mouth open, sound asleep; he arrived at Newfield, on a stretcher, mouth open, sound asleep. Maybe this was the end after all? It certainly looked that way.

Newfield House sits on top of a hill, with views of Plymouth Harbor and the ocean. It's less than a mile to Plymouth Rock and the Pilgrim burial grounds. It's a spectacular location, even during the winter months. The grounds were bare and muted, but you could tell they were well tended during the warmer months, and I was struck by the property's inherent beauty. As I drove up the long drive, to the top of the hill, I felt a calm overtake me. I wasn't nervous or anxious. Something just felt right about the place.

The EMT staff brought Dad to his room, still on a stretcher, eyes closed. John was right; the place was old and dated, but it was apparent from the moment they wheeled my dad in through the front door and took him to his room that the care would be exceptional. And it was.

Despite sleeping for nearly a week in the hospital, Dad remained asleep the entire time I was with him that Tuesday afternoon. Perhaps I should have said my goodbyes, too, as John had days earlier, but something in my gut held me back. I stayed with him for hours, and he remained asleep the entire time. I was so discouraged by the time I left the building. I sat in my car and could not control the tears.

And I prayed to God, yet again, to take my dad peacefully in his sleep.

RISING

The following day, my dad's first as a resident at Newfield, the staff had him dressed and in a wheelchair for breakfast. I wasn't with him, but my brothers sent photos. Wow. I have no idea what transpired overnight, but within twenty-four hours of his arrival at Newfield, he was not only awake but was alert and eating again. I was stunned. It was a complete 360-degree turn from just two days ago. Before leaving that day, the nurses had him walking and eating solid food for the first time in eight days.

Should we have had him here months ago?

Within a week of his admittance to Newfield, he was back to eating finger foods by himself. When I was with him, he had no trouble eating muffins and small sandwiches. Drinking was still somewhat tricky because of his depth perception issues, but he managed.

Despite the distance to Plymouth, I didn't mind the drive. It was relaxing and gave me time to think. I also didn't have to do anything once I arrived at Newfield. Meaning, I didn't have to help my dad in his room, refill his meds, put on a happy face for the residents, help get the coffee ready in the dining room or take him out to get things at the supermarket. My only job was to spend time with my father.

Two, three, sometimes four days a week, I visited my dad. We talked as much as we could. Sometimes we just settled for solitude. I could sit next to him, put my hand on his knee, and hug him goodbye. Sometimes I shaved his beard, walked beside him in the recreation room, or watched TV with him. Most importantly, he still recognized me, as evidenced by his calling my name out or smiling upon seeing me enter the room. There was no greater feeling.

The month of February passed quickly. Dad used a wheelchair most of the time, but the staff ensured he walked at least twice a day. The weather was cold and dreary. As we sat together near the large windows in the recreation room overlooking Plymouth Harbor, I often thought about future visits taking place outside on the deck during the warmer months. Maybe late April or early May. I could wait. My former thoughts of him lasting only a few weeks at Newfield were gone. Each visit with him was a blessing, and I intended to keep this schedule for as long as God would allow.

My new visitation schedule lasted less than a month—only it wasn't God who stopped me from making the drive to Plymouth to see my dad. It was something else entirely.

When I hugged my dad goodbye on March 12, 2020, the day before my birthday, I had no idea it would be our last hug for several months. The plan was to see him the following day, on my actual birthday, but I decided to push off the visit until the weekend at the last minute.

I never got the chance to see him, though. By Sunday, the nursing home suspended visitations due to the COVID-19 pandemic. Nursing homes across the country were doing the same, as the virus was ramping

———

up with a vengeance. It was the beginning of a very long lockdown for Newfield and the nation.

I had no idea how tough things were about to get. Welcome to 2020.

March 13 through the end of June, when Newfield allowed visitors to return, was the longest period without seeing my dad since his Alzheimer's diagnosis nearly five years ago. For the first time in almost a year, my schedule didn't revolve around my visits with Dad. The lockdown brought our fast-paced lives to a crawl, and I accepted it in every way but one: seeing my dad. It was an unsettling feeling, but there was nothing I could do about it.

College students were sent home mid-semester, and schools at every level pivoted to remote learning. The private sector followed suit. Even the churches were forced to close their doors and provide services virtually. No industry or individual avoided the wrath of this virus.

I was relieved when Newfield began to welcome visitors sometime in early June. In most ways, my dad looked the same. He was thinning out, but not so much as to concern me. His beard had thickened up quite a bit. One of my favorite things to do before the COVID shutdown was trim his beard. It was still somewhat neat, but it was much thicker than normal.

Physical contact wasn't allowed, so I still couldn't hug my dad, but I did get my outdoor visits with him—just not as many as I had planned. Over the summer months, I only made it to Plymouth six times. The guilt overwhelmed and saddened me.

On Sunday, September 13, I visited my dad for the first time in three weeks. It was a beautiful September day, with blue skies, a warm sun, and ever so slight breeze; background music played lightly from the patio speakers, and a nearby water fountain soothingly gurgled. Face masks on and sitting eight feet apart, Dad mumbled for a few minutes, maybe three or four in total, then closed his eyes and nodded off for twenty minutes. I didn't mind. I sat there peacefully and watched him. He stirred once, and then looked up.

I said, "Hi, Dad."

He nodded and dozed off again.

As lovely as the view and ambiance were outside, I intentionally switched to indoor visits, which allowed me to, on occasion, cheat the social distancing guidelines and sneak in a hug. I also pushed back my visit times to the afternoon, shortly after his nap. I found him much more alert and talkative. It was always difficult to hear him but was especially difficult due to the masks. Still, I asked him how he was sleeping, eating, and getting along with everyone. I have no idea what part of the conversations he understood, yet there were glimmers of recognition, either in response to me or what I had said. Small wins—but wins, nonetheless.

There's a difference between being alone and loneliness, but it's a fine line. The Resnicks have straddled this line our entire lives. At times, it has been a strength, allowing us to acclimate and embrace new settings and situations without much thought or discomfort. For example, unlike most kids, I wasn't sad about leaving home to be by myself in college. Sure, I was nervous about finding my way around campus and doubted my preparedness for the academic rigor of college, but I was never worried about being alone. I imagine some of my father's transitions, whether to bootcamp or Boston University, were much easier for him than most of his peers as well.

But being alone for prolonged periods has drawbacks, too. When my dad's marriage failed and he had to raise his three boys alone, I am sure he felt lonely quite often, even surrounded by his three boys. Yet this kind of loneliness pales compared to what he experienced during his Alzheimer's battle.

Dad was alone for most of the day in his Pembroke condo. His driving days behind him, all he could do was wait for us to show up. Our visits were the highlight of his day. After we left, he was back to dealing with the hallucinations by himself—that is, until I got him out of there for good.

During his stay at Whitney Place, he was surrounded by fellow residents and staff day and night, but I think he felt more alone there than at any point in his life. I saw him between 8 and 10 a.m. We ate breakfast, chatted, and took walks together. Once I left him, the rest of his day was spent wandering the halls, trying to look busy but never really doing anything.

The progress Dad made at Newfield was remarkable, but unfortunately, there wasn't enough time to establish a routine together. Due to the pandemic, we only had one month of regular visits before the nursing home was closed to visitors. The three months spent apart were painful to endure for me and detrimental for him. Confined to his room most of the day, my dad's only interaction with people was a small handful of staff, dressed in full PPE.

I never felt like he was nearing the end of his life, just the end of our relationship as I knew it.

It doesn't matter what age your kids are, the fall is busy. Still, I made it to Plymouth every Sunday for the next two months. I didn't have strong feelings or premonitions about how long my dad's battle with Alzheimer's would last. It was likely that his aortic stenosis or cancer would be the primary cause of his death, whenever the time came, and I had long since acknowledged that each visit was a gift. But there was still one more inevitability that had to be reconciled—and that day had arrived.

On Saturday, October 17, I finished up a visit with Dad and said my usual goodbyes.

"Same time, same place, next week?"

No reply.

"Have a good week, Dad. I love you."

No reply.

His aide, Shannon, started to wheel him away, back to his room.

"I love you, too, Mark."

Shannon turned to look at me, and we both started to cry. I watched her slowly wheel him down the hall, his feet lightly shuffling along. It would be yet another last for Dad and me.

It was the last time he recognized me as his son.

ROCK STAR

My father's Alzheimer's battle lasted seven years. It began in 2014 at Pembroke Primary Care with his nurse practitioner, who recommended he see a specialist for forgetfulness. It ended in 2021 at Newfield House, with Bill, his oldest son, holding his hand and wondering which breath would be his last.

The months leading up to his passing were not filled with uncertainty or despair, at least concerning my dad's Alzheimer's, weak heart, or colon cancer. My brothers and I continued to visit him, knowing full well that he no longer knew we were his boys. That fact alone wasn't going to stop us from spending what precious time we had left with him.

Our biggest concern was financial. We were running out of money, and the thought of moving my father out of Newfield House terrified us. The staff, from the owners on down, truly cared for my dad and every other resident. We fell in love with the team on day one and relied on their exceptional care and compassion until he died. I wish we had moved him there sooner, but that's one of the realities of dealing with Alzheimer's: *you don't know what you don't know.*

I always had the impression that my dad was winging it most of the time. Not with his career or in taking care of his customers, but with us, his boys. Work was the easy part of his day. Raising us by himself was hard.

But he did have a plan. Despite our constant pleas for him to take more vacations and spend more on himself, he wanted to pass on his savings to us. That was his goal all along. He knew the amounts weren't going to be life-altering, but they might be enough to help with our own children's college tuitions. Unfortunately, his plans were derailed by Alzheimer's, and we used almost every last dollar of his $300,000 of savings to cover his care and expenses.

The money he put aside may not have gone to us directly, but because he saved enough to cover his entire Alzheimer's care, we did not have to cover the cost from our savings. Not every family has that luxury, and I'm grateful for his selflessness. To the very end, his priority was his boys.

By the time Alzheimer's reached the advanced stages, and my greatest fear of not being recognized by him had occurred, the days, weeks, and months following that fateful moment were a mixed bag of emotions. I never formally said my goodbyes to my dad on any visit, but that's essentially what I had been doing for more than a year. If I missed a visit, I didn't have the same overwhelming guilt as before, as I knew I had been there when he needed me the most: during his darkest days fighting the dementia demons, moving to assisted living, and during each hospital visit.

Removing my dad from his condo was an impulse decision but a wise one. It also marked the beginning of a journey for both of us.

During the last eighteen months of his battle with Alzheimer's, something happened to me that I can only now appreciate.

Despite the heartbreak of his disease and the pandemic, I was happy—not about my dad or the virus, obviously—but with how my life was trending on a personal level. The changes I was implementing in my life—eating better, working out, meditating, and a better balance between my work and personal life—were paying dividends. In some ways, I felt as if my journey was just beginning.

Unfortunately for my dad, his was about to end.

On Sunday, August 1, *something* happened to my dad in the early hours of the morning. It's possible he suffered a hemorrhagic stroke, which likely resulted in some vomiting during the episode, but I am merely speculating and don't know for sure. They were able to get him dressed in the morning, in his usual khaki trousers and polo shirt, but once they had him comfortably resting in his recliner, he shut his eyes for what seemed to be a nice morning nap.

Somehow they realized it was more than a usual nap. The staff tried to gently awaken him, but he was unresponsive. He remained unresponsive the rest of the morning, at which time they called John to inform him of the situation. I didn't receive phone calls from the nursing home. John did, as he lived so close to Newfield and was my dad's healthcare proxy. I can only imagine the range of emotions that coursed through his body after hanging up with the nurse.

John, in turn, made calls to Bill and me. The issue I was facing was COVID—not with me, but Coleen. She was very sick with it, bedridden and quarantined. The news was filled with stories of older people dying alone due to COVID. Some people had to say goodbye via an iPad. I called to see what Newfield's latest policy was and almost collapsed. The nurse on duty wasn't going to allow me to come say goodbye to my dad.

There was no way in hell I was letting COVID stop me from saying goodbye to my dad. My sister-in-law, who is an infectious disease doctor at Johns Hopkins, told me to call the owner directly, which I did. He calmly assured me that I could come see my dad, only I had to do a rapid COVID test and be in full personal protection equipment, or PPE.

My test was negative. *Phew.*

After I checked in with the nurse shortly after noon, donned in protective gear from head to toe, Dad was in his bed. He looked like he was resting comfortably, but there were telltale signs that he was experiencing pain, including frequent moaning and labored breathing. It was likely his cancer that was causing it, and they began giving him morphine to keep him comfortable. He remained unresponsive throughout the day—the slow, deliberate, and dreadful deathwatch had begun.

I sat with my dad for the remainder of the day. I held his hand, watched his chest slowly heave up and down, and stroked his face. Most of my communication with him was silent. Staff members were in and out, rolling him onto his other side every two hours, administering morphine, and checking vital signs. Uncomfortable gurgling sounds emitted from his throat. His eyes never opened.

After the staff carefully turned him onto his right side in the late afternoon, my dad suddenly awakened. His blue eyes popped open as wide as I've ever seen them. Full, deep breaths came one after another, faster and faster.

Right now? I thought. *This is happening now?*

Tears ran down my cheeks as fear and helplessness consumed me. I shot a text to John to tell him it was happening and then got right next to my dad's face and held his hand.

"It's okay, Dad. You can let go now. You've fought so bravely. It's time to let go."

He wasn't trying to communicate and showed no signs he knew I was with him, but I felt as if he was saying his final goodbye to me in my heart and mind. For just a minute, I forgot anybody else was in the room with me.

"You're okay, Dad. You've been a rock star. It's time to be with Linda and Shirley now. I love you so much. I'm so grateful for everything you did for me."

I held him tight and kept repeating how much we loved him and how proud we were to be his sons. Then, just like that, he closed his eyes again. The quick bursts of breaths were replaced with softer moans. His body began to relax again, and the episode was over. I texted John the update, then called my cousin Sara, Dad's niece, to ask if she could come down and say goodbye. She left her job in Brighton immediately to make the one-hour trip south to Plymouth.

After Sara had some alone time with her uncle, we took a break to grab dinner in Plymouth Harbor. I ordered a gin martini, *extra, extra, extra dry,* exactly how my dad used to order his, and Sara got a margarita. We toasted my dad and spent the next two hours talking about him and Sara's mom, Linda, who passed away from cancer three years prior.

———

After dinner with my cousin, I took over the watch from John. Over the next several hours, I held his hand, said prayers with him, and talked to him. Only this time, I spoke aloud, as if two best friends were sitting by the fire pit, talking the night away. I was instantly brought back to our many late-night hospital chats, which were some of the best conversations we shared. His breathing continued to labor and slow, to the point where I had to get right in his face to make sure he was, in fact, still breathing.

He wasn't a religious man, but I read both Catholic and Jewish prayers to him. I didn't know any Jewish prayers but found them easily on Google. My favorite one was a poem called "Life is a Journey" by Alvin Fine. I must have read it aloud five times. The beginning has stuck with me:

> Birth is a beginning
> And death a destination
> And life is a journey:
> From childhood to maturity
> And youth to age;
> From innocence to awareness
> And ignorance to knowing;
> From foolishness to discretion
> And then perhaps to wisdom.
> (Alvin Fine, "Life is a Journey")

After prayers, I took out my laptop and began writing something akin to an obituary. I had been putting it off for months, starting and stopping, waiting for inspiration to strike. Well, that time had come, and the words flowed easily that evening. An hour later, I finished. I shut my laptop, kissed my dad good night, and said my prayers.

And I prayed that God would take him peacefully in his sleep.

John arrived early the following day, August 3rd, with coffee for me and doughnuts for the staff. There was no change in my dad's status. I drove home in silence. No podcasts, radio, or audiobooks. Today was the day my dad was going to die. I just knew it. *I felt it.*

I checked in with my family and responded to some work emails. Today was also the day of Coleen's beloved Aunt Annie's wake. We had to attend via Facetime because Coleen was still in isolation from COVID. I packed an overnight bag just in case, then headed back to Newfield, leaving my house around 2 p.m. I was not rushing to get to Plymouth. Don't ask me why; I just had a feeling that he was going to die later that evening.

I was right in that it was my last trip to Newfield House but wrong on the timing of his passing. Bill texted me when I was about fifteen minutes away: *He just passed*.

As director of alumni relations at Fairfield Prep, one of my roles was to represent the school at wakes and funerals for alumni who had died. That was more than twenty years ago, but I can still recall sitting in the pew, usually alone, thinking about my dad. It didn't matter whose funeral it was or how well I knew the person; my thoughts naturally drifted to my dad's mortality. I don't know why. He was still in his late fifties and quite healthy, but he was the only person I could think of while the melancholy music played and incense floated toward the ceiling.

There's no easy way to say goodbye to a parent when they die. I used to believe the anticipation would be worse than the actual passing, but it's not. If you're in the room when it happens, or shortly after like I was, there's an odd sensation of finality and disbelief. *Is it really over?* You don't want to leave, but you can't stay.

It's not that anybody is rushing you, but suddenly, things need to happen. People need to be notified, arrangements made, and accounts closed. The sadness and mourning will hit you whenever it so desires, whether you are ready for it or not. It is inescapable, no matter how hard you try to push the feelings aside.

Later that night, I posted my obituary on Facebook. For the next several hours, I was glued to my laptop's screen, watching people post heart emojis or make comments.

Obituary:

My dad's seven-year battle with Alzheimer's ended peacefully today at Newfield House in Plymouth. Barry, Dad, Papa, Big D, Papa Smurf, Coach Resnick . . . and my hero, was eighty-four years old. He is survived by his life partner, Jane McMorrow, my brothers Bill and John, his grandchildren: Campbell, Erin, Sean, Matthew, Alice, and Ryley, his niece, Sara Robinson, and all of the McMorrow clan.

Born and raised in Brighton, he was a four-year starter on the varsity hockey team. After high school, he joined the Navy, where he served in the 4th Regiment, Company 69, at the Bainbridge United States Naval Training Center in Maryland. His bootcamp was from November 1955 through January 1956, and he was assigned to the Dental Technician School. The longest stretch of his service was on the USS Vulcan AR-5 out of Norfolk, Virginia.

He put his dental training to good use. One weekend, when the ship's dentist was not present, a young sailor sought my dad out. "Doc, Doc, you have to help me. This one tooth is killing me!" My dad didn't have the heart to tell him that he wasn't the dentist. He figured he had watched the dentist do it enough times that he would give it a shot. He cleaned out the rotten tooth with a drill in hand, mixed the cavity filling, and patched up the hole. The next day, the patient went out of his way to find my dad and said, "Doc, thanks for taking care of that tooth. I feel much better!"

He brought his hockey equipment to the Navy and managed to skate at the local rinks whenever his schedule allowed. It would prove to be a wise move. After leaving the Navy in 1957, my dad returned to Brighton and enrolled at Boston University. He convinced the hockey coaches to let him try out for the team. Dad started on the freshman team and practiced with the varsity. The coaches loved his speed, and he was on track to make the varsity team his sophomore year. Unfortunately, finances were tight, and my dad had to leave the program after his first year to help pay for his tuition. He received some money from the G.I. Bill but funded the balance of his degree on his own.

Upon graduating from Boston University with a degree in business administration, my dad took his first professional job with Standard Register. He sold business forms, labels, and stationery. Dad worked for several different printing companies before launching his own business in 1999, Proforma Printing & Promotion, at age sixty-two. Starting a business with my dad was the honor of a lifetime. Before long, Bill and John joined us, and together we built a successful company, one which continues to thrive today. From raising his three boys alone to running a business with them was something none of us ever imagined. I would say he was a lucky man, but we were the lucky ones.

Hockey was the most important part of our lives growing up on Beers Ave in Norwell, thanks to my dad. He taught us how to skate on Jacobs Pond and coached all three of us at various times. His former players would remember his Ten Commandments of Hockey. Some of them included:

I will keep two hands on my stick and my stick on the ice.

First man in takes the puck carrier; the second man takes the puck.

I will always headman the puck.

Puck carrier is never the last man to leave the zone.

We recited the hockey commandments before every game. One player was assigned to shout out a commandment, and the team would scream it back to him. My dad always strived to be a better coach. Not afraid to try new things or steal concepts from other coaches, he was one of the most successful coaches within the South

Shore Seahawk program. He coached kids from Norwell, Scituate, Cohasset, Marshfield, and Hull. Outside of the Seahawks, he coached at Derby Academy in Hingham, Plymouth High, and many all-star and travel teams. His former players loved my dad, and many went on to play college hockey.

My brothers and I were in the rinks constantly growing up and traveled all over the Northeast, to Lake Placid, New York, Philadelphia, Pennsylvania, and local rinks. My dad was the founder of high school hockey in Norwell, at least according to us. He was the first to create a club hockey team in the mid-'80s, scheduling games against other high school teams. Years later, the town would formally make ice hockey a high school sport at Norwell High.

My dad appeared to be a quiet man, but that's because he never needed or wanted to draw unnecessary attention to himself. He was humble, kind, and generous to friends and strangers alike. His good nature, humor, and hard work resulted in a successful business career, but his most outstanding achievement was his steadfast support of his three boys. Even now, I have no idea how he managed to balance his responsibilities as a salesman and single father.

Despite not having much cooking experience, he became quite proficient in the kitchen. Like his coaching, he never stopped trying to perfect his skills. He was proud of his meatballs, meatloaf, and chocolate chip cookies. Except for one or two mishaps, Dad owned our annual Thanksgiving feast. He prepped for days to make sure his unique potato, squash, and stuffing recipes came out just right. For many years, he got assists from my kids, but he was our all-star chef on game day.

———

When I think of my dad and the life he lived, here's what will come to mind: his gardens on Beers Ave; watching him study the racing form at the track; his presence behind the bench as my coach; the drives to Lake Placid and his singing "Puff the Magic Dragon" while pretending to be asleep, and his big win over Compuware in 1980; seeing him at a Xaverian soccer or hockey game, usually by himself and away from the crowds, or at a Fairfield University hockey game; his enjoyment sitting at the tables in Las Vegas, playing blackjack, and the time I won $1,500 with him when he taught me how to play Let it Ride; the smile on his face when he received his first Proforma Million-Dollar Club Award; looking up from behind the bench and seeing him in the crowd watching Sean play hockey, Erin basketball, or Campbell on the soccer field; his pre-meal remarks when looking over the menu: "What looks good, guys?" or how he ordered his martini, "extra, extra, extra dry with a twist"; the ten days with Dad before he moved to assisted living and the 200-plus meals we shared together during his time at Whitney Place; the team of incredible caregivers at Newfield in Plymouth; his love and dedication to his sister Linda and niece Sara; and his remarkable, selflessness commitment and love for his boys.

A celebration of his life party is forthcoming. Together we can toast Coach Resnick—my hero, friend, business partner, and father.

My dad had died around 4 p.m. that afternoon.

Coleen was so sick with COVID that she had to text Campbell, Erin, and Sean that their Papa had died. She wasn't able to tell them in person. It was heartbreaking.

By the time I finished brushing my teeth that evening and refreshed my Facebook page one last time, I could barely keep my eyes open. The exhaustion from the past seventy-two hours had hit me hard.

I willed myself to say a few quick prayers, the last of which, before drifting off to sleep was, *Dear God, please let me hug my dad one more time.*

In some ways, the day after my dad died was a little easier. I spent most of my time bouncing back and forth between reading Facebook posts and replying to work emails. For the next two days, I kept an eye on the comments, refreshing my browser to see new ones. I have to say, the responses were unbelievably beneficial in helping me heal. The outpouring of support touched me deeply.

Family, friends, colleagues, classmates, teammates, former players of my dad's—almost 900 comments or heart emojis in total. Dad was a quiet, humble man, but I know he would have been touched by the affection from so many people.

Some of the hundreds of comments posted on Facebook about my dad's passing:

> *He was a great man and you and your bros are a great representation of the legacy he left behind.*

> *This is so beautiful ... And now I completely understand Ryley (John's three-year-old son) shooting pucks at 2 years old!*

My heart goes out to you all. I used to enjoy hanging out with your Dad at conventions. Our talks about everything. Good hearted person. I respected him and his knowledge of the print industry as well. His receptive nature. Been missing Barry at previous Proforma events. GOD Bless Barry, and your family at this difficult time.

Barry was the friendly face in the crowd that I looked for when I joined Proforma. He had a genuine nature about him and a great laugh. He's the guy that I looked to to build confidence starting my business. Deep condolences to the Resnick family.

This is such an amazing tribute to your dad. What an amazing man. I lost my mother to Alzheimer's last October and can appreciate what you've gone through the last 7 years. Happy he is now at peace. Treasure your memories.

Your Dad was such a special person and an amazing coach. I remember NHS hockey and all the street hockey battles we had on your street and around town like it was yesterday. So sorry to hear this very sad news. My thoughts and prayers are with the Resys and family.

So sorry to hear this boys!! He was a fantastic coach, so knowledgeable, passionate, caring, and yes the 10 commandments! I have so many memories of him and how he helped me grow! I was fortunate to know your Dad, RIP Coach!

Mark, we're so sorry for your loss of your Dad. We know how close you were. You were a wonderful son to him taking such great care of him over the last several years. Love your beautiful tribute to him. Sending our love and prayers to all of you ❤

Such a beautiful reminiscent of your dad and how much he enriched his, yours and everyone he touched in life. I'm so sorry for your loss. He lived a full life and that's all any of us can ask. Prayers to you, your brothers and extended family as you celebrate his life and mourn your loss.

What an incredible tribute to your dad. He was an amazing father, coach, and mentor. I loved reading about the Ten Commandments! My heart goes out to you and your brothers.

You guys are a reflection of all his life teachings in your own unique and individual ways as we all tend to be most influenced by loved ones. At times he probably didn't even realize he was teaching you by leading by example but you guys soaked it all up such as his character and morals as a human being.

So sorry for your loss! Great memories shared in this post . . . so well written. He was a great man and you and your bros are a great representation of the legacy he left behind.

There are no words no matter how heartfelt to erase your sorrow. I am so very sorry for your loss. Having gone through the same experience with my dad, I totally feel your heartache. Find strength in knowing there are many who love you. Find comfort in your years of happy memories. I will keep you and your family in my prayers.

I'm so sorry for your loss. I didn't know him but feel like I did thanks to this beautiful, heartfelt tribute to him. What an amaz-

ing man he must have been ♥ *. I hope your memories help you through the hard days.*

Mark beautiful words about Bazza ♡ *I have such great memories growing up from him teaching me how to play darts in my grandparents basement and making fun of sitting next to him on holidays in which I called the Barry splash zone. Thinking of you, Billy, and John at this time.*

So sorry for your loss John. Your old man sounds like a hell of a guy, one I would have enjoyed playing for! Thinking of you & your family, Rez. Be well brother!

So sorry to hear about your dad. I loved Barry. He was a single parent like me and we looked out for each other. I remember when Nicole got bit by the neighbor's dog when he came after my dog, on your back stoop. Your dad was so helpful. And he helped me not feel guilty because I was at work at the time. He was an angel. And he is now your angel. ♥

I admired Barry greatly. He was an early mentor to me in Proforma. "sales feeds egos, profit feeds family". Those words from him still sit with me. Godspeed Barry. Condolences Mark, Bill, & John.

Mark, John, and Bill, I am sorry to hear this sad news. I am glad that I had the opportunity to know a man who was such a great inspiration to his family and all of those around him. Keep those memories alive and share those lessons with your family.

Bill, Mark and John - I am so sorry for the loss of a great mentor to so many of us. He is a great example to all of us dads. He made every sacrifice to raise three very successful boys. I think of him often and will continue to think of him in the most random of times. He was the best hockey coach I ever had. And who can forget those 10 commandments? Rest In Peace Coach Rez. You leave behind hundreds of better people because of you.

Ohhh, I am so very sorry to read this Mark. What a beautiful tribute to your dad. I have fond memories of him on Beers Ave, with all those hockey bags lying around . . . . ♥ You were blessed to have such a loving and dedicated father. May he Rest In Peace. Keeping you all in my thoughts and prayers during this sad time. 🙏 ♥

A month later, we said formal goodbyes to Dad at a private ceremony at the Bourne National Cemetery. It was beautiful and brief, just as he would have liked.

However, the "celebration of his life" event—his party, as he had called it—would be anything but brief, and that's exactly what he would have wanted as well.

"I put money aside for my party, you know, for when I die."

"Anything special we should do?"

"No—just invite lots of people and have a good time."

"Consider it done."

"Thanks, Markus."

PART SIX:

FINDING PURPOSE,

PASSION, & PEACE

THE COMMANDMENTS OF LIFE

There isn't a former player on my dad's South Shore Seahawk teams who would not remember his Ten Commandments of Hockey. His commandments summarized the fundamentals of the game. In all my years of playing organized sports, I can't recall another coach who came close to preparing his players the way my dad did. I was never the most talented player on my college team but was always one of the smartest—thanks to my dad's training.

If you put a bunch of his former players in a room together, I bet we could list most of the commandments. Probably not all twenty-nine of them, but most of them. How he got his players to recite them enthusiastically before every game was a testament to our respect for him as our coach.

We didn't just recite the words before the game, either. Coach Resnick reinforced them at every opportunity during practice. One without the other wasn't going to be enough to bring about real improvement in our game.

Caring for my dad these past few years brought me closer to him than ever before. I saw sides of him that I never knew existed. He was always kind and generous, but I saw him demonstrate compassion and concern for his fellow residents, a warmth and tenderness he seldom shared with his boys. He got emotional at times, which was difficult for me—not because I wasn't used to seeing him show emotion like this, but because he didn't understand why he was so sad and lonely; he was unable to put his finger on his predicament—Alzheimer's. *There's something wrong with me,* he was thinking. *I just don't know what it is.*

In a completely different manner, I could relate. I had just gone through some of the darkest days of my life, watching his memory disappear and dignity fade—and yet, I was discovering for the first time since I was a child how to be happy again.

There's something right with me. I just don't know what it is.

It was after I finished writing his Facebook obituary that it started to make sense. Suddenly, my dad had the stage to himself. After a lifetime of caring for other people, it was his turn to let go, as in letting go of everything. Our time together on Earth was ending, but the next chapter in our stories had already begun.

The hockey commandments were the rules of the game. Their purpose: help us become better players. But I realized that my dad had unwritten commandments for living his life, too. He didn't intentionally teach or share them with me, nor did he know he even had such commandments. Yet all along, they were there, with a similar purpose: help us become better players in the game of life.

My dad's ultimate legacy was showing me how to overcome my demons to live a more purposeful, passionate, and peaceful life. No matter how difficult a situation may be, it is not only possible but likely that you can do the same.

The ten commandments of life my father taught me aren't unlike the hockey commandments. If followed, you will see improvement—greater happiness, balance, and fulfillment in your life—but only if you practice them daily.

1. *Never give up.*
2. *Be kind.*
3. *Forgive others.*
4. *Be yourself.*
5. *Always give more.*
6. *Be mindful.*
7. *Expect less.*
8. *Never make excuses.*
9. *Be grateful.*
10. *Forgive yourself.*

1. NEVER GIVE UP.

It takes about eighteen months before you get to know someone—at least that's what Laura Schlessinger, more commonly known as Dr. Laura, says on her weekly radio show. My dad was eighty-four when he died. I lived with him for the first twenty-two years of my life, then had the unique opportunity to co-run a business with him for another fourteen years. Yet, I never felt like I knew who he was until he moved out of his home and into assisted living—until we spent nearly every day together for, well, about eighteen months.

It's not that he was uninvolved in our lives—he just wasn't *emotionally involved*. He knew my close friends, especially Sean Fogarty, as I spent the majority of high school alternating between sleeping at his house and mine on weekends. But there wasn't much guidance, advice, or supervision provided. He did the best he could with the tools in his toolbox; he simply didn't have some other tools, like empathy, compassion, positive reinforcement, and the ability to understand and support our emotional needs.

He was the ultimate submarine parent, in stealth mode most of the time but surfacing when required. The important work was done below the surface, out of sight, like grocery shopping and cooking, arranging rides to practices, coaching and attending hockey games, and paying tuition bills. My dad provided opportunities—to play ice hockey, live in a fabulous town, and attend private schools.

Losing my dad the way I did wasn't even on my list of possibilities. I always assumed it would be his heart, stemming from his alcohol use, meat-and-potatoes diet, and high blood pressure and cholesterol. Somehow, his heart kept humming along, and instead, we watched his mind decline in slow motion. That is, until COVID hit. Then his decline was anything but slow.

By the end of 2020, the worldwide COVID death total was 1.8 million, and more than 80 million people contracted the virus. By the end of 2021, the numbers surpassed 5 million and 250 million, respectively. The COVID death toll in the United States topped the Spanish flu as the deadliest on record for a pandemic. As if my dad's Alzheimer's wasn't already pushing the limits of my mental health, I had to deal with this, too?

Because of COVID, Newfield House suspended visitation three times during my father's eighteen-month stay there. Their longest stretch without visitors was the original shutdown in March of 2020, which lasted nearly three months. During that time, the wonderful nursing home staff managed to coordinate virtual "visits" through Face-Time, which I appreciated, but it was the first time in almost a year that I could not be by my dad's side, hug him, and laugh with him.

Like all Newfield residents during COVID's peak, my dad was mainly in isolation, confined to his room. The extended absence of his three boys allowed Alzheimer's to take absolute control of his memory and recall—only we didn't know it was happening. While he was increasingly spending more time alone, I was blessed in a way to get more time with my family during the lockdown. I loved the time with my family, especially the ninety-eight consecutive dinners we shared. But at the same time, I had the same dismal image in my head each night before going to bed and upon waking in the morning. It was my dad asking me, *"Where have you been, Markus?"*

I wondered if I was ever going to see him in person again.

When visitors were allowed back to Newfield in June, his voice was softer and barely audible at times due to the mask and social distance guidelines. I didn't receive the same attention from him each time I walked into the room, which was gut-wrenching. There were times his face would light up in recognition of me for maybe six, seven seconds—slivers of humanity for us both—but they were gone before we could acknowledge them. It went on like that until the day he died.

COVID didn't just impact my dad's Alzheimer's deterioration. The kids had to adjust to remote learning on the fly, which was handled well by all three of their schools. Still, the Richmond basketball team was denied the opportunity to play in the NCAA tournament, as the event was canceled. Campbell was in his second year as a student manager and was crushed along with the coaches and players. It doesn't get much bigger than that for a college hoops team.

Erin missed out on her junior and senior proms, senior year soccer season, high school ring ceremony, college visits, hanging out with friends, and scheduled sweet seventeen birthday trip to Disney World. If this doesn't sound difficult to deal with, you don't have teenage girls.

These were monumental events, and as parents, we were in uncharted territory. It was the first time we experienced a global pandemic, too. There's only so much you can say to console someone who had missed out on so many quintessential high school experiences.

"It's going to disappear. One day, it's like a miracle—it will disappear," said former President Trump at the start of the pandemic.

Well, after many months of downplaying the virus at every turn, it caught up to him, and he contracted COVID. For nearly a year and a half, my family, including my dad, escaped it, but it eventually caught up with us, too.

Coleen contracted COVID the day after we returned from our annual July vacation in 2021. Out of the twenty fully vaccinated adults living under one roof for the entire week, she was the only one to test positive. Not only was Coleen a breakthrough case, but she was also a long-haul COVID case as well. Her illness lasted more than seven months. Beyond the usual symptoms of fever, sore throat, cough, fatigue, and loss of smell and taste, she suffered respiratory problems. Her breathing struggles were scary. She went from walking two miles a day to barely making it to the end of our short street.

Days after Coleen's COVID diagnosis, her beloved Aunt Annie lost her battle to cancer. Coleen was still in quarantine, alone and heartbroken. I put two masks on and entered the bedroom to hug her, but she wouldn't let me because she was still contagious, symptomatic, and bedridden. Not being able to console her—even hug her—was awful.

Unable to attend the wake and funeral, we live-streamed the funeral mass from separate rooms within our home. The kids were naturally upset, watching their mom suffer from COVID, unable to support her. We were the ones who relied on her to lift our spirits when needed, and now that she needed a lift, we were helpless to reciprocate.

A week later, my dad died.

I thought I was emotionally prepared for this eventuality, but I wasn't. Crying during an emotional movie is one thing, but when it came to crying over real-life events, well, that was a different ball game altogether. How is it that I can openly cry watching a comedy but can't seem to do so while grieving the death of my dad?

Coleen was still in her ten-day isolation period, so we maintained her strict quarantine measures. She was just too sick to take a chance on relaxing them, and now it was my turn to grieve by myself. The net result was either no emotion or an uncontrollable flood of emotions. The problem was, I had no idea when to expect either. There was no obvious trigger or reason for the tears—they seemed to come at the most random times. And always when I was alone.

I believe two things kept us from further despair during the pandemic: *perseverance* and *progress*. Scientists, researchers, doctors, businesses, and the federal government found a way to get safe vaccines to market in record time. Not just any kind of record, either—this was full-on *warp speed*, as the project was aptly named. New vaccines usually take years to develop, but with COVID-19, it took under a year. Suddenly, what was previously thought to have been impossible was made possible.

Before writing *Ten Days With Dad*, I didn't think much about progress or perseverance. If I am honest with myself, I spent years dwelling on events and experiences that somehow negatively impacted my life or people who wronged me. I blamed my past, including my parents' lack of emotional support, for my perceived lack of success, recognition, and happiness.

No matter how much I accomplished personally and professionally, it was never enough to make me feel proud or satisfied. It didn't matter if I had raised more than $250,000 for my children's schools, founded or co-founded multiple businesses, played college hockey, raised three beautiful children, celebrated twenty-five years of marriage, or published a book.

Not only did I not feel successful, but I battled other demons, some of which had been with me since childhood, including insecurity, lack of confidence, and at times, a perverse lack of joy and fulfillment in my life. I couldn't appreciate my blessings or success. The lifelong craving to *do something* and *be someone* was all-consuming. I constantly compared myself to other salespeople, friends, my siblings, and former classmates. Why wasn't I as successful as them?

It wasn't until I helped my dad beat back his demons that I began to defeat my own. I stopped making excuses and started to let go of grudges, regrets, and misguided expectations. Passions from my youth, like baking and writing, were reignited. I began exercising regularly, established a meditation routine, and struck a greater balance between my professional and personal life. Even though I was entrenched in suffering and sorrow while dealing with my dad's Alzheimer's and a pandemic, something extraordinary happened to me.

Disney World's Carousel of Progress attraction is one we rarely miss when visiting the theme park. Not because it is thrilling or even exciting, but because it gives us a break from running around the rest of the park.

I'm not sure whether it classifies as a ride, show, or something else. The Carousel of Progress follows an American family of animatronic characters throughout the twentieth century. Seated in comfortable chairs, the audience rotates around four main stages, representing four generations of progress. From the invention of ice boxes to keep food cold longer and water pumps in the kitchen at the turn of the century to virtual reality gaming and voice-activated smart appliances at the end of the century, the audience sees how technology has transformed their lives. It's not an exciting attraction, though its theme song, "There's a Great Big Beautiful Tomorrow" by Rex Allen, will stay with you long after you leave it.

What does a Disney attraction have to do with my story?

The concept of the attraction, that being progress, was omnipresent throughout my life over the past three years. Only my progress was emotional, not technological. By the end of my story, I had come full circle: I saw the people, places, and experiences—the rotating stages of my life—so clearly. I experienced a transformation in my priorities, passions, and purpose in life. There was no script, plan, or expectation for change, either positive or negative. No preparation or warning. It just happened, albeit gradually—so gradually, in fact, that those closest to me probably didn't realize or recognize the transformation.

But I did.

A once-in-a-century global pandemic and my dad's Alzheimer's pushed me to the brink of despair. And yet, I managed not only to endure, but thrive. I rediscovered my childhood passions, came to peace with my past, and accepted and embraced my purpose—to live my life to the fullest in the moment, help others pursue their passions, and accept and embrace my role as husband to Coleen and father to Campbell, Erin, and Sean.

The demons we face may never disappear. Mistakes and failures are inevitable. And yes, excuses will still sometimes be made. But we can still find purpose, passion, and peace during even the most challenging of times.

In his book *Getting Undressed: From Paralysis to Purpose*, my brother-in-law, David Cooks, writes, "Our ability to endure is always greater than our willingness to endure." In other words, if we follow the first commandment of life: Never give up—we can endure anything.

When it got tough for my dad to raise three boys on his own, when the responsibility pushed him to the absolute limit, he didn't give up. Instead, he persevered and raised three amazing men. When his partner Jane became ill and was in rehab for six months, he showed up every day with a smile on his face. And after his Alzheimer's diagnosis, I never once heard him complain or place blame. Instead, he listened to his medical team and carried on with his life. *He never gave up.*

Maybe that's why I didn't give up when nothing went right in tenth grade, or more poignantly, when my friend Marty committed suicide. Or when I had to choose between my brothers and the business I co-founded with my dad. Or when I had to be there every day for my dad, watching Alzheimer's steal his dignity, then his mind, then his life.

Don't you think I wanted to give up?

Every dark, cold, wet winter morning when I woke up before the sun to deliver newspapers, I wanted to give up the job. The second time I broke my wrist playing hockey, I wanted to give up playing hockey. When my boss took a new job, and I wasn't promoted to his position, I wanted to give up. Watching my son experience panic attacks, not being able to help him, I wanted to give up. When my commissions were cut and my colleagues were acting like high school bullies, I wanted to give up.

And when my dad stood in the corner of his room and stared at the wall for almost ten minutes straight, I wanted to give up.

But in choosing to persevere, I maintained a purpose despite my challenges and obstacles. Even during my darkest days, I believed there was light within me—somewhere. I couldn't summon it sometimes, even when I needed it most, but it was there. Before meeting Coleen, I didn't have anybody to lean on or turn to. It sucked in every way, but I never quit. Even with a best friend and wife of twenty-five years, sadness still occupies a small part of my insides. I don't expect it ever to fully go away, but I will never let it control my happiness ever again.

Because if it does, then I know I will have given up. And that is not going to happen.

To never give up means:

> *You are willing to persevere, no matter how hard things get.*

> *You wake up each day believing you have a chance to start anew.*

You are open to changing your habits, routines, and beliefs to improve yourself.

You will accept help, even if you don't want to.

You have more to give this world.

You are capable of doing whatever you set your mind to.

You matter.

2. BE KIND.

I will never know the full reasons behind my parents' failed marriage. My mom told me that my dad was drinking too much, that he shut her out emotionally, and was gambling. That's not what surprised me. To hear that he was not very nice to my mom—now that surprised me.

My grandfather was addicted to alcohol and gambling. He abandoned my dad and his sister at such a young age that they barely acknowledged his existence to me. I never knew his name until I started working on this book. There's no doubt my dad inherited some of the demons and sins of his father, but to hear that he was not nice goes against every shred of personal evidence that I witnessed in my life with him. Without hesitation, the first three words I use to describe my dad are kind, gentle, and generous.

When Mom left the house, my dad had no choice but to change his lifestyle and habits. When faced with his new reality of raising three young boys alone, he beat back some of his demons, even if they never left for good. Dan Harris wrote in his book *10% Happier*, ". . . I tried to keep in mind something a friend once told me: 'Your demons may have been ejected from the building, but they are outside doing push-ups.'"

My dad may have been unkind in my mother's eyes, but he certainly changed for the better. The comments on my dad's obituary on Facebook were heartwarming. So many people took the time to share their opinions of him, and hundreds mentioned his kindness. My dad's smile put people at ease, along with his easy-going personality and sense of humor.

Having a mentor in a particular field of study or occupation can be extremely helpful. I had many when I worked in fundraising and a few as a salesman, too. I've also had kindness mentors my whole life. Mrs. McCann, my first-grade teacher, was so kind to me when I showed up the first day of school with a cast on my arm that I still talk about her today. Mrs. Blake's kind words to my dad about my writing skills are the reasons you're reading this book.

My dad was the ultimate kindness mentor. I can't recall when I saw him being rude, disrespectful, or mean to someone. He sometimes interrupted me to tell me what was on his mind, but not because he was rude. At the Flamingo resort in Las Vegas, he treated everyone with kindness. Even behind the bench, he was primarily good-natured with refs, though I did witness a few harsh words from time to time. I can say with certainty, he didn't go out of his way to be nice just to get something—it's just how he was wired.

I was lucky to get that kind of wiring, too. I smile and say hi to strangers every day. I don't think about it or plan it out; it's just natural to me. As a student at Fairfield, I got friendly with the people behind the scenes: the kitchen staff, maintenance crew, mailroom clerks, and bookstore employees. I may not have remembered every name, but I said hello, smiled, and chatted with them every day. They reciprocated that kindness, and we became friends.

Is it just me, or are people less kind than they used to be? Things took a turn for the worse during the rise of Donald Trump's prominence. Love him or hate him, I don't care, but you can't deny that his rhetoric was anything but kind. It was downright nasty, most of the time.

It doesn't matter which side of the political aisle you fall on. Trump's words, whether on Twitter or TV, made it acceptable to say whatever you wanted about another person or topic. From Lincoln's time through today, politicians have used nasty words to describe one another, but it's not just politicians who are fair game nowadays—it's anybody. I don't like it. Not only do words matter, but kindness does, too. Perhaps now more than ever before.

But why does it matter?

One morning, I was with Sean, my youngest son, getting coffee and doughnuts at the local doughnut store in Walpole. I'm a huge doughnut guy but had made a conscious effort to limit my doughnut intake to once a month. Well, it was my one day of the month to get my glazed chocolate stick, so I was excited.

The state mask mandate had just been instituted by Governor Baker, which required customers and store employees to wear masks. Walking to the entrance, ahead of us were four young guys, none of whom were wearing a mask. Right away, I knew there was going to be a confrontation. Sean knew it, too. He asked me to let it go, but I couldn't help my-self. I was tired of the excessive anti-mask rhetoric and falsehoods being promoted on TV, Facebook, and at the local market.

"Excuse me," I said to the group of guys. "Why aren't you wearing a mask?"

They looked at one another before one of them said, "Because we don't have to."

"Actually, you do. The governor is mandating it, and there's a sign right there on the door."

"We don't have to wear them if we don't want to."

They left the store and returned to their company truck, but I was livid. I even asked the store employee why she didn't ask them to put on a mask.

"Well, we have a lot of seniors who come here, and some of them have difficulty wearing the mask," she said. "So we don't enforce it."

Flustered and pissed off, I turned and left on the spot. Sean followed me to our car, but he was upset with me for saying something to the guys.

"I asked you not to say anything, but you did anyway."

"Sean, I can't go see Papa because of COVID. People are dying from it, and these jerks will get people sick by not wearing a mask. I don't care if you're mad; it's wrong."

Before he could reply, we heard the four guys taunting me from across the parking lot, which only annoyed and angered me further. I snapped and started yelling back at them. Sean was even more visibly upset with me. Which only made me angrier.

———

"Get back in your truck before you make a bigger fool of yourself," I shouted at them.

"You're the damn fool!"

Back and forth we went until I drove off, shouting, "I hope you all fucking get COVID!"

The brief moment of satisfaction I got from *doing the right thing* was immediately replaced by shame and embarrassment for my words and actions—both with my son and the teenage store employee at the doughnut shop. I was the opposite of kind; I was rude, disrespectful, and nasty. I could have gotten my message across to the young men in a manner that wasn't hostile or aggressive. Instead, I threw civility and kindness out the window. I'm still embarrassed by my behavior almost a year later.

If we're not going to be role models for our children and treat others with respect, how can we expect them to show respect and kindness in return? When we see political leaders get in front of a camera and eviscerate an opponent, journalist, or even a voter from the opposing party, we wonder: why can't we do the same?

"Well, that's just politics."

"It's locker room talk."

"Politicians have been doing that forever."

"They're only saying that for the camera; they don't really believe that in private."

"Of course it's not okay if a teacher or coach talks that way."

"Blame cable news for giving their words so much airtime."

You bet your ass kindness matters. There's no acceptable rationalization or justification for nastiness, hatred, or outright lying just to win an argument, secure one more vote, or prove a point. At least, not in my book.

How can we show kindness?

Be a kindness mentor to your children, spouse, and siblings. Smile more. Say hi to people you pass on the street. Hold the door open for others. Quit using the horn on your car when you're merely frustrated. Be more patient. Reject the harmful language that people use against one another. Think before you speak. Text, email, or call someone you haven't talked to in a while. Make breakfast for your family. Offer to pay the dinner check. Write a handwritten note to a friend. Take out the garbage. Stop judging others. Stand up to bullies. Say please and thank you. Ask someone how you can help them.

And let's not forget to be kind to ourselves, too. There are enough people in this world who will try to beat the crap out of you—there's no need for you to do the same.

3. FORGIVE OTHERS.

My favorite television show is HBO's hit series, *Game of Thrones*. In season two, Arya Stark listens to Yoren, a brother of the Night's Watch, share why he has a kill list. It was Yoren's practice to repeat the name of every one of his enemies each night before he went to sleep, to kill them at some point. From that night on, Arya started reciting her kill list: "*Joffrey, Cersei, Walder Frey, Meryn Trant, Tywin Lannister, The Red Woman, Beric Dondarion, Thoros Of Myr, Illyan Paine, The Mountain . . .*"

Before you think I am losing it, I don't have a kill list. Quite the opposite. I have a *forgiveness list*.

In my mind, forgiveness is giving yourself permission to let go of resentment toward those who have caused you pain. Both physical and emotional pain, the latter of which tends to linger the longest. Even the mere perception of being wronged or snubbed remains with us—well, forever—unless we give ourselves permission to let it go.

We don't have to wait for others to ask for forgiveness. Rarely do any of us want to admit that we were in the wrong, or somehow caused another person pain and suffering. Many times, we don't even realize that we offended, hurt, or insulted someone.

As my dad's health declined, I became more aware of the resentment in my life. From professional colleagues to former coaches to friends and family members. I needed to forgive them—to let go of my resentment—whether it was well placed or not. I no longer saw the point in harboring grudges and regrets or fueling the fire of grievances, some of which went back to middle school.

Leaving my family business in 2013, the one I co-founded with my dad and ran with my brothers, Bill and John, was pure agony. I never *wanted* to leave, but for reasons already mentioned, felt it was necessary.

Three months after that fateful decision, I was working for my friend and fellow Fairfield graduate. I was grateful for the chance to run a brand-new division for him, and he quickly became more than a friend and boss; if anything, I saw him more like a big brother.

What excited me most about joining this new company was his customer service team. I was going to spend 100 percent of my time selling products, rather than running a business like I had done during the past fourteen years for my family business. Between the customers I was bringing with me and his printing customers who were not yet ordering promotional products, the potential for success was huge.

The support I needed from the customer service team never came, as they didn't want to learn a new product line. It was a difficult reality to face my first week on the job, but I was able to hire my own team. In six years at the company, we grew promotional product sales to $1.5

million. The growth outlook remained strong for the foreseeable future, but unfortunately, my time at his company was coming to an end.

The main reason was because I realized how much happier I was owning my business, rather than working for someone else. By *owning*, I mean owning the responsibility for my success—the strategy and vision, yes—but ultimately, it was the ability to decide with whom I wanted to work, including colleagues, customers, and vendors. The majority of my stress points either came internally from various colleagues or externally from inherited customers.

Internal stresses happened because my division within the company operated much differently than the printing one, which required difficult accommodations to the order-entry, accounting, inventory, and shipping programs already in place.

Six years of swimming upstream was enough to make me realize that it was time to work for myself again. Unlike the situation with my family, compensation wasn't a factor in my decision. In fact, by leaving my friend's company, I was walking away from a six-figure salary, which was no small amount.

The decision to leave coincided with my dad's decline in health. I was dealing with enough hurt, anger, and suffering over my dad's Alzheimer's—the added stress at work was unhealthy. No amount of money was worth continuing in that difficult environment.

When I gave my notice to leave, my friend seemed genuinely surprised. It was eerily similar to when I left the family business. I thought to myself, *How can this be a surprise?* But Jack, like my brothers, was family—and working with family is never what it seems to be.

———

My former boss was the first person I added to my forgiveness list—I was letting go of any lingering resentment and pain.

Before bed, sitting in traffic, in the shower, or whenever I felt like it, I recited my list. Some nights I felt like Arya Stark reciting the names on my forgiveness list: "*Jeff, Bob, Jon, Will, Annie, Alison, . . .*"

By this point, my dad was now living at Whitney Place in Sharon. A few things happened over time as I saw him every day. I realized forgiving people made me feel better. Letting go of grudges was an immense relief. The more people I stopped resenting, the better I felt—all because I finally gave myself permission to do so.

The memories associated with the people on my forgiveness list might never go away, but there's no more lingering pain. It's not that I have chosen to block out the wrongdoing, but I no longer give it oxygen to live inside my brain. Instead, I choose to focus on things that I can control. In other words, I still have the scar on my thumb from when I sliced it open with my French chef knife, but it no longer hurts. If I think about the incident long enough, I quiver and *almost* feel pain, but it's emotional, not physical pain, and a hell of a lot less emotionally painful than before I started the list.

The second thing I realized about my forgiveness list was that not everyone belonged on it. Take Coach McCarthy, my college hockey coach, for example. Why did I need to forgive him for something that was my fault? His decision to play me less was a direct correlation to my decision to skip offseason practices. From his point of view, it looked like I didn't have the commitment and dedication to the program. He was still friendly to me; he just didn't give me as much ice time. When I thought about it, I realized that I owned this pain, not my coach.

Forgiving people and letting go of grudges does more than lower anxiety, stress, and anger; it can also improve your mental health, promote a more robust immune system, and improve self-esteem. Do a quick Google search on the topic, and you will be amazed at what you find. Again, not a cure-all for past misgivings but a massive step in the right direction.

Please know that I didn't add people to my forgiveness list lightly. I left off the coach who cut me from the Squirt A hockey team because that's just silly. But others were added with a fierce reluctance. My dad was one of them.

I forgave him, not to make myself feel better but because he deserved it. He didn't give me the encouragement, guidance, or emotional support I desired growing up, nor did he always possess the ability to show empathy or compassion. And yet, despite his flaws, mistakes, and demons, my dad rose above them all to ensure his boys were successful, healthy, and respected men.

When I skated onto the ice for my next shift, I could always find my dad standing in one of the corners, away from other parents but intently following the action. While playing for Fairfield, he drove two and a half hours for almost every single game, then headed home after saying goodbye.

As a boy, I not only wanted to be just like my dad, but I wanted to be with him as much as I could. My Uncle Jim and Aunt Linda owned cabins in Maine. On one trip to the cabins, there was a giant carnival in town. My dad was going to the race track instead, and I begged him to take me with him. I was too young to know what gambling was—I just wanted to be with him. When he barbecued on the grill, I was usually the only one with him, watching him light the grill and cook the meat. I tried to make things easier around the house for him, whether it was doing the lawn, laundry, or taking out the garbage.

While my love for him never once diminished, there was a time, as I got older, that I realized I didn't want to be exactly like him. Not who he was as a person, mind you, but some of his habits. I never felt at ease with him having a couple of drinks after dinner and then falling asleep watching TV. I remember hockey road trips to Lake Placid and Philadelphia, he had a six-pack of beers in the front seat and would sip his beers while driving. I never said anything but knew it wasn't right. I was concerned about his weight, blood pressure, and high cholesterol from overeating. I came to accept his trips to Las Vegas but didn't condone them.

Dad's demons were "out of the building, but doing push-ups in the parking lot" for most of his life. And yet, despite his flaws and weaknesses, despite the demons he overcame both early on and later in his life, he will forever be my hero. Regardless of the circumstances that led to their divorce and despite his true motivations at the time of their separation, I am, and will forever be, grateful for his sacrifices for my brothers and me.

As I matured, got married, and started a family, my love and appreciation for my dad only grew. As business partners for fourteen years, we disagreed on some issues but were basically on the same page. We built a great business together, along with Bill and John, and I would miss working alongside him the most after leaving the company. I agonized over the decision and wished I had talked it over more with my dad before making my final decision.

Yet, it wasn't until Alzheimer's came into our lives that I realized how much I *did* want to be like my dad.

No, he wasn't perfect. I wanted him to attend school art shows, concerts, and fundraisers. I wish he had picked me up when I fell into the pond in second grade or written notes to the school nurse explaining why I didn't need to take the eye exams. I wanted him to pat me on the back, give me encouragement and motivation, and ask why I was sad or having a bad day. I forgave my dad for not being the father I *wanted* him to be. But he never needed my forgiveness.

I'm the one who should be asking for his forgiveness. He gave us everything he had—everything he was capable of giving. And that's all that we can ask of our parents, isn't it?

My mom is on the forgiveness list because I felt abandoned by her. Not literally, mind you, but emotionally. I was reluctant to forgive her because I was reluctant to acknowledge that it wasn't her fault my parents got divorced, at least not entirely. I was too young to understand the situation's complexities—before, during, and after she moved out. When I got older, I had only one side of the story: *my own*. How I went my entire life without seeking answers, without knowing what happened, still mystifies me.

My relationship with my mom is complicated. I love her because she is my mother—she brought me into this world. But I don't love the emotional roller coaster of a relationship I've endured with her for the past forty years. Tormented by my middle-child brain, I always give her the benefit of the doubt, even when the facts don't imply that I should. I want to see her side of the story but never get the whole side, only bits and pieces that seem to either go against all logic or have enough missing parts to conclude that she's telling the story she wants me to believe.

I don't know the exact number of hockey games I've played in since I was a boy, but I would estimate the number to be well north of 500. I don't think my mom saw me play more than five times. My eighth-grade girlfriend saw me play more times than her.

When my mom stopped coming to see us regularly, it was a turning point in our relationship. Her decision hurt me. I may not have given it a ton of thought at the time, but it was a big deal. I would later wonder what was so important that she couldn't continue seeing us regularly. It turned out that she didn't see the point in coming to Beers Ave if we were busy with hockey or friends. I never used the word *selfish* to describe her decision, but that's what it was.

She has been putting her needs and desires above ours her entire life. No matter how many times I tried to defend her, the facts proved me wrong. Deciding it was not a good use of her time coming to Beers Ave because we were active teenage boys was selfish. Not coming to watch us play hockey, the thing that was most important to my brothers and me, was selfish. She never once initiated a visit to see her grandchildren. Instead, she waited for an invitation, even though I told her she had an open invitation. Coleen and I have already warned our kids, invitation or not, nothing is going to keep us from spending time with our grand-kids!

My Aunt Janet once tried to get me to see it from my mom's point of view: her boys abandoned *her*. She didn't use those words, but that's what she was saying. We should have had her back instead of my dad's; we didn't appreciate the things she did for us; we never included her in our lives; we shut her out; we unfairly blamed her for the divorce.

Needless to say, the victim card was her power play.

I don't believe in irreconcilable differences when it comes to mother and son. Long before my dad got Alzheimer's, and long before my forgiveness list was created, I tried to forgive her. Each time I silently forgave her, something else would happen between us.

Is it even possible to forgive someone who has caused you so much pain?

The short answer is yes, it is possible to forgive someone. In its simplest form, to forgive someone is to stop resenting them. There's much more to the definition, but in terms of forgiving my mom, I no longer resent her for the choices she made and how those choices negatively impacted me. I chose to stop resenting her after my dad got sick, but mainly, I decided to forgive her because I wanted to—because I *needed* to—so I could come to peace with my past.

And I finally have.

The choice to forgive people who have hurt or wronged us somehow is deeply personal, but I'm willing to bet that we give the notion of forgiveness very little thought. I mean, how often does it even come up? If my dad hadn't gotten sick, I wouldn't be writing about forgiveness at all, which means I would be carrying around with me loads of unnecessary resentment toward people.

The goal of the ten commandments of life is to help us become better—better people, yes, but also better in the buckets of life that matter most to us. Even if this commandment isn't your most pressing area of concern, it's important.

Drop the resentment, grudge, or ill will toward someone in your past or present. You will feel better and free up space in your mind to focus on more positive things. Redirect this unhealthy energy from holding on to the past toward more useful and productive priorities.

It's not perfection—but it's progress.

4. BE YOURSELF.

As a kid living in a time without the internet and cell phones, I watched a lot of cable television. I imagine my brothers and I watched more TV than most kids, especially when we were home alone after school or on the weekend. We watched sports, especially the Boston Bruins, but we also watched horror movies, inappropriate comedies, dramas, and action thrillers. And of course, we watched the holiday movies.

My favorite Christmas movie came out my freshman year at Fairfield: Chevy Chase's *Christmas Vacation*. I have no recollection of the film causing sadness or provoking an emotional reaction, but after I had kids, I couldn't watch the movie without tearing up. *Yes, I know, it's a comedy*. Remember when Clark gets stuck in the attic and is watching his old movies; or the little girl when she tells Clark she doesn't think Santa is coming; and when Clark recites *Twas the Night Before Christmas* surrounded by his family? Instant tears.

Don't even get me started on the scenes from *Home Alone* that make me cry.

Christmases have always been challenging for me. Subconsciously, I suppose that is because of the absence of both parents contributing to making Christmas "happen" each year: the annual buildup to the big day,

---

decorating as a family, wrapping presents, having Christmas music playing in the house, and especially, having people genuinely prepare us for the magic that is Christmas. We didn't have much of that growing up.

We spent Christmas Eve with my mom and her family in South Boston, dining on Chinese food and dessert from Mike's Pastry, a North End favorite. It was one of the few occasions that we saw our younger cousins, and the highlight of the night—for my cousins and me, anyway—was the annual story I made up for them after we opened presents. I think they looked forward to the stories even more than the presents. I never planned it out; I just created something on the fly and usually tried to incorporate every crazy family member I could.

If I got stuck, I renamed Rudolph's reindeer with some of their names and planned a story where we had to make a return trip to Dorchester because Santa forgot to deliver a few presents: "Only Santa was sick, so he appointed Uncle Pete to drive the sleigh—but because he had a few too many beers, Aunty Rosemary took over. Then she got sick from eating too much Chinese food, so Aunty Janet became the driver, only she fell asleep while flying over California because she had too many cannolis from Mike's Pastry . . ." We laughed and giggled until I ran out of ideas.

The tradition lasted well into my college years, and I always looked forward to seeing their reactions.

After presents and storytime, we headed back to Norwell to wake up on Christmas morning in our beds. Our ritual wasn't unlike other families, except that we only said good night to one parent on Christmas Eve. I still listened intently for Santa throughout the night but never once heard him.

My dad arrived at the house early Christmas morning, before we got up. Then we opened presents in the room off of the kitchen, which we called the family room. It was the coldest room in the house. The room had no heat, which is an odd place to put a Christmas tree. I assume we put it there because it was a big room, but still, why didn't we put the tree in the living room—you know, the part of the house that had heat?

Coleen and I have our own Christmas traditions for the kids, including each having their own colored wrapping paper each year. Campbell's presents are green with red ribbons and bows; Erin's are red with silver ribbons and bows; and Sean's are wrapped in silver, with green ribbons and bows. After the presents are wrapped and perfectly presented under the tree, I usually spend some time by myself admiring Coleen's work.

Every year, although the sight isn't remotely reminiscent of my childhood Christmas, my mind can't help but wander back to Beers Ave. We may have lived with my dad full-time during the year, but Mom got the Christmas holiday. She spent the night with us at Beers Ave, and then my dad came from Jane's apartment on Christmas morning to see us open presents. Later in the day, we hosted the extended family dinner, so both of them stayed until dinner and dessert were finished. It only lasted a day, but it was special.

The contrast between my childhood Christmas and my children's is dramatic. It makes me appreciate what we have now that much more. My Christmas Eve sit-by-the-tree ritual is emotional, but in a good way. If there are tears, they are not all tears of sadness.

It isn't just Christmas that triggers emotional swings. I could conceal a little crying watching a movie or television show, but as I got older, it became harder to avoid the sadness or rushes of emotion that overcame me in specific situations. The first time I broke down in public was in college, the night of my inauguration as FUSA president. I was so overcome with emotion that I couldn't get through my acceptance speech. I attributed the night's overwhelming feelings to "the moment," but I knew it was more than that.

When we moved to Massachusetts, Coleen landed a great job at Boston University, running the annual giving program. Her colleague, Ryan, shared a book with her entitled *Delivered from Distraction: Getting the Most out of Life with Attention Deficit Disorder'* by Edward M. Hallowell, M.D. and John J. Ratey, M.D.

To clarify, the book wasn't for her; it was for me. When Coleen gave me the book, I put it on my bookshelf, where it sat for five years.

I didn't want to read the book. I certainly wasn't interested in the possibility that I may have ADHD, even though I knew I likely did. Mostly, I didn't want to medicate myself as part of the treatment. That's what held me back from reading it or taking any action. However, one day years later, I was cleaning my home office and came across the book. I didn't go looking for it, but there it was, staring at me.

Five pages in, I knew I had ADHD.

The core symptoms of ADHD are excessive distractibility, impulsivity, and restlessness.

The authors then list about thirty bullet points under Advantageous Characteristics and Disadvantageous Characteristics [of ADHD]. I highlighted all but three characteristics under both categories.

Advantageous:
- Original, out-of-the-box thinking.
- A tendency toward an unusual way of looking at life, a zany sense of humor, an unpredictable approach to anything and everything.
- Remarkable persistence and resilience, if not stubbornness.
- Warmhearted and generous behavior.
- Highly intuitive style.

Disadvantageous (too many to list, but here are some of them):
- Difficulty in explaining themselves to others.
- Achieves at a high level, but they know they could be performing at a higher level if only they could "find the key."
- Trouble with time management; they typically procrastinate and develop a pattern of getting things done at the last minute.
- Impatience. People with ADHD can't stand waiting in lines or waiting for others to get to the point.
- Alternately highly empathetic and unempathetic, depending upon the level of attention and engagement.
- Poor ability to appreciate own strengths.

Reading bullet after bullet, my head started to spin. *Oh my God, this is so me*! Simultaneously, I was energized and distraught. On the one hand, it was a huge relief to understand some of the reasoning behind my behaviors, habits, and perceptions of myself. Yet it also brought me sadness. I thought, *Where would I be in my life had I known about my ADHD sooner?*

My risk tolerance is above average. Okay, that's a lie. It's off the charts high. Not just because I grew up with my dad and three brothers and had to fend for myself for the first twenty-two years of my life, but because of my ADHD.

As a twelve-year-old boy, I rode my bike to a farm two miles away during rush hour traffic to earn $4 an hour, then rode home after a day toiling in the sun. In middle school, I showered, dressed, ate breakfast, and then hid under my bed until my dad went to work, just so I could stay home to sleep or write a paper, then forged his signature on my absentee note, which I wrote, and handed it in to the office the following day. I may have been afraid to kiss girls but had no fear when I rollerbladed across town, sometimes in the middle of the day and at other times in the middle of the night, to visit Sean or Kim.

When one of my brothers-in-law was looking into buying a franchise and asked if I had heard of it, I went out and bought one myself. It failed.

Ten years ago, I wanted to buy a brand-new condo in Maui. It was expensive, yet the rental income it would have generated was going to cover our costs. We didn't end up purchasing it, but I spent hundreds of hours researching and planning for it.

When I was at my wit's end running a business and raising two kids simultaneously, I got the insane idea to try out for a reality TV show—twice. You may have heard of it. It was called *The Apprentice*.

Speaking of Donald Trump, when he first ran for the presidency, every fiber in my body was pushing me to run for political office. Not the local selectman's office—the United States Congress. I must have spent three hours a night for eight months planning for an eventual run. I even wrote a book called *Weird Brags: From the Halls of Cole Elementary to the US Capitol*. I wrote it for Coleen, to explain to her why it was so important for me to run.

As I wrote in *Weird Brag*s, I was running for Congress *because the country needs honest, transparent, and accountable leaders who are motivated by doing the right thing for the people they serve—not themselves—even if it means crossing party lines to build consensus and promote common-sense legislation.*

Because the country needs leaders who follow their hearts and minds; people unafraid to stand up for what they truly believe in and not what their donors, lobbyists, or party leaders tell them to support.

Because I am frustrated by career politicians who continue to ignore corruption, greed, and waste in Washington—or are themselves corrupt, greedy, and wasteful.

Because I see a process that heavily favors incumbents, and incumbents who heavily favor special-interest groups and lobbyists.

I thought of Ted Kennedy because of his efforts to work with the opposing party. And because he stayed in office too long, it was a reminder that the country needed to "pass the torch on to a new generation of

Americans," like his famous brother once said.

Every few years, I found a new obsession to lose myself in, only to move on when I realized I was chasing the wrong thing.

This is what it's like to live with someone with ADHD—and why Coleen is a saint!

I thought ADHD was just an excuse parents used for their children's poor behavior in the classroom. While this may have been accurate for some kids, I now know that ADHD is very real, powerful, and thankfully, treatable. In my case, medicine wasn't the answer. I have been able to overcome the liabilities ADHD can present by changing my habits, whether it is by leaving my keys and wallet in the same place every day after work (instead of leaving them in the car overnight) or planning my workday the night before to help keep me on task. I've read books, listened to podcasts, and even hired an ADHD coach to help maximize the positive attributes and traits.

There's a common misconception that people with ADHD are too distracted, unfocused, or lazy. In most adult cases, this couldn't be further from the truth. An article I read on www.inc42.com entitled "The Ten Most Successful People with ADHD" pointed out:

> *When people with ADHD can find something that they're passionate about, they will dedicate themselves harder than anyone else could even imagine - often crushing the competition.*

It's been fifteen years since the diagnosis, and I have learned to thrive with my ADHD. I wish I had been diagnosed as a kid, for I now realize that having it is a blessing. I can't imagine my life being remotely the same without it. People with ADHD are some of the most creative, energetic, innovative, independent, and successful people on the planet. Athletes, CEOs, entertainers, and geniuses use their ADHD to dominate their respective industries—people like Michael Phelps, Richard Branson, Michael Jordan, Walt Disney, Simone Biles, and Albert Einstein, to name a few.

I always believed that my approach to a challenge or problem, my willingness and ability to look at an issue and come away with a completely different perspective than my peers, was unique. Not special. Not always better, either. Just different. One former colleague of mine used to tell me how good I was as the devil's advocate because I could see both sides of a situation, even when people in the room didn't want to hear the other side. I've been like this as long as I can remember, and it's mainly because of my ADHD.

If there is one constant throughout my professional career, it's this: I have never been afraid to speak my mind for the betterment of a company or organization. Whether as a professional fundraiser, business owner, or volunteer, I never shied away from providing feedback, suggestions, ideas, or even constructive criticism—so long as it helped achieve our goals and mission. Not because I had an ego, thought I was smarter than everyone, or needed to be right, but because I believe ideas are meant to be openly shared and discussed—not behind closed doors, destined to remain in the dark.

More than one person has said to me, "Mark, you sometimes make a bad first impression. But once people get to know you and where you're coming from, they love you. You come from the heart and are genuine."

———

I took that as a compliment. That's not to say I haven't worked hard on making better first impressions. Nobody wants to intentionally leave a bad first impression, even if it's short-lived.

At least those less-than-ideal first impressions were social. I don't believe my words or actions could be construed as lapses in moral character or malicious intentions. I just said what I felt, and since most people don't appreciate hearing someone else's ideas and only want to hear things that back their point of view, I can see how I may have ruffled some feathers, especially earlier in my life.

I was never a stay-at-home dad but was the parent in our family who did the most volunteering at our kids' elementary school. I served on the school board for six years, ran major fundraising events, and volunteered at many other events. I was a permanent staple at the school and interacted with hundreds of parents.

Most of the parents I worked with were women. Very few dads volunteered during the day at Blessed Sacrament. Remember, I grew up in a household of guys; we didn't sugarcoat our thoughts and feelings, we simply said what was on our mind. I have never been afraid to speak my mind, but more than that, I always want people to know where I stand, either with them personally or with an issue. I also hadn't been diagnosed with ADHD yet, so I said some things that were very likely misconstrued as negative or offensive over the years.

I had never heard of the term "emotional intelligence," and nobody ever mentioned the phrase to me, but when I discovered it, a hand grenade went off in my brain.

Wikipedia defines emotional intelligence as "the ability to perceive, use, understand, manage, and handle emotions." I wish I could give credit to the article and author by which I first encountered the term but can't recall the details. For adults like me who tend to speak before they think, emotional intelligence is huge. It's the difference between making a good first impression and a terrible one, being labeled a great listener or poor one, or being an effective or ineffective leader.

For me, the big takeaway on emotional intelligence as it applies to my life is asking myself three questions:

1. Does something need to be said?
2. Does it need to be said now?
3. Does it need to be said by me?

I lived my entire life believing that yes, yes, and yes was better than keeping quiet and not saying anything—or worse, holding back your opinion for fear of what others might say. Truthfully, I never gave it much thought. Why wouldn't I want to share my expertise, idea, or concern with others? I never concerned myself with making other people feel good; I just wanted to do what I thought was the right thing and get results.

I used to get upset at the parents who thought I was being critical or too vocal on a topic, but after years of making less-than-ideal first impressions—and after learning about emotional intelligence—I don't find myself in as much trouble when talking to people, including my wife and my kids. I have a long way to go, but I am figuring it out.

I was diagnosed with depression and ADHD at the same time, in my mid-'30s. My mom suffers from depression, and I should have been more aware of the potential hereditary nature of the disease—but I wasn't. I felt the sadness, loneliness, and uncontrollable emotions build up at certain times in my life and should have known there was something larger at play. Between ADHD and intermittent depression, I was consistently fluctuating between high and low points.

My friend Peter Shankman is a media entrepreneur, best-selling author, keynote speaker, podcaster, and single dad. His book and podcast, both entitled *Faster Than Normal*, embrace the concept that having ADHD is a gift, not a curse.

> *Having ADHD allows you to supercharge your brain when you need it, letting you hyperfocus on tasks, solve problems in untraditional ways, and come up with ideas that haven't been thought of before. (Peter Shankman, Faster Than Normal)*

Unfortunately, for a long time, I didn't have the tools, hacks, and resources to manage it properly. I made bad choices, created awkward moments, and had more misguided expectations than I care to recall—all stemming from my ADHD. Peter gave me some of the tools I needed to harness the "gift" of ADHD, and the rest I figured out on my own.

Instead of losing my keys all the time, I put up a key hook in the hallway. I created a binder to house all my important documents, things like purchase receipts, insurance, financial statements, travel documents, and more.

Since it's my role to manage the finances, if anything should ever happen to me, Coleen would have all the information she needed in one place.

The best thing I did, however, was create a system to manage my email inbox. Instead of keeping hundreds, if not thousands, of emails in the main "inbox," I act on each and every email. How? Rather than letting them build up, staring me in the face each day, reminding me of all the work that needs to be done, I now delete, file, or act upon each one in real time. At the end of the day, I never have more than five emails showing in the main inbox. This new system was the ultimate efficiency hack for my ADHD brain. Life-changing, actually.

My ADHD is not a full-blown superpower yet, but the more I learn to use it effectively, the greater my productivity, creativity, and output becomes.

As for the mistakes along the way, and there have been many, I no longer let them define me as a person. The best I can do is learn from them and move on. Failure is feedback, isn't it?

The biggest takeaway about my ADHD is that it has allowed me to *be myself*. The only thing I would have changed is that I wished I had known about it sooner. I'm grateful to Peter for his help, and to Ryan, who shared Hallowell and Ratey's book with me.

It's very easy for me to tell my children just to be themselves—and mean it. I don't understand why they worry so much about what other people will think of them. Unfortunately, the whole notion of being yourself disappeared with today's obsession with social media. Instead of showing our true selves, we post things that garner thumbs-up or heart emojis. Young people, in particular, are afraid to be themselves for fear of being judged. Or worse, ridiculed. It's such a shame.

To be yourself is to use common sense to know right from wrong without analyzing or overthinking a situation. Coleen and I always tell our children before they head out for the night: "Make good decisions." My litmus test is simple: *Am I going to regret this decision the next day?*

Being yourself means doing more of what you love to do—and not letting fear, stress, and worry about people judging you get in the way of your interests and passions.

Nowadays, I'm proud of my ADHD, and I love being myself—and I'm okay shedding a few tears while watching *Home Alone.*

5. ALWAYS GIVE MORE.

More than one coach has gotten in my face and screamed at me to give him 110 percent effort. It wasn't so much a threat, just encouragement to give more. It wasn't as obnoxious as the hockey parents at Sean's games who screamed all game long, "Skate, Johnny. Skate!!"

I had a few games growing up during which, I believe, I left it all on the ice. When the final buzzer went off, I had nothing left in the tank to give.

Or did I? Is it even possible to give 100 percent effort? As soon as the brain registers that you hit max effort, wouldn't it automatically expand your ability to endure more?

Like when a runner competes for the first time in the Boston Marathon, after months or years of training, only to hit Heartbreak Hill—and then he simply can't finish the race. The hill broke him. But then he comes back the following year and finishes because he found a way to give more.

The only current situation I can think of when I gave close to 100 percent is when I was taking care of my dad. I gave him almost everything I had during those first ten months at Whitney Place, seeing him every day, sometimes twice a day. Could I have given more? Yes, but at a price that would have broken me—and my family.

Always giving more doesn't mean giving 100 percent at everything you do all day long. We know that's not possible—or at least I do. But we can give more, even 1 percent more, to the areas of our life that matter most.

As James Clear prescribes in his book, *Atomic Habits*:

> *If you're having trouble changing your habits, the problem isn't you. It's your system. Bad habits repeat themselves again and again not because you don't want to change, but because you have the wrong system for change. You do not rise to the level of your goals. You fall to the level of your systems.*

James Clear is an expert on changing habits; I am not. His book outlines tools and strategies to improve your life each day. He tells you how to *give more* of yourself, even just 1 percent more. When we give more to ourselves, even in the smallest increments, we see tremendous benefits in the long term, like compounding interest.

Yet doing more on principle alone isn't effective, just as the expression "practice makes perfect" isn't really true. Repetition will give you results, but it might not be the results you are desiring. If our practices or daily approaches to changing a habit are being done poorly or without purpose, that's a setup for disappointment. *Doing the same ineffective things over and over again and expecting a different result?*

The definition of insanity, yes.

One of the challenges of living with ADHD is patience. I just want to dive into something, get going right away. I don't like reading instructions or mapping things out. I have learned the hard way that not having a plan or purpose before beginning a new task, project, or dream can be counterproductive—or worse, a recipe for failure.

It's important to know the specific outcome or result we are trying to achieve beforehand—to see the finish line. Whether that's to lose weight, get out of debt, start a new business, get stronger, eat healthier, find more clients, get A's in school, worry less, win more games, or publish a book, always have the end in mind. Know where you want to go. See the ending of your story. Visualize the intended result.

Long into his seventies, my dad began his day with push-ups, sit-ups, and leg lifts. It's one of the clearest memories I have of him from Beers Ave, in his bedroom, on the floor, working out. If getting in shape is one of your goals, start with one push-up a day. I can pretty much guarantee that you will do more than one, but you don't need to crank out ten, twelve, or fifteen. Start with one.

The goal is to create better habits—to start with 1 percent improvement each day or week. One push-up, one small overpayment on your credit card, one minute of breathing, one extra email or text to say hi to someone, five extra minutes of studying, one less cup of coffee, a short walk around the block, a few less minutes of screen time before bedtime, one Netflix show instead of three, one hello to a stranger, one prayer at night, one person on your forgiveness list, one thing for which you are grateful.

Always give just a little more of yourself, and the rewards will follow.

After reading *29 Gifts* by Cami Walker several years ago, my friend Stephanie Jones decided to embark upon her gift-giving journey. Stephanie's definition of a gift was something you can give and expect nothing, not even a smile or thank you, in return. What she did next blew me away. For more than 500 consecutive days, she gave a gift.

From giving away free tickets to the local Kiwanis pancake breakfast to buying pizza for college students to arranging for a friend to meet Condoleezza Rice at a function, Stephanie was making a difference in her community, one person at a time.

She had this to say about it: "I couldn't stop seeing opportunities to give and help others. The possibilities were all around—everywhere I went. What I discovered was incredible. I didn't expect the journey to change my life, but it did. My relationships strengthened, I found more ways to be thoughtful and encouraging, and I became more grateful, patient, and generous."

Her giving journey resulted in a book: *The Giving Challenge: 40 Days to a More Generous Life*. She wanted to inspire others to go on their own giving journey.

Stephanie followed her giving challenge with a gratitude challenge and wrote another book: *The Gratitude Challenge: 41 Days to a Happier, Healthier, and More Content Life*. In the book, she shares personal stories involving the people she was most grateful for, from her pediatrician to local police to her supportive running group. At the end of each chapter, she suggests writing a personal thank-you note to the people who have made a difference in your life. I think if you were to write just one thank-you note a month, you'd be making someone very happy.

———

I'm a sucker for challenges like this—probably because of my ADHD—so naturally, I went on my own giving challenge. It began in 2020, during the peak of COVID, and is ongoing today. My goal is to give a gift once a week. Usually, I pay for the Dunkin Donuts order for the car behind me in the drive-through line, but that's not all I do.

Erin got to witness the experience once at the Verizon store. The store clerk was super helpful. She went out of her way to see if she could save me money on our family plan, which she did. I was genuinely grateful for her assistance. After leaving the store, we went to Bed Bath & Beyond next door and purchased her a Panera gift card worth $25. Then we walked back to Verizon and gave her the card. She didn't want to take it at first, but I insisted. She was thrilled.

"That was cool," Erin said when we were walking back to the car.

"Yeah, it was, wasn't it?"

In Hawaii this past year, I bought drinks for a couple on their honeymoon, just as someone did for Coleen and me twenty-five years ago. At the airport, a woman's credit card was not working and was about to give up on her purchase of bottled water and gum for the plane. I stepped in and paid for her items. I have purchased books for friends and mailed them with a note of thanks for something they have done for me in the past. On my writing journey, I have purchased books from first-time authors and wrote reviews on Amazon—the key to long-term success for aspiring, and accomplished, authors.

Start your giving journey and see how much more you get in return. If you can't give one gift a week to someone else, how about one gift a month for twelve months? The gift doesn't have to be a monetary one.

———

You can make something or give your time, which is likely even more meaningful to both the recipient and the giver.

⌣ ⌣ ⌣

Coleen and I recently celebrated our twenty-fifth wedding anniversary with the kids in Maui. I wanted to hire a local minister to renew our vows, but Coleen had her own vow: "If you do that, I'll walk the other way. Vows don't need renewing!" I settled for a video montage that Erin helped me put together. We both cried in front of the kids while taking in the sunset at Pacific 'O, one of our favorite restaurants in Kaanapali.

Cheers to twenty-five more, Col.

Meeting at Fairfield and our experiences during four incredible years together as students were only some of the reasons why Coleen and I choose to make annual donations to the university. In fact, we've made a gift every year since 1994, our graduation year. As former and current fundraising professionals, we know why our gifts, and others' gifts, matter so much. I would not have been able to attend Fairfield had I not received financial aid. Most of my good friends also received assistance. To ensure that other students can have the same experiences we did, or better ones, we'll continue to give more.

When we *give more* to nonprofits, our alma maters, or local community groups, we acknowledge that we can make a difference. Our investments in people and organizations, no matter how small, are also cumulative.

⌣ ⌣ ⌣

———

Years ago, I read Tim Ferriss's book, *The 4-Hour Workweek*. I hated it. I thought he was full of shit, that he lived in a fantasy world that was unattainable for most people stuck behind a desk. He conveniently skips most of his hard work and struggles to get to the point where he could automate his business. Mostly, I kept saying to myself, *This isn't relevant or relatable to my life.*

When I was cleaning the basement one day, deciding which books to keep or donate, I came across Tim Ferriss's book. *Why was I still resenting this man?* I quickly skimmed the book, then tossed it into the donation pile. But something was nagging me, so I picked up his book and began reading it, right then and there. ADHD at its finest!

When I was finished, I resented him less. A lot less, actually. I completely missed the point of his messages the first time I read the book in 2011. Ten years later, I can see that what he was getting at was pretty relevant. Here is my own summary of his points:

- Define your goals.
- It's not what you want; it's what excites you.
- Eliminate parts of your life that can free up time to do what's important to you.
- Be effective or purposeful in your hours each day.
- Focus on the 20 percent of your activities that move the needle.
- Say no to interruptions.

To be honest, I still don't agree with *The 4-Hour Workweek* and its "step-by-step guide to the luxury lifestyle," but at least I was able to find some messages within the pages that resonated.

———

To *always give more* means you want to be the best version of yourself—eventually. It doesn't mean you have to create fifteen new habits today. That is unlikely to work. Not impossible, but unlikely. Likewise, Tim Ferriss wasn't suggesting a four-hour workweek could happen instantaneously, but over time.

Giving more to others will make you feel great, whether you go on a giving journey, donate to meaningful organizations, or volunteer your time.

But giving more to yourself is equally important.

Whether it's 1 percent, 5 percent, or 10 percent—give more to the buckets of your life that matter most to you. Is it your health, personal relationships, career, passions, finances, or something else? Write your goals down and make sure they are as specific as possible. I suggest keeping them in a place where you see them every day. Even better, create a vision board and put it in your office, kitchen, or bedroom.

What's a vision board?

A vision board is a collage of images, pictures, and quotes of a person's goals, dreams, and desires. The board serves to inspire, motivate, and remind you of what's possible. According to Inc.com writer Marla Tabaka, a 2019 study showed one in five successful entrepreneurs use vision boards—and the results are backed by neuroscience.

> *Your brain is malleable and trainable; it can even rewire itself. This remarkable capacity is referred to as neuroplasticity, and it allows you to train your brain for success. Visualization is one of the most powerful and efficient ways to do this. (Marla Tabaka, "A New Study Shows 1 in 5 Successful Entrepreneurs Use Vision Boards. The Results Are Backed by Neuroscience")*

My dad wasn't *that* coach, always in your face, barking at us to *give more* effort, hustle, and commitment. His hockey commandments helped us prepare for each game, but it was up to us, the players, to execute them.

Of all the commandments of life, I think "Always give more" might be the one that defines me as a person. I can't say it was because I learned it from my dad—that I witnessed him always giving more to his boys—because in some ways, I didn't.

I wish he had shown me more compassion, empathy, and verbal support, but he didn't. I wish he had shared more about his life, his struggles, his story, but he didn't.

I know my father had limitations. It's not that he wasn't willing to show love or share his story—I'm just not sure he was capable. The things he gave us were often unglamorous, like paying tuition as a single parent, finding a way to make hockey a priority for each of his boys, and leaving his former printing company at age sixty-two to buy a business that remains very successful to this day.

He gave all he could. I wish he was still alive so I could hug him, thank him, and tell him how much I love him, but I can't.

6. BE MINDFUL.

It was after 8 p.m. on Friday, January 31, 2020, when I left my office for the last time. It was another long and stressful week. While I was relieved to have decided to cut ties permanently upon my return from Texas, there was still plenty of angst in my life.

Several things happened while I was in Fort Worth. Barely a day into the trip, I received a call from my brother John, who told me that my dad had fallen and was now in the hospital. The doctors found nothing wrong with him and planned to send him back to Whitney, but fortunately, John convinced them that he was unfit to return. Which he was. The search for a nursing home was on.

Yet despite the stress over my dad's fate, the conference was incredibly productive. You could even say life-changing.

On the second-to-last morning, I woke up early to see my business partner, Lynda, be recognized for her certification as a promotional products expert within our industry. I wanted to sleep in (and told her I was going to), but I was mindful of how hard she had worked to earn this certification, and there was no way I would miss her well-deserved recognition. She was thrilled (and surprised) to see me in the audience.

———

Waking up early that morning resulted in another surprise. The keynote speaker was Jesse Itzler. I had never heard of Jesse, but they introduced him as an entrepreneur, business owner, songwriter, best-selling author, ultra-marathon runner, part-owner of the Atlanta Hawks NBA team, husband, and dad of four.

His biggest career win was co-founding Marquis Jet, which allowed customers to book private planes with just six hours' notice from anywhere in the United States. It was hugely successful, and Jesse and his partner sold the business to Warren Buffett. In all likelihood, you're probably more familiar with Jesse's wife, Sara Blakely, the founder and owner of Spanx.

Over the next thirty minutes, the audience lapped up his energy, enthusiasm, and passion. I not only liked how he delivered his message, but I was digging the message, too. Here are some highlights:

> *"Add at least one winning habit that will invigorate your business and personal life."*

> *"Don't wait until everything is perfect. No one came this far only to come this far."*

> *"Our biggest challenges are self-imposed limitations."*

> *"Nobody wants to be the 80 percent version of themselves."*

> *"Maximize the time you have from now until when your life's bus ride is over."*

Soon after I got home from Texas, we were consumed with moving my dad to Newfield House in Plymouth. I forgot all about Jesse Itzler and his advice. For a few weeks, anyway.

Listening to a podcast while driving home from visiting my dad, I heard Jesse's voice through my car's speakers. He was discussing his brand-new coaching program, the Calendar Club (formerly known as the Big Ass Calendar Club).

Jesse's goal in creating the program was twofold. He wanted to share his system for managing his business, family life, and personal adventures. His plan was to openly share his habits, hacks, and routines to be more productive, successful, and fulfilled. Additionally, outside speakers and guests were to share their own expertise and talents on a wide range of similar topics.

The second goal of the Calendar Club is to challenge its members to identify and schedule three to four meaningful experiences that you wouldn't have done otherwise, which are called Kevin's Rules.

Examples of Kevin's Rules include planning a weekend alone with each of your children, then one with your spouse. A guys' weekend with college friends. Spend the day with your mom or dad doing something different, like a cooking or grilling class. Treat yourself to a weekend yoga or meditation retreat. Go with your sibling to a college football game somewhere you've always wanted to go.

It doesn't have to be a weekend, but the point is, over a ten, fifteen, twenty-year stretch, you'll have created thirty or more life experiences or memories with those you love. Instead of looking back on your life with regret for not spending time with loved ones, enjoying life, and crossing off items on your bucket list, you can look back with a sense of pride and joy over having such meaningful experiences.

I joined Jesse Itzler's club that day. Like Abraham Lincoln said, "It's not the years in your life that count—it's the life in your years."

It wasn't that I wanted to learn Jesse's system per se; I just felt a connection to him and what he was trying to espouse. I remembered his words from the keynote: "Maximize the time you have from now until when your life's bus ride is over." My dad's bus ride was coming to an end, but I felt like mine was just beginning. Jesse's program was what I needed in my life, and the investment has been paying off.

In addition to Kevin's Rules, there is one other experience members are challenged to undertake—a misogi.

A misogi is taking on a life-altering challenge that expands your notion of possibility. In real simple terms, it means committing to doing something way outside your comfort zone. Some people write a book, create a podcast, run their first marathon or ultra-marathon, or start a business. It is supposed to push your limits and remove your limitations. You can find an article written by Charles Bethea from Outside magazine on my website, www.markjresnick.com, under Resources. It is a must-read article for understanding the concept of a misogi.

I immediately knew that my misogi was writing and publishing Ten Days With Dad. I've wanted to be an author my whole life but never got around to acting on that dream. I believe I would have written this book eventually, but joining Jesse's Calendar Club made it a reality much sooner. I had a coach keeping me on track and was even motivated by Jesse, a best-selling author himself.

Each week the Calendar Club celebrates successful misogi accomplishments. I was proud to see my name on the list with hundreds of other members. More than 700 people have completed or are in the process of completing their misogi challenges. Here's a small sampling of wins:

- Earned yoga certification.
- Opened a restaurant.
- Lost sixty pounds.
- Left my current job and started my own company.
- Flew a Cessna plane.
- Launched my online course.
- Ran my first ultra-marathon.
- Booked my first speaking gig.
- Launched a podcast.
- Turned my part-time job into a full-time job.
- Took an RV trip with my family to Alaska.
- Learned to speak Spanish.
- Got out of debt.
- Published a book.
- Became a foster parent.
- Bought my first commercial property.

Seeing the massive list of misogis online was so inspirational that I decided to add a second misogi: write my first screenplay. It had nothing to do with being born in the same hospital as Mark Wahlberg, but my love of movies, my *emotional attachment* to them, was something to which I have always been drawn. Who knows, maybe I'll even find a role for Wahlberg in *Five Kisses*, which is the title of my screenplay.

Since joining the Calendar Club, I have learned from experts on health, exercise, nutrition, memory, marketing, coaching, meditation, business, productivity, and more each week. Because of my active participation in the Club, I have experienced significant changes in my mental, physical, and emotional mindset.

One of the more meaningful mindset changes revolves around my definition or expectation of what makes a *great* day. I no longer define greatness as experiencing monster success or something grand happening. Instead, I take my "daily vitamins." Not vitamin A, C, and E, but daily tasks that supplement my happiness, gratitude, and personal greatness, like vitamins.

In other words, in order to have a truly great day, what needs to happen? What makes me happy, excited, or fulfilled? My initial list of daily activities—vitamins—that I needed to take or experience in order to have a great day included:

1. Writing—at least five minutes but optimally twenty.
2. Reading—from one of the several books on my Kindle or bookshelf.
3. Prayer—both set prayers and individual ones.
4. Meditation—my goal is thirty minutes a day, but the duration isn't the focus.
5. Exercise—walk for at least twenty minutes outside or on the treadmill.

Closing a business deal is great, too, but my daily vitamins happen to be more personal than that. There's no such thing as a right or wrong vitamin; whatever needs to happen for you to experience a great day is your vitamin. Of course, if you have a list of ten or more items, it may not be possible to do them all, so my advice is to start simple and build up the list over time.

Each month, I try to add a new winning habit to my life. Examples have included drinking five glasses of water daily, reaching out to three people via social media, email, or text each day, and writing at least two handwritten notes to friends or customers each month.

Here's what I discovered: I may not always complete every single vitamin on my list, but I consistently have great days. Stuff happens all around us—taking care of aging parents, sick children, COVID, relationship problems, rude people, missed opportunities at work, bad exam grades, lost games, or fill in the blank. Yet most, if not all, of those things are beyond our control, aren't they? So don't let them spoil a good day. Create your list of vitamins. Start small. Do them every day. Then watch the positive feelings you receive by accomplishing them each day—the compounding interest on your great days—spill over to the other areas of your life.

- - - - - -

My Texas trip resulted in one more positive outcome: my introduction to Transcendental Meditation®. Often interchanged with the term mindfulness, meditation is a proven technique designed to decrease stress, anxiety, and even depression by training our minds to observe thoughts and feelings without emotion or judgment. Stay with me here!

One day, I was catching up with Charley, one of my vendors at the time. He asked about my dad's Alzheimer's. The pain was visible on my face, which prompted him to ask if I would be interested in learning about Transcendental Meditation®. I had known Charley for a few years and always admired his intelligence, calm demeanor, and outlook on life. Now that I knew he practiced meditation, it all started to make sense at a high level.

According to Charley, the primary issues we face—our fears, stresses, insecurities, doubts, and other unhealthy thoughts—come from our minds. Essentially, the mind is in constant conflict—we look to the mind to solve our issues, even though the mind created them in the first place. When we attack our problems at the mind level, we are simply rearranging the deck chairs on the Titanic.

Most people never think about or ask themselves these questions: What is past the mind? And how do we get there? The thought had never crossed mine either, and why would it? Mainly because it's a strange question! If I may dare say, it's a little *out there.*

As a practicing Catholic, I know firsthand that some of our beliefs are a little out there, too; and I believe that parts of other religions are out there as well. But I still believe in the foundation of my faith, and more importantly, it is an essential part of my life.

Transcendental Meditation® is a mantra-based meditation practice, and while it may be seen by some as being *out there*, it has been extremely beneficial during my emotional transformation. The goal of each meditation is to leave our fears, worries, and insecurities—all of which are thoughts—behind us. On a typical day, tens of thousands of thoughts run through our minds, and the only ones that concern us are the ones we become attached to—the sticky thoughts.

Just think of all the thoughts that keep you up at night—those are the sticky ones that cause you the most stress and anxiety. Work pressure or expectations, self-doubt and self-worth insecurities, or worrying about things like getting COVID, receiving a bad grade, or missing the cut in a golf tournament. I had thoughts like, *Will my book suck? What if nobody reads it, or my family hates it?* It goes on and on.

How do we create less stickiness in our minds?

Think of it this way: Imagine a piece of sticky tape, like duct tape, being applied to a table. It is going to be quite tough to get the tape off due to its strong adhesion. The duct tape represents stressful, negative, and anxious thoughts, all of which originate in our minds. For many people, these thoughts are always present, as in all day or night. Some people self-medicate to rid themselves of these thoughts, but that doesn't work.

The mind is very good—too good—at reapplying that tape, causing those bad thoughts to come roaring back. Each time we meditate, we *rip* off the tape, removing those unhealthy sticky thoughts, but soon enough, our mind reapplies it. We rip it off, then the mind reapplies it again and again and again.

What happens to the tape over time if we keep ripping it off? It loses its stickiness, and at some point, it will not stick at all. The same applies when meditating each day—what bothers you now, what sticks in your brain, won't stick to you in the future as long as you remain consistent with your meditation.

———

Like any good ADHDer, I started meditating that evening and have been practicing it ever since. I was more than satisfied by the extensive studies completed on Transcendental Meditation® and its proven benefits. Increases in calmness, creativity, energy, and clarity of mind were of particular interest, but perhaps even more meaningful and timely were the meditation studies touting improved brain function and cardiovascular health. Relieving stress and anxiety was only icing on the cake.

Here's what I have noticed about myself since Charley introduced me to Transcendental Meditation®. Overall, I find myself far less agitated by the simple (and smaller) aspects of my daily life: traffic, inclement weather, rude people, waiting in lines, incorrect coffee orders, or things my kids sometimes do (or rather, don't do) around the house that used to annoy me.

The coffee shop scene from earlier—when I lost control of my emotions over the guys not wearing masks—most likely would not have happened. I am generally calmer than at any point in my life and am experiencing a healthier balance in my perspective, optimism, and self-confidence. Bad news still disappoints me, but I no longer dwell on it. I don't see the point in stewing over things that are out of my control. Do I still lose my temper sometimes? Of course. But only briefly.

Meditation has made an enormous impact on my mental health and happiness. It took more than a year to notice the benefits, but I see them clearly now. And while it isn't known whether meditation can reduce the risk of Alzheimer's, it does improve conditions known to increase the risk of Alzheimer's, including stress, anxiety, insomnia, and blood pressure ("Meditation – its effect on cognition and general well-being," Alzheimer's Drug Discovery Foundation, alzdiscovery.org).

———

Despite the pandemic and my dad's Alzheimer's, my life is feeling just a little less *sticky*, and the meditation a lot less *out there* than before.

And yours can be less sticky, too.

My advice to you? Be mindful, or aware, of the feelings of others in your life. Ask about their day before telling them about yours, and try to be present in your conversations. Put the phone away at dinner or while in the car with your family.

Reach out to a struggling friend through text, email, phone—or if you really want to show you care, send a handwritten note. Congratulate or compliment others when you hear about their achievements and resist the urge to reciprocate with your own. This will show them you are a good listener and care about them.

Remember that you don't have to win every argument. I used to believe that I needed to win them all—even if I never realized that's what I was trying to do. It wasn't that I was looking to *win* them; I just felt so strongly about my views that I was being unreasonable or exhausting.

It's okay to "agree to disagree" sometimes, in a cordial manner, but don't bully or ram your opinions down someone's throat—they are only going to resent your actions (or you).

Be mindful of *your* feelings, too. Most people want to help you, but you have to ask for it. If you need help, seek it out now, rather than waiting until the problem is out of control.

What needs to happen to make your day great?

Be mindful of your potential, promise, and purpose.

Come up with one or two Kevin's Rules for the year—text some ideas to yourself or write them here in the book. If you're not currently meditating but might want to try it, start with a popular app like Calm. I prefer mantra-based meditation, only because I struggle to focus on breathing alone. I find using a mantra works better for my ADHD, but both types are effective.

And if you're really inspired, come up with your misogi. I promise you that nobody ever looks back on their life and says, "I wish I had done fewer Kevin's Rules with my children—or didn't undertake my misogis, like running that marathon, writing my book, launching a podcast, learning a new language, or starting a business."

If anything, you'll look back and wish you had done more of them.

7. EXPECT LESS.

My father was a creature of habit, from ordering his food and drinks in a restaurant to beginning his day with push-ups and sit-ups to conducting his business affairs.

During appointments with customers, I witnessed his selling, communication, and presentation styles. What I quickly learned, however, was that all three were the same. He never oversold, overpromised, or lied to his customers. If he didn't have the answer, he promised to get right back to them with it. His meetings were always about the person in front of him; he didn't look past anybody, which explained why he retained most of them for more than thirty years. And even though my dad eventually learned how to use the computer to email and place orders, he still kept hard copies of every purchase order, invoice, and sales report.

The first few years as business partners, we met regularly for lunch. If alcohol was involved, he would always order his martini *extra, extra, extra dry*. Then, without fail, he would turn to me and ask, "What looks good, Markus?" when perusing the menu. By the time we finished eating, Dad would inevitably add, "I ate too much again."

"Dad, you don't always have to eat everything on your plate, you know."

"That's just how I grew up. My mom always made us finish the plate."

"That was what, fifty years ago?"

"Old habits die hard, my man."

On vacation in Las Vegas, at the Flamingo resort, of course, Dad treated those around him as if they were customers. He was friendly, attentive, and appreciative of the little things they did for him. "Welcome back, Barry!" a few of them would say, with large handshakes or hugs. Dad was home at the Flamingo. He liked the location, pool, and people, but really, I think he most enjoyed the comfort and familiarity the Flamingo provided.

Dad was consistent in other ways as well. He was content to drink his low-end scotch, gin, or vodka at home. (My brothers and I made sure we brought the good stuff to Thanksgiving or Christmas dinners.) Getting him to try a new vacation destination was challenging; he simply preferred the comfort and routine of Las Vegas, Maine, or Nova Scotia. He listened to conservative talk radio in the car on the way home from work, even though he wasn't conservative. And he loved sharing his truisms with me: "It could always be worse," or my favorite, "You're only getting screwed if you think you're getting screwed."

I never ascertained whether the latter expression was his own or borrowed, but it was at the front of my mind when my kids used to say, "The coach screwed me," or "My teacher gave me a bad grade." I just never thought to apply the phrase to my own life until my dad got Alzheimer's.

As a freshman at Fairfield, I started on the varsity hockey team's first line—not initially, but I earned a spot about midway through the season. The guy I replaced, a senior, felt he "got screwed" by the coach. But the reality was that I put myself into that position through hard work.

As a member of the top line, I skated more than any other player, except for my two linemates. I was part of the power play and penalty kill units and would often be the extra skater when we pulled our goalie late in the third period. Unfortunately, it would be the highlight of my four-year career on the team. I never saw the first line again. The reason?

Coach Doc McCarthy "screwed" me.

When I returned to campus for my sophomore year, I didn't participate in the offseason practices held by our captains. I didn't attend a single one. It wasn't because I thought I was too good or didn't want to participate. I was short on cash and couldn't pay the ice fee. That's what I told myself, and that's what I told Coach McCarthy when he asked about my absence. But now I realize Doc didn't actually screw me. *I screwed myself.* The blame goes to me, not my coach.

I blamed him for my stupid decision. I didn't have a *reason* for not attending the practices; I had an *excuse*. And a poor one at that. My dad would have paid the fee; hell, Coach McCarthy would have, too.

I continued to play hockey at Fairfield for the next three years but never got off the coach's shit list. The truth is, I held a grudge against Coach McCarthy for twenty-five years because he didn't accept my excuse.

My dad had lots of habits and routines that both irked and intrigued me, yet I seldom heard my dad make excuses in his life. Not about work, coaching, his health, and especially not about the choices he made. It was another aspect of his life that I paid little attention to until he got sick. He could have complained the moment he received his diagnosis, and nobody would have questioned it. But he didn't.

I believe my dad didn't complain or make excuses because he didn't have high expectations. I don't mean he didn't have hopes, dreams, and goals; I mean he didn't expect those hopes, dreams, and goals to happen automatically. I suspect it was because he prioritized his sons' happiness and success over his own, but either way, he seldom had to contend with misguided expectations. I, on the other hand, did.

I *expected* my girlfriend to stay with me in tenth grade because I was the nicer guy. I *expected* to remain on the first line of the hockey team because of my prior success. I *expected* the recognition for bringing a pub worth $400,000 to campus because nobody had ever done that. I *expected* to get the top job after my boss left because I was next in line. I *expected* to be the breadwinner for my family because that's what society expected of me.

When we expect things to happen and they don't materialize, we do one of two things: we harshly judge ourselves, or we judge someone else. *I stink. I'm stupid. My boss is a jerk. My teacher is out to get me.* Or worse, we train our brains to fear uncertainty, which leads to anxiety. *What if I say the wrong thing to my friends, boss, or customers? What if I fail the test? What if I screw up the job interview? What if I don't make the team? What if I lose the election? What if I get sick?*

This is an excellent time to remind you that I am not an expert on anxiety and am not offering medical or professional advice on the topic. I've never had a panic attack, though unfortunately, I have witnessed my son endure them. Even though I was diagnosed with depression in my mid-thirties (and was dealing with it for much longer before then), I am not an anxious person.

But was I scared to kiss a girl in middle school, to debate with my opponent when running for student government president, to bathe a naked homeless man at Mother Teresa's Home for the Dying, or to officiate my younger brother's wedding in front of close family and friends? *Hell, yes.* I was terrified. My voice faltered, my knees shook, and my stomach churned incessantly. But my fear and nervousness during those moments weren't so all-consuming that I could not breathe, think clearly, or ultimately take action.

It wasn't the expectation of a particular outcome that nearly paralyzed me with fear; it was the years of emotional baggage—my demons—I had carried with me since I was seven that held me back. Low self-esteem was chief among these demons, and it impacted nearly every aspect of my life. *Was I ever going to be successful? Why am I not happy? Is this all there is to my life?*

After my dad got Alzheimer's, God knows my dad had every right to complain, make excuses, or just quit. But he didn't. He stuck to his mantra that it could always be worse, much to my chagrin. Of course it could always be worse—so what? What he was saying, I now realize, is that maybe I should appreciate the things I have in my life right now. My health, family, career, and friends, for starters.

I didn't consciously decide to limit my expectations. After all, that sounds sort of like protecting a lead during a hockey game, doesn't it? Rather than sticking to the game plan, which got you the lead in the first place, all of a sudden you're now playing so as not to lose the game. Isn't that what we do when we stay in our comfort zone instead of trying new things? When we don't pursue things we are passionate about or that make us happier, we are protecting the lead rather than playing to win.

I like my job and career, but it's not what I am most passionate about and is certainly not my purpose. I used to tell my kids that when I get older, I am going to be a writer. It took an incurable disease and global pandemic to help me see that I can be a writer *and* have a successful sales career.

Expectation is the degree of probability that something will occur, but it's not an either/or outcome, so stop treating it as such. Prepare and practice to get an A on your exam, land that job, make the team, shoot under par, or write that book. Just don't expect it to happen automatically. Obstacles might slow you down, but don't let them stop you.

Don't wait—like I did—for a life-altering event to inspire you to change. It won't happen overnight, but it will happen, as long as you stop protecting your lead and focus on playing the game.

8. NEVER MAKE EXCUSES.

I used to have a full array of excuses at my disposal for not getting what I wanted—what I *deserved*. Whether it was the girl, grade, roster spot, award, college acceptance, job offer, large order—you name it, I seemed to have an excuse for everything.

My parents' divorce, my ADHD, and my nystagmus. Those were the big three excuses throughout my life.

I never openly shared these excuses, to my credit, but they were widely used inside my head. One particular ADHD characteristic, in the negative column, kept rearing its ugly head: *Achieves at a high level, but they know they could be achieving at a higher level if only they could "find the key."*

I searched long and hard for that key but never found it. When my dad's Alzheimer's worsened to the point where he had to move into assisted living, I stopped looking for the key. The priority in my life was being there for my dad every day. Between taking care of him and my family, there was no time to look for the key to my success.

And that's exactly when I "found" it.

I didn't just drink coffee with my dad during his time at Whitney Place; I also *made* my fair share of it when the aides were too busy running around at mealtimes. I poured it for his friends when their cups needed to be topped off. It became part of my routine, and I enjoyed it.

Pouring coffee for the residents gave me the chance to get to know them better. I learned some of their stories, where they were from, how many children they had, and what they did for a living. It didn't take long to know who was a complainer and who would never complain, no matter how cold the coffee, food, or room was that morning. And those are the people I naturally gravitated toward.

More often than not, the complainers are the ones with all the excuses. Nothing is ever right in their world. Once a person is outed as an excuse-maker, either knowingly or not, they might as well have a giant X on their forehead, like those put on the outside of buildings so firefighters know not to put themselves at risk for a building deemed unworthy of saving.

My dad didn't make a single complaint during his time in assisted living—unless you include his complaint that I was not tipping the staff. I don't recall him ever making excuses for his mistakes, missteps, or misunderstandings.

According to the site lifehack.org, here are some of the top excuses most people make that stop them from achieving their dreams:

- I'm too old to start.
- I'm not talented enough.
- I come from a poor background.
- I'm not smart enough.

- I don't have the support.
- I don't have enough time to discover what I like.
- I'm just not lucky enough.
- I'm not destined to succeed.
- I can't handle failure.
- I'll start tomorrow.
- I'm not ready.
- I don't believe I can do it.

These are heavy excuses. Perhaps you've even used some of them yourself. I certainly have. Remember the key to success that was missing from my life all these years? Well, I didn't actually find it, but that's because it doesn't exist.

I learned so much about my dad under tragic circumstances. I regret not taking the time to know his story sooner. I'm not going to make excuses, but the *reason* I never learned his entire story is because I thought I knew everything there was to know. I mean, how much more is there to know about the person who raised me since I was seven, who coached my hockey teams, drove me to practice, school, and college, who worked alongside me for fourteen years, who hosted Thanksgiving dinners for as long as I can remember, who went to my children's sporting events, and who let me take care of him during his greatest time of need?

It turns out, there's plenty to learn. Far too much to fit into a few chapters of a book.

Campbell, Erin, and Sean: this book was written for you. It's a legacy memoir, but please consider it the first of many volumes. Your grandfather, Papa, had many idioms or truisms, including, "It goes by quick, man," "It could always be worse," "Don't ever get old," and my favorite, the aforementioned "You're only getting screwed if you think you're getting screwed."

I've also weaved in several borrowed truisms "of my own" into the book, such as: "Your ability to endure is always greater than your willingness to endure" (Uncle Dave). "The best four years of your life are always in front of you" (Fr. Kelley). "Our biggest challenges are self-imposed limitations" (Jesse Itzler). "It's not the years in your life that count—it's the life in your years" (Abraham Lincoln).

I love them all.

Papa had us read the hockey commandments before each game. They've stayed with me for more than thirty years, and as you saw from the Facebook comments from Papa's obituary, I'm not the only one who remembers them.

They made us better players, but they only make sense for hockey players.

I never set out to create a list of life commandments, though that's what has happened. I didn't even intend to write a book. I simply needed a way to express my emotions and feelings, which had been building up since Papa's original Alzheimer's diagnosis in 2014. I turned to writing because that's what I did growing up; unlike you guys, I didn't feel like I could talk about my feelings with my parents—or anybody, for that matter.

———

Why have I waited until now to share this with you?

While there's no proper sequence or meaning behind how the life commandments are listed, I wanted to pause here, on the "never make excuses" life commandment, to remind you that I used to make excuses all the time for my perceived lack of success. I'm not ashamed of myself for making excuses, but I'm ashamed of myself for believing them.

There's only one life commandment that can prevent you from remembering, practicing, and benefitting from all ten—and it's this one. Through the stories in this book, the love and support you receive from Mom and Dad, and plain common sense, it should be easy to follow and live by them. By keeping them at the front of your mind, you will be a better person, son or daughter, sibling, friend, teammate, player, teacher, and eventually, husband or wife.

Just promise me three things:

1. Never make excuses for who you are.
2. Never make excuses for doing what you love to do.
3. Never make excuses for your failures.

Hey, at least I kept my commandments to ten. Papa had twenty-nine of them to remember.

9. BE GRATEFUL.

Even before I knew what the word "grateful" meant, something within me told me I had things in my life for which to be thankful. Norwell was beautiful and wealthy, and although Beers Ave contained some of the smallest houses in town, they were a step above the trailer park homes down the street.

Shuffling between Norwell and South Boston as a little boy only heightened this invisible feeling of gratitude. Visiting my grandmother's apartment in the projects was unlike any other place I would stay. I keep coming back to the memories of the smells, whether the burning trash from the incinerators, exhaust from city buses, or plumes of subway steam rising from the grates on Broadway, seemingly out of nowhere. To this day, I avoid walking over those grates. Even the smell of the ocean at low tide caused me to wrinkle my nose.

I don't recall saying, "Thank God I don't live there all the time," but I'm sure it was a near-constant unspoken sentiment.

By the time we entered middle school, it was hard not to notice how wealthy some of my friends were. I honestly don't think I was jealous of them, though I was undoubtedly envious of how much food the Fogartys had in their kitchen pantry. My brothers and I never expected new hockey equipment, bikes, video games, or even a family car, but that doesn't mean we didn't want those things.

Norwell didn't have a high school hockey team at the time. My dad could have easily said, "Too bad. You're going there anyway." Instead, he found a way to send me to a private school. He borrowed money using the equity in the house, watched his spending, and dug into his savings jar, which was supposed to be for vacations. It seldom was.

Teenagers aren't supposed to notice these kinds of sacrifices, but I did. I was grateful to my dad for sending me to Xaverian from day one. I didn't have predefined expectations about what it would be like; I just knew I was lucky to be there. I worked hard to earn good grades and make the teams. I had no idea how good of a hockey player I was, but I think my dad did, even if it was because other parents told him as much. So I was grateful for them, too.

Creating a forgiveness list was helpful, but it only takes up a small portion of a single stage on my carousel of progress. The creation of a forgiveness list was instrumental in helping me find inner peace. It was a great start, anyway. Unloading so much negativity and emotional pain was liberating. But perhaps more importantly, it led me to my gratitude list. There's a much bigger stage for the people in my life I am most grateful for than those I need to forgive.

I hardly remember Mrs. Blake, my fifth-grade English teacher—not her class, teaching style, or even what I learned that year. But I remember her kind words to my dad that prompted a lifelong passion for writing. Mrs. Blake will be on that gratitude stage for the rest of my life as a reminder that kindness matters and that nothing gives me more joy than when I am writing.

———

Stage lights shine brightly on Mr. Dalton, the Xaverian teacher who brought Hugh O'Brian into my life; mentors like Fr. Kelley, S.J., Jim Fitzpatrick, Janet Canepa, and George Diffley; my best friends, Dave and Deirdre; my dad's caregivers from Whitney and Newfield; John and Cathy Fogarty; Eleanor; Tony McLaughlin; Bill Lincoln and his dad; Fr. Higgins; Jeff; Br. Kevin; and my family: Sara, Bill, Heather, Johnny, Kerri, the Campbells—all 30 of them— and even Mr. Davis from Kingston, Jamaica.

Gratitude is mental magic. I wish I could take credit for the phrase, or at least give proper credit to the phrase's source, but I don't remember when or where I first came across it. But it truly is.

If you don't believe me, do the following: write down ten things for which you are grateful. Try it right now. It doesn't matter if it is a person, object, experience, or memory. I promise you that after writing out the list, you will smile. Your attitude, mood, and outlook will instantly improve. Do it every single day, and you'll be amazed at how it makes you feel.

There are only so many times you need to recite a forgiveness list. Eventually, you either forgive someone or you don't. Don't get me wrong, I still review the list, and it helps. But gratitude is the Holy Grail of happiness!

When I started with my new company in January 2019, one of the first key decisions was selecting the right daily planner. Over the years, I had tried, unsuccessfully, many paperless organization systems. It was too much for my ADHD brain to manage. I would inevitably forget to update my task lists and wasn't very good at being tied to my phone like most people are these days. It was time to go old school, to pencil and paper.

The only trouble was, I couldn't find a planner that worked for my needs. They included way too many "planning" sections for me to complete each day, which only made me more inefficient—or they didn't give me enough space for the areas that I rely on most: action lists and notes. So I created my own color-coded planning page, which features: appointments, top three tasks, an action list, notes, health tracker (water, exercise, mediation, prayer, reading, kindness, and writing—my daily vitamins), and most importantly, a gratitude section.

Before leaving the office at the end of each day, I fill in my appointments, top three tasks, and action list for the next day. In the morning, the first thing I do is complete the ***today I am grateful for*** box. I don't do anything else until that's done. I don't stress or dawdle over what to write; whatever comes to mind at that moment is what I write down: people, places, events, and emotions. Examples include Col, Campbell, Erin, Sean, Dad, American Solutions, Fairfield, Xaverian, HOBY, and Woodloch. Or I might write out a sentence like, "I'm so happy and grateful that I get to take my family to Hawaii this year."

There's a lot more to gratitude than you think. Like forgiveness, gratitude has a multitude of well-documented and scientifically proven mental and physical benefits. Amy Morin's 2015 article on psychologytoday.com highlights some of them, including better sleep, improved relationships, enhanced empathy, reduced aggression, and stronger physical and mental health.

We all have the ability and opportunity to cultivate gratitude. Rather than complain about the things you think you deserve, take a few moments to focus on all that you have. Developing an "attitude of gratitude" is one of the simplest ways to improve your satisfaction with life. (Amy Morin, "7 Scientifically Proven Benefits of Gratitude." Psychology Today, 3 April 2015, www.psychologytoday.com/us/blog/201504/7)

Putting gratitude front and center in my life helped me deal with the grief I experienced with Dad's Alzheimer's. I mean, it *really* helped. Instead of focusing on everything that was wrong, both with his disease and COVID, I was able to see and appreciate some of the good taking place in my life.

For example, when COVID prompted the nationwide lockdown in March of 2020, and schools and companies went remote, this allowed Coleen and me to enjoy 98 consecutive dinners with our family! This meant I could cook homemade meals, including fresh bread, each night. What an incredible blessing that was. We will likely never get to experience that family time again.

It was during this same time that I began writing this book. My work routine was drastically different under quarantine. Because there were no in-person appointments, I had time to block off an hour or two each day to write. I took advantage of the situation and committed to the process of writing every day. Working on the book and running a business kept me engaged and energized on both fronts, and certainly helped me cope with the pandemic devastation and my father's Alzheimer's.

In addition to writing *Ten Days With Dad*, I also wrote my first screenplay. I juggled the book, movie script, and business for two months—and was never happier. The screenplay is now complete. It's a romance movie that needs fine-tuning, but it felt great to dive into something brand new and see it through to completion in short order.

COVID shut down my gym, but my family and I took daily walks, even during the winter. While working from home, Coleen and I walked and ate lunch most days together, which energized our relationship. To say that my respect and appreciation for Coleen continues to grow would be a massive understatement. I can say without bias that Dean College is lucky to have her. I have learned more from watching and listening to her than ever before. I am continually amazed at how well she communicates with colleagues, parents, and alumni, and I am most impressed with how she manages conflict, of which there is no shortage.

If writing was my coping mechanism, then baking was my outlet for relaxation. Although I am not an expert, my family and I enjoyed fresh sourdough bread, cookies, pizza, doughnuts, and cinnamon buns. Making fresh bread from scratch is so satisfying! I even did a Facebook Live demonstration on making it, which I would never have done before.

Practicing gratitude allowed me to put aside my past grudges and regrets, like not attending the Captains practices at Fairfield. My list of regrets was extensive, even if some were unfairly categorized as such. I always wondered why I felt the need to constantly remind myself of my mistakes and poor decisions—or worse, lack of "success."

Letting go is easier said than done, I know. I still beat myself up whenever the credit card bill gets too high or when I say the wrong things to one of my kids. Or after an argument with Coleen, when I should apologize right away but don't. Or when I am unproductive, even though I have a long list of tasks to get done.

I *used* to beat myself up anytime I said "yes" to others, even if that meant saying "no" to myself, skipping a day of meditation or writing, and worrying about things that were out of my control. But I don't beat myself up as much anymore.

Before my dad's disease, I held on to grudges going back to middle school. Some were pretty silly; others were significant. Reducing the amount of mental and physical energy required to bear these negative feelings was huge. Adding forgiveness and gratitude lists, daily exercise, and meditation was like a double leap forward in my mental health.

To be grateful is to genuinely appreciate kindness or benefits received. I will be eternally grateful to my dad. Not only for his sacrifices, but also for putting our interests over his own, and for teaching me the very definition of kindness through how he treated people throughout his life. From a young age, I emulated his behavior without realizing I was doing so. Kind and generous, humble yet heroic, my dad was indeed grateful for the love and devotion of his three boys—and I carry that example of gratitude with me today.

Beyond appreciating others' kindness toward me, I am grateful for what I *have* in my life. In particular, I have a job that gave me the flexibility to take care of my dad when he needed me. My job also allowed me to be present for my children, whether to watch one of their games, golf matches, attend an event at school, or take them to appointments. I can't imagine how much harder it would have been for Coleen and me if one of us was not able to be there for Campbell, Erin, and Sean throughout the years.

Each night before I go to bed, I pray for the happiness, health, safety, and success of my family—and then thank God for having them in my life. Whether you use the term blessed or something else, like fortunate, or even lucky—it's all the same, isn't it?

Be grateful for the things you have rather than focusing on what you don't have.

And remember, we all have magic powers—gratitude is yours.

10. FORGIVE YOURSELF.

I set out to write *Ten Days With Dad* to express my sadness, anger, and disbelief over my dad's Alzheimer's, but the more I wrote about *his* story, the more I realized that this was *my* story all along. I didn't just come to accept my dad's fate or his flaws, limitations, and demons—I was also accepting *my* flaws, limitations, and demons.

My story is one of forgiveness; that much is clear. But it is not about forgiving my dad or others from my past. It is about forgiving myself.

My entire life, I not only believed that I was different from most of my peers but that I was inferior to them. Growing up, I didn't know a single person (other than my brother John) who had nystagmus, which meant we were the only two people in the world whose eyes and heads shook every second of every day. Now that Erin has it, that makes three of us who have this highly noticeable but rarely recognized handicap that we've lived with from birth.

On the first day of first grade, I showed up with a cast on my arm. In second grade, I fell into Hatch Pond. My friend Marty was the only friend I had with divorced parents. I intentionally skipped school dances in middle school because I was embarrassed by my clothes and dreadfully afraid to kiss a girl. And when one of those pretty girls finally saw me as more than a friend, my so-called crush of all crushes, I was unable to let her go long after we broke up.

In all my years of playing hockey, I was never a captain of my team. I thought I had the talent, work ethic, and dedication, but not the "C" on my shirt. I let that fact torment me, mainly because it made me feel unrecognizable.

At Fairfield, I was the first varsity athlete to serve as student body president. By the end of my term, I presented the largest student-led initiative to the Board of Trustees and successfully gained approval to build a new campus pub. I certainly wasn't the most accomplished president, nor was I a star on the hockey team, but it was more than a grind to manage them both and land on the Dean's List. I didn't seek recognition for any of my accomplishments, but deep down, I wanted it. I was, again, not recognizable.

When the campus pub, The Levee, opened in the fall of 1995, I attended, though I don't recall any mention of my team's efforts to make the building a reality, no recognition of our work by name—there wasn't even a chance to say a few words. So I held on to that grudge, too. Noticed but not recognized.

Instead of writing checks to my kids' fundraisers, I *ran* the fundraisers and spent twenty, sometimes thirty hours a week collecting donations, securing ads and sponsorships, running committees, and grinding it out. The two most significant events I co-ran at Blessed Sacrament raised more than $100,000 apiece, and yet, I never allowed myself to feel a sense of pride or accomplishment. The school and my friends appreciated the efforts, but I couldn't enjoy them or feel satisfied. Noticeable achievements—but not recognizable ones.

Last year, over drinks late one night with my brothers-in-law, Tim and John, I confided in them that I didn't see myself as a successful person and that this perception has troubled me for as long as I can remember. They were shocked and assured me that I was beyond successful in every measure that mattered. I objected but appreciated their kind words.

A day or two later, I received a text from Tim.

"I was thinking about something you said, about not feeling successful. According to my definition, you are the epitome of success: your dad and the beautiful relationship you had with him, your family—you are beyond respected and loved by all, from your kids to spouse to in-laws to nieces and nephews—your cooking, writing, and career. You are the best friend that lives upstairs, and the fact that you don't see it just reinforces it. You rock. I admire you. And you are my definition of success."

Tim's text was the impetus for my transformation. It was underway long before I read his message, but it was the final blow that brought down the wall of inferiority. His genuine kindness and affection toward me were just enough to turn the spotlight on my carousel of progress toward center stage—only this time, I was the one front and center.

For the first time in more than forty years, I allowed myself to bask in the spotlight long enough to realize that slipping off the log and falling into the pond in second grade was never about the lack of empathy and concern I received—or didn't receive. It was about letting go of the shamefulness of an event that had no importance or meaning in my life—except in my mind.

The persuasive pull to punish myself for making bad choices, to feed regret and resentment, to hide behind pains of my past, and to question my success faded under those bright lights. Instead, those feelings were replaced with the understanding and sincere belief that the only recognition I needed was provided by my dad—every time I visited him.

I not only took care of him, but I was able to return the devotion, sacrifice, and commitment that he gave me all those years. I spent hundreds of hours with him—shared more than 200 meals with him—and got to know him for the first time in my life. I sat next to him, and we smiled, laughed, and cried together. I was there for him when he needed me most. He *noticed* and *recognized* me daily.

Forgiveness is powerful. Forgiving people is empowering. But forgiving yourself is the ultimate gift. I know that forgiving yourself and letting go doesn't eliminate every pain from your past. It is, however, a required first step if you want to have more peace in your life.

It took a seven-year Alzheimer's journey, a global pandemic, a well-timed text, fifty years of living, and this book to transform my priorities, define my purpose, reignite lost passions, and feel true inner peace.

Don't wait for tragedy or a life-altering event to begin your transformation. If you're having a rough day, write down what you're grateful for. Start your own giving journey. Stop judging other people. Don't let other people define your happiness. Expect less and give more. Be mindful of how long your bus ride might last. Smile. Resist the temptation to make excuses. Take charge of your story. If you're stressed or anxious, ask yourself this question: *Are these thoughts really useful?* Forgive people who have wronged you. Persevere. Establish a meditation or breathing routine. Become a kindness mentor. Construct your carousel of progress.

———

Embrace the parts of your past that brought you joy, pride, confidence, and fulfillment—but don't let a handful of mistakes, regrets, and obstacles define your present. Permit yourself to change, for you are under no obligation to be the person you were five years ago, one year ago, or even a month ago. Know that the people, places, and experiences you have in your life can only *influence* change.

To transform your priorities, build better habits, become the person you want to be, and find *your* purpose, passion, and peace . . . well, that's entirely up to you. Only you have the ability to take control of your story. Nobody else is going to do it for you, so don't wait for the right time in your life to begin the journey—and definitely don't wait for a tragedy or a terminal disease, as I did.

It's been a remarkable journey in my role as a sandwich parent, taking care of my dad and three teenagers. In many ways, nothing has changed. I still cut my thinning hair too short before events and vacations, still believe anything is possible, and am still always in a rush to do something and be someone.

But thanks to my dad—beginning with his hockey commandments and continuing with the commandments of life—I am living with purpose, following my passions, and for the first time since before that fateful night on Beers Ave, when my parents announced that they were separating, I am at peace with who I am.

It's not perfection, but it sure is some serious progress.

EPILOGUE

"You either walk inside your story and own it,
or you stand outside your story and hustle for your worthiness."

-Brené Brown

Dad's initial diagnosis was in 2014, weeks—or maybe months, I am not sure—before my brother John's wedding. Seven years later, Dad's journey ended. Mine is only beginning—at least that's how I feel in many ways. I am the happiest I have been in a very long time, even though the past few years have been the most challenging, hurtful, demoralizing, sad, and painful—because of Alzheimer's and COVID-19.

Did you say you are happier now, or happy?

The answer is both. I can't emphasize the point enough: 2021 was a lousy year. But it was also my best. It wasn't the same kind of year as my 1987–88 sophomore year at Xaverian. Remember all the bad stuff that happened to me then? I had hepatitis and two broken wrists, I was dumped by my girlfriend, and I was cut from varsity hockey, only to end the year with being chosen for, and subsequently attending, the Hugh O'Brian Leadership Conference.

Unlike high school, 2021 was filled with more serious events—such as car accidents and deaths, including my dad's. Yet it was also filled with extraordinary accomplishments, including the completion of my final edits on *Ten Days With Dad*—a successful misogi indeed—and something far more extraordinary.

The year started to unravel in March, when a teenager blew through a stop sign and we collided. I never saw him coming. He couldn't have been going more than thirty miles per hour, but it packed a powerful punch. The airbag imploded into my face, causing whiplash symptoms that remain with me today. My Kia minivan, only a few months from being paid off, was totaled.

As detailed earlier in the book, Coleen contracted COVID after our July vacation. Seven months later, she is still recovering from long-haul COVID. Once the typical symptoms passed, she battled respiratory issues, ear and sinus infections, shortness of breath, severe coughing, and vocal cord issues, and more.

Coleen's Aunt Annie died in late July. In the throes of her COVID battle, bedridden and fevered, she watched a live-stream of the funeral. (Coleen was able to attend a celebratory funeral mass in Annie's home parish a month later, giving her some closure.)

A week later, my dad died.

In the fall, the new COVID variant, omicron, was ravaging the world. *Was this really happening again?*

November 2021 stood out as a bright spot in my year. *Ten Days With Dad* was finally ready to be sent to my editor. The book was heading into the home stretch, and I was excited.

———

Then, the week before Thanksgiving, I met up with my closest Norwell friends at The Fours, a restaurant and bar located about a half mile from Beers Ave. Catching up with people who once dominated the physical landscape of my world, but now exist primarily within the confines of social media, text messaging, and my memory, was full of surprises, some sorrow, and kinship.

This intimate group of lifelong friends from the tiny town of Norwell all knew my dad—and all understood that what he and I experienced during our time on Beers Ave was indeed special. For some in attendance, it was the first time in twenty-five years that we saw one another, and yet, it was like a day hadn't passed. After warm hugs and genuine condolences about my dad, we launched into endless conversation about our lives, both old and new, until the manager kicked us out around 11:30 pm.

The news of my dad's death probably hit Sean Fogarty the hardest. My best friend throughout middle school, high school, and college, Sean spent more time with Big D than all of my friends combined. Losing touch with him after college was tough for me. It didn't matter—once we hugged it out and shed tears over my dad, all was good, and any doubts that he had forgotten me during our prolonged separation were gone.

Like it never happened.

Eleanor, my first serious girlfriend and closest Norwell friend, organized the gathering. Like my dad was with his Brighton crew, Eleanor is the glue that keeps us together. More like super glue! Despite having a hundred things going on in her life, running a successful law practice, and raising two middle-school boys, she makes the time for her friends. I heard her laugh across the room while mid-conversation with others and couldn't help but smile. She bounced casually from conversation to conversation, like we were back at Beers Ave, infecting us with her enthusiasm and affection.

I wasn't the only person in their glory that night.

I learned for the first time that Rachel, my friend who let me *borrow* her eighth-grade music paper on Whitney Houston, had been in the same preschool class with Mrs. Bandara. She had also received a purple hippo stuffed animal from our teacher. Her two boys are the same age as my Sean and compete against one another in golf tournaments, unbeknownst to either of us.

Remember Anne, my super-crush in high school? I had no idea she attended Cole Elementary for one year before moving to the other side of Norwell—and, she was in my class— with Mrs. McCann. No surprise, Mrs. McCann was also Anne's favorite elementary school teacher. I guess it wasn't the broken arm after all that caused her to be so nice to me. Mrs. McCann was loved and adored by everyone lucky enough to have had her as a teacher.

The eighth-grade dance came up in conversation, and Anne and I both laughed about how special it had been for us. I gave her a hard time for dumping me for another guy and got her to admit, rather easily, that he was kind of a jerk. She didn't remember breaking up with me after I broke my wrist, but she did remember the rest of our story.

Tony McLaughlin, my oldest friend, still stands out, due to his six-foot, five-inch frame and relaxed demeanor. Our dads had coached together for the South Shore Seahawks, including the team that upset Compuware at Lake Placid in 1980. We had learned to skate at the same time, beginning on Jacobs Pond, but his hockey career had given way to basketball, football, and baseball. He had captained all three at Norwell High before going on to play basketball for Roger Williams College in Rhode Island.

In honor of his dad's hockey coaching career, Tony wanted to get his boys playing hockey early. His oldest son, Charlie, had followed in my footsteps, leaving Norwell to play for a catholic conference high school. A sophomore at Archbishop Williams in Braintree, he had made the varsity hockey team as a freshman. Tony is the most solid, consistent guy friend I have. He's worked for the same company for twenty-six years now and is successful in every area of his life.

Oh, how fun it was to laugh with Carolyn DeCoste, my *girlfriend* at Cole from grades four through six. Fortunately for me, she didn't remember how I broke things off. I recounted the story, just for kicks—how I had written her a note, folded it up, then turned it into a paper airplane and zoomed it across the hall to her.

She remembered Camp Wing, including holding hands by the campfire, but did not remember (or see) me climbing the highest tree so I wouldn't have to talk to her when she visited my neighborhood in the summer. Her son is a junior at Thayer Academy, where my oldest, Campbell, attended.

Keith MacDonald lives in Duxbury, across town from my brother John. His oldest is getting close to high school years, and he and his wife have Xaverian on their list of schools. When I had told my friends that I was going to Xaverian in 1986, very few had heard of it, and when they found out how far it was, they thought I was crazy. Today, kids from the South Shore routinely make the trip to Xaverian, and his son would be the third from our close group to attend the school.

Unfortunately for Keith, we share another common reality—his parents are both experiencing early-onset dementia. He's in for a rough journey, but he knows I will do whatever I can to help him, even if it just means listening or taking him out for a beer.

Kate Gennelly gave me the biggest hug and the warmest congratulations on my book.

"I'm so proud of you—I'm so, so happy for you. It's going to be amazing!"

Later in the evening, I pulled Kate aside to tell her that it was *me* who was proud of *her*. It took me my entire life to find purpose and passion, but not Kate. She was the only person in the group who had pursued her true passion—art—from the very beginning. I've watched her amazing talents as an artist from afar, but have truly admired her all along for pursuing her dream to create, draw, paint, and inspire people.

We cried. The tears were happy ones, though.

After returning home to Walpole sometime after midnight, I walked into the kitchen and saw the sink still full of dirty dishes. I smiled, rolled up my sleeves, and loaded the dishwasher. The kitchen is my domain. I cook the meals, clean up the mess, and take care of the dishes. That's one of my roles in our household, and I embrace it. And on that particular evening, I don't think I was ever happier to do the dishes.

It was a glorious night, indeed.

———

Coming home to a dirty sink didn't always make me smile or feel grateful. Not too long ago my thoughts would have been, *Why am I the only person who has to do the dishes, cut the grass, take out the trash, cancel a meeting, cook dinner, clean the garage?* And the list would go on and on.

Prior to my dad's Alzheimer's, I was *standing outside my story*—chasing my worthiness. Worse, I battled demons, made excuses, blamed my past, searched for new roles, and sought a definition of success that I didn't create or desire. I was desperate for recognition and respect, but what I was really searching for was love—a type of love I never experienced at home on Beers Ave in Norwell and love from friends and family.

Then it hit me that November night, beginning with my Norwell friends, who have been with me during this entire journey, from Mrs. McCann to my dad's passing. They had loved my dad and the time we spent on Beers Ave, but what I didn't know—could never see—was that *they loved me.* Their love was right there in front of me this entire time, but I couldn't see it.

Whether it was from my Norwell friends or Fairfield, Mrs. Blake or Fr. Kelley, John and Cathy Fogarty or Mr. and Mrs. Campbell, nieces and nephews or in-laws—and especially, Coleen and my children—*I have been loved all along.*

Seeing my dad's reaction each time I showed up to see him while he was sick was further proof that I was not only loved but was *noticed* and *recognized.* I couldn't see it at the time, but it was so obvious in hindsight.

And then there's Coleen, the one person in my life whose love has never wavered or diminished. No matter how many impulse decisions I made or attempted to act on, missteps or mistakes made, businesses I wanted to start, or poorly timed lapses in memory and judgment—she's been walking beside me this entire time. From Campion to Bellarmine, Sunnyridge to Lamplighter, Mt. Laurel to Maui—nobody has shown me more love.

I see it now, Col. Believe me, I do.

In December 2021, Sean and I spent five days in Richmond, and we were able to see two men's basketball games on campus. After the second game, and a brief stop in Baltimore to see Coleen's brother and family, I drove eight hours home to Walpole, arriving at 4:30 in the morning. We had a lot to get done, as our rescheduled Hawaii family vacation (it was canceled the year before because of COVID) was in a few days.

We were worried that the entire trip would be canceled, again, because of COVID. The omicron variant blazed through college campuses. Campbell managed to avoid it, again, but Erin was not so lucky. She was in quarantine the day before Christmas. Our flight was on Christmas night. Coleen's dad and brother had just tested positive, so their Christmas plans were already on the fritz.

More than 10,000 flights were canceled over a span of five days surrounding our trip. Not because of passenger safety but because too many airline staff were getting COVID and had to call in sick. A flight attendant on our first flight to Las Vegas was included among the sick, which delayed our flight for two hours. We had a long layover in Vegas before the next segment of our trip, so we had more than enough time to catch our next flight to Maui.

That was until the pilot announced that we had to stop and refuel the plane in Denver before getting to Las Vegas. *WTF, seriously?* I have flown to

Las Vegas probably a dozen or more times and never heard of such a thing. Why would JetBlue use a plane that couldn't make it all the way to Nevada?

Suddenly, our four-hour layover in Vegas before the flight to Maui was causing some panic. *Are we going to make it?*

We missed the flight to Hawaii by two minutes.

No joke. Hawaiian Air had a firm cutoff for receiving luggage at the terminal counter, or so they said, and would not let us check our luggage at the gate, unlike every other airline in the world.

"Sorry, there's nothing we can do."

"Please, *please* help us," Coleen pleaded—no, she *begged*.

The amount of stress and anxiety she was experiencing in December was truly at the breaking point. I had never seen her face so pained as when the Hawaiian Air employee casually shrugged off our begging.

"There's nothing I can do about it."

The next flight was at 9:45 a.m., so we spent the next eight hours in uncomfortable chairs outside security at McCarran International Airport. People have asked why we would travel so far to go to Hawaii.

"It's the only place I've been where the stress literally drains from my body the moment I step off the plane," I tell them.

"But the flight is sooo long."

"Yeah, but I'm going to Hawaii—I'm excited on the way there and exhausted on the flight home. No big deal for me."

This time, it was a big deal. The exhaustion Coleen and I felt during the next eight hours was like the days after your first child was born—it smacks you in the face and your entire body aches. *How am I going to make it through this without collapsing from exhaustion?*

We made it. Thirty-six hours after waking up on Christmas morning.

After an early breakfast in the room the next day, we made it down to the beach. I walked to the water and created mental snapshots of the two looming mountain islands in front of me, Lanai and Molokai. I took in the crashing waves, paddleboarders, the beach views, Black Rock and the Sheraton to my left, blue skies to the center, and Honua Kai and condos to my right. I burned the images into my subconscious for easy access in the future, for when I find myself under stress.

I laid my yellow and white striped Westin beach towel in the sand, positioned my body toward the sun, and put my back on the towel. I closed my eyes and took in the sounds around me. Waves crashed. SSSH-HHWWHHHOOOOPFfffsshhhhhsssss. Odd-sounding birds chirped off to my left in the protected dune grasses. Even the conversations taking place around me:

"You're hungry already?" "Can you put sunscreen on my back?" "Incoming!" "Whoa, did you see the spray from that whale?" "Those people over there said a sea turtle just swam by." "Honey, can you bring an extra beach chair when you come down from the room?"

Then I meditated.

My eyes were shut, but I was still seeing flashes of bright orange sherbert—or some sort of deep orangish-reddish canvas of brightness in front of me—like molten lava, or Mars. *Mars? I don't know what Mars looks like.* I took a few deep breaths and began my mantra: *Shri-Shri, Kirring-Kirring, Namaha-Namaha—am I supposed to be sharing my mantra with the world?* No matter, the words and brightness were of no significance, but because of my nystagmus, the golden canvas in front of my closed eyes shook gently from side to side. *Or up and down?* The little vision floaters appeared like fallen fragments of fireworks. *Does everyone have floaters?*

The waves crashed in front of me. SSSHHHWWHHH-HOOOOPFfffsshhhhhsssss.

My eyes had adjusted to the brightness on the other side of my lids, but I could *see* the waves in my mind. And Lanai and Molokai. *Shri-Shri, Kirring-Kirring, Namaha-Namaha.* Birds were close but not really. Small talk. Laughter from the pool a hundred yards behind me. SSSHHHWWOOOOPFfffsshhhhhsssss. *Shri-Shri, Kirring-Kirring, Namaha-Namaha.*

My right hand touched the sand, but I didn't care. Nor did I try to keep the sand off my towel. SSSHHHWWHHHOOOOPFfffsshhhh-hsssss. *Shri-Shri, Kirring-Kirring, Namaha-Namaha.* Soon, the conversations around me gradually faded. Not entirely, but enough not to notice every word of what was being said. Nothing bothered me. Nobody asked me any questions—as if they could tell I was in a blissful state.

The stress was draining from my body. It took a little longer this time due to our extended travel itinerary—but it drained.

I cut the first meditation short. Only twenty minutes instead of thirty. That happens. Besides, ideas came quickly. I was flooded with things I wanted to add to my book. I forgot my phone, which would have made me upset a year ago but was no big deal that day. I borrowed Erin's and wrote myself notes for later use.

The unemotional Hawaiian Airlines rep from the day before was long forgotten—forgiven, actually. *Just doing her job.* I can only imagine my reaction a couple of years ago. Actually, it would have been similar to the time I lost it with those guys not wearing masks at the local doughnut shop.

After writing my thoughts down, I dove into the Hawaiian waters and couldn't wipe the smile off my face. Each time I entered the waters I said silent prayers to the Gods of the Sea—*please, please let 2022 be better for Coleen, Campbell, Erin, and Sean.*

It's not that I didn't need the prayers, too—but they needed them more. Coleen's and Campbell's health, Erin's continued happiness at Fairfield, and Sean's prayer was for a breakthrough year with his golf game prior to his college recruiting next year.

I'm not proud to admit that I haven't been inside of a church more than twice in two years, because of COVID (that's what I tell myself); but at the same time, in that ocean, I felt closer to God than ever before. I pray more often to Him and feel, somehow, that my meditation actually helps me stay more focused.

My dad and I didn't talk much about religion. My mom would only marry him if he consented to raise us Catholic, with which he had no problem. He was a Jewish man who celebrated Christmas—both because of us and Jane, his life partner of forty years.

If priests were allowed to marry, I don't think it would have been out of the question to say that I would have considered it as a vocation. Then again, I say the same thing about serving my country in uniform, something I was unable to do because of my vision impairment.

But it wasn't my purpose to serve God or my country in that way.

Everyone *has* a purpose in life. Some figure it out early on, while others, like me, need some help—or may go their entire lives without

———

ever figuring it out, which makes me sad. I think that's because we don't always want to acknowledge our purpose. *That can't be my only purpose, can it?*

So let me ask you this: What's the one thing that makes you most happy? The interest or passion that keeps you up at night? When you wake up, it's the first thing you think about. When you go to bed at night, it's the last thing on your mind.

That's what writing has become for me once again. I am not naive enough to think I can quit my day job and become a writer overnight—you know, pay the mortgage and tuition through book sales. But it's definitely what makes me the most excited—the most alive. And it's been there all along. Well, since the fifth grade, anyway!

How do you know if it's a seasonal obsession or passion?

I don't have the answer to that question. I can only tell you that this is how writing makes me feel, and if I'm honest with myself, it's how I've always felt. I also don't believe God *gives* us our purpose, nor do I believe we are destined to have just one purpose in life. I'm not suggesting that you don't turn to God for answers. By all means, you should. I'm just saying I don't believe he's going to *tell* you what that purpose is—at least not in a manner in which you're expecting.

This is why I was reluctant to use the term *commandments* when sharing my ten commandments of life. Nothing we do is going to guarantee happiness, purpose, passion, or peace. But something kept pulling me back to my dad's hockey commandments. After more than thirty years, most of his former players mentioned them when they reached out to express their condolences.

Reverence to God aside, I came to the conclusion that my ten commandments of life—or living—were a fitting tribute to the man I respected and loved so much.

I never realized that I was practicing some of these life commandments my entire life—*because of my dad*. In watching, emulating, and admiring him up close and afar, I was becoming the best version of *myself*. Not the best version of my dad, but *my* best version.

Of the ten commandments of life, only one escaped my dad's reach: number 10, forgive yourself. I believe he would have embraced it eventually—had Alzheimer's not robbed him of that opportunity.

It took my dad's terminal illness and the COVID-19 pandemic for me to find my purpose in writing. Taking care of my family comes first, followed by my writing, specifically, writing to remind and motivate others that it's never too late to pursue your passion—or perhaps, more importantly, it's never too early. In doing so, you will change the trajectory of your life forever.

Baking bread, cookies, cinnamon buns, and pizzas give me tremendous joy, but my true passion is writing. My next writing project has yet to be determined, though I can promise you this is only the beginning of my storytelling journey.

As for finding peace, forgiving myself was the first step, but ultimately, it wasn't until I began to love myself that I began to experience inner peace. In order to love myself, I had to accept and genuinely embrace my roles—as a middle child, supportive husband, doting dad, and now, as an ambassador for helping others find and live their passion.

Now it's your turn to own your story, pursue your passion, and love yourself. Believe me, if I can do it, then so can you.

———

HAT TRICK SPONSORS

**Take photo
of QR code
to visit website**

The Right Senior Living Decision Is An Informed one

**Take photo
of QR code
to visit website**

Haba Wealth Management

**Take photo
of QR code
to visit website**

HAT TRICK SPONSORS

BELCHER FITZGERALD LLP
COUNSELLORS AT LAW
BUSINESS • LITIGATION • TRUSTS & ESTATES

**Take photo
of QR code
to visit website**

Leon V. Rosenberg & Family

*"Mark wrote a book. That's a good thing.
Back to shrimps and rusty nails with Barry...
delicious!"*

- John, Dan, Tim, and Jim Campbell

GOAL SPONSORS

Fairfield
UNIVERSITY

Alumni Relations

PRO*f*orma®
Printing & Promotion
Bill Resnick   **John Resnick**

Assist Sponsors

Charles River Apparel
www.charlesriverapparel.com

J.DERENZO
Properties, LLC
www.jderenzoproperties.com

Newfield House
www.newfieldhouse.com

Walpole Chamber of Commerce
www.walpolechamber.org

Salmon Health & Retirement
Whitney Place Assisted Living, Sharon, MA
www.salmonhealth.com

Pete DeFilippo & Rob Malley

ACKNOWLEDGEMENTS

To my wife and best friend, Coleen, for taking a walk with me.

To Campbell, Erin, and Sean: own your story, pursue your passion, and love yourself.

To Bill and John: we'll always be partners in life.

To the Campbells—all of you—for loving me for who I am and making me feel like family from day one and throughout our time growing up.

To my Norwell friends, teachers, and coaches, I wish I could list every single one of you here, but if I do, I am going to unintentionally leave someone out—which I will regret.

To my Fairfield family, especially Dave and Deirdre, Fr. Kelley, Fr. Higgins, Janet Canepa, Jim Fitzpatrick, George Diffley, and hundreds of others who impacted my life during my four years of college, I also wish I could list every one of you here.

To my Xaverian teachers, coaches, classmates, and teammates.

To Jesse, Laurie, and the Calendar Club family.

To Brett and the Self-Publishing School family.

To the American Solutions for Business family.

To the Walpole Writing Group: Molly, Elizabeth, Bob, and Eric.

———

To Sara Robinson, The McMorrows and The Griefs

To my hat trick and goal book sponsors, I am grateful for your support and belief in my book: 2Sisters Senior Living Advisors, American Solutions for Business, Justin Zavadil, Belcher Fitzgerald LLC, Leon and Richard Rosenberg, Haba Wealth Management, Proforma Printing & Promotion, Namaksy-Zammito Insurance Agency, Fairfield University, and John, Dan, Tim, and Jim Campbell.

To those no longer part of my life on earth: Marty, Mike, Johnny, Kevin, Grammy, Grandpa, Uncle Pete, Maureen, Aunt Annie, Linda, and of course, Dad.

ABOUT THE AUTHOR

I've wanted to be a writer since the fifth grade, when Mrs. Blake, my English teacher, encouraged me to consider writing outside the confines of her classroom. She put me on this path and I'm grateful for her kindness. I hope she is proud of my work, wherever she may be.

Growing up in Norwell, Massachusetts wasn't special, but sharing a house with my dad and two brothers was. Most of the time we didn't know what we were doing, both literally and figuratively, but we found our roles and fulfilled them the best we could. I've remained true to my middle child mold ever since, which has served me well more often than not.

Ten Days with Dad was originally written as a means to express my anger, disbelief and sorrow over my dad's Alzheimer's. It quickly became something much larger. Although the book is described as a memoir, it goes beyond the traditional boundaries of the genre–which, if you know me, makes perfect sense.

I currently live in Walpole, MA with Coleen, my wife of 25 years. We are in the throes of putting our kids through college and high school. From Richmond to Fairfield, and locally to Xaverian Brothers HS, we bounce back and forth, offering counsel as needed, encouragement when allowed, and nourishment–which is always enthusiastically accepted!

––––––

I invite you to visit and connect with me at *www.markjresnick.com*. Remember, it's never too late—or too early—to pursue your passion.

-Mark

CAN YOU HELP?

Please take a few minutes now to leave a review on Amazon.

www.markjresnick.com/review

Reviews don't need to be lengthy, formal, or perfect---just honest.

Leaving an online review will only take a few minutes but will help others make an informed purchase.

Reviews also make a significant impact on my book's long-term success.

Thank you so very much.

-Mark

NOTES

NOTES

NOTES

Made in United States
North Haven, CT
21 March 2022

17401193R00207